STUDIES ON THE CHINESE ECONOMY

General Editors: Peter Nolan, Sinyi Professor of Chinese Management, Judge Institute of Management Studies, University of Cambridge, and Fellow of Jesus College, Cambridge, England; and Dong Fureng, Professor, Chinese Academy of Social Sciences, Beijing, China

This series analyses issues in China's current economic development, and sheds light upon that process by examining China's economic history. It contains a wide range of books on the Chinese economy past and present, and includes not only studies written by leading Western authorities, but also translations of the most important works on the Chinese economy produced within China. It intends to make a major contribution towards understanding this immensely important part of the world economy.

Titles include:

Thomas Chan, Noel Tracy and Zhu Wenhui
CHINA'S EXPORT MIRACLE

Xu Dixin and Wu Chengming (*editors*)
CHINESE CAPITALISM, 1522–1840

Christopher Findlay and Andrew Watson (*editors*)
FOOD SECURITY AND ECONOMIC REFORM

Samuel P. S. Ho and Y. Y. Kueh
SUSTAINABLE ECONOMIC DEVELOPMENT IN SOUTH CHINA

Kali P. Kalirajan and Yanrui Wu (*editors*)
PRODUCTIVITY AND GROWTH IN CHINESE AGRICULTURE

Bozhong Li
AGRICULTURAL DEVELOPMENT IN JIANGNAN, 1620–1850

Alfred H. Y. Lin
THE RURAL ECONOMY OF GUANGDONG, 1870–1937

Dic Lo
MARKET AND INSTITUTIONAL REGULATION IN CHINESE INDUSTRIALIZATION

Jun Ma
THE CHINESE ECONOMY IN THE 1990s

Guo Rongxing
HOW THE CHINESE ECONOMY WORKS

Sally Sargeson
REWORKING CHINA'S PROLETARIAT

Ng Sek Hong and Malcolm Warner
CHINA'S TRADE UNIONS AND MANAGEMENT

Michael Twohey
AUTHORITY AND WELFARE IN CHINA

Wang Xiao-qiang
CHINA'S PRICE AND ENTERPRISE REFORM

Xiaoping Xu
CHINA'S FINANCIAL SYSTEM UNDER TRANSITION

Yanni Yan
INTERNATIONAL JOINT VENTURES IN CHINA

Wei-Wei Zhang
TRANSFORMING CHINA

Xiao-guang Zhang
CHINA'S TRADE PATTERNS AND INTERNATIONAL COMPARATIVE
ADVANTAGE

Studies on the Chinese Economy
Series Standing Order ISBN 0–333–71502–0
(*outside North America only*)

You can receive future titles in this series as they are published by placing a standing order.
Please contact your bookseller or, in case of difficulty, write to us at the address below with
your name and address, the title of the series and the ISBN quoted above.

Customer Services Department, Macmillan Distribution Ltd
Houndmills, Basingstoke, Hampshire RG21 6XS, England

China's Trade Patterns and International Comparative Advantage

Xiao-guang Zhang
Lecturer in Economics
University of Melbourne
Australia

First published in Great Britain 2000 by
MACMILLAN PRESS LTD
Houndmills, Basingstoke, Hampshire RG21 6XS and London
Companies and representatives throughout the world

A catalogue record for this book is available from the British Library.

ISBN 0–333–74087–4

First published in the United States of America 2000 by
ST. MARTIN'S PRESS, INC.,
Scholarly and Reference Division,
175 Fifth Avenue, New York, N.Y. 10010

ISBN 0–312–22571–7

Library of Congress Cataloging-in-Publication Data
Zhang, Xiaoguang.
China's trade patterns and international comparative advantage /
Xiao-guang Zhang.
p. cm. — (Studies on the Chinese economy)
Includes bibliographical references and index.
ISBN 0–312–22571–7 (cloth)
1. China—Commercial policy—Econometric models. 2. China–
–Commerce—Econometric models. 3. Comparative advantage
(International trade) I. Title. II. Series.
HF1604.Z24 1999
382'.1042'0951—dc21
99–26132
CIP

This book is printed on paper suitable for recycling and made from fully managed and sustained forest sources.

10   9   8   7   6   5   4   3   2   1
09   08   07   06   05   04   03   02   01   00

Printed and bound in Great Britain by
Antony Rowe Ltd, Chippenham, Wiltshire

To Xinhua, Jing and Bo

Contents

List of Figures

List of Tables

Preface

This book is an empirical analysis of the impact of China's recent economic reforms on the commoditiy patterns of trade and structure of international comparative advantage. It originated from the doctoral dissertation I completed five years ago at the Australian National University (ANU). The study was undertaken out of a strong feeling of the need to understand how foreign trade and domestic industries have interacted with each other in an era of fundamental economic transformation. The original work covered the first decade of China's reforms up to 1987. However, the rapid growth and structural changes that have taken place in the Chinese economy and the radical reforms introduced since 1987 warranted a thorough updating and revising of the original analysis. In this book, I have extended the investigation to include the second decade of the reform period up to 1995–6. The results have confirmed the findings of the original study and shed some new light on the impact of the reforms on China's dynamic foreign trade and comparative advantage structure.

This study would not have been possible without the help and encouragement I have received from numerous people over the years. First, I would like to express my deepest gratitude to the members of my dissertation committee, Peter G. Warr, Ross Garnaut, Rodney E. Falvey and David Wall for their advice at every stage of my dissertation. The original study also benefited from intellectual support from several other people, in particular, Will Martin, K. P. Kalirajan and Frances Perkins through helpful discussions at various stages of the research. I benefited also from Thomas Rawski, who made a careful reading of an early draft and gave invaluable and constructive comments. The thesis could not have been undertaken without financial assistance from the National Centre for Development Studies. I am particularly appreciative of the support of Helen Hughes, the executive Director of the Centre, during the years I spent there. The help of other staff members and my fellow students in the ANU is also gratefully acknowledged.

As this research relies heavily on the quality of quantitative data, without the help of those people who provided the data, the research would not have proceeded. I am most grateful to Dai Guoqing for providing China's price data at a very early stage of this research and the other officials and the academics whom I contacted directly or indirectly in various government departments, research institutes or universities in China for assisting me with data collection. Thanks also go to Prue Phillips for providing access to the international trade data at the International Economic Data Bank of the ANU.

Since I began updating the original study and rewriting it as a book early this year, many people have helped me. Among them, I would like to express my special gratitude to Zheng Yuxin, Wang Li and Ma Gang of the Institute of Quantitative and Technical Economics (IQTE) at the Chinese Academy of Social Sciences, who provided some of the latest trade and price data and introduced me to the Chinese State Statistical Bureau and some other government departments.

I have also benefited immensely from the critical and constructive comments that Nicholas R. Lardy, Kenneth Klements and Yun-Wing Sung made on my original dissertation. In addition, Fan Mingtai of the IQTE, who visited the Department of Economics in the first half of 1998, helped me with analyzing some of the empirical results. In the past few years, some of the results of this study were presented in a number of seminars at the University of Melbourne, Monash University and the ANU. The comments that I received from seminar participants helped me further clarify some of the basic ideas, which was very useful in preparing this book; the financial support I received through a research grant from the Economics and Commerce Faculty of the University of Melbourne has facilitated this. Thanks are also due to Maree Tait and Dayaneetha De Silva for their editorial assistance, to my commissioning editor at Macmillan, Sunder Katwala, for guiding the manuscript to publication and Peter Nolan for including this book in the series Studies in the Chinese Economy.

Finally, my greatest debt goes to my wife, Li Xinhua, whose understanding and constant support have contributed enormously to the completion of this study. I owe a great deal to my family who have not only supported but also actually assisted me in this endeavour in many ways. Therefore, it is to my wife, Xinhua, and our two children, Jing and Bo, that this book is dedicated.

Department of Economics
University of Melbourne
Melbourne

XIAO-GUANG ZHANG

List of Acronyms and Abbreviations

ACFB	Almanac of China's Finance and Banking
ACFERT	Almanac of China's Foreign Economic Relations and Trade
ANU	The Australian National University
AQP	above-quota procurement price
CCP	Chinese Communist Party
CICNEA	China's Industrial Classification of National Economics Activities
c.i.f.	cost, insurance, freight
CRS	contract responsibility system
DRC	domestic resource cost
DRP	domestic resource productivity
ERR	effective exchange rate
EIR	export–import ratio
EPR	export performance ratio
ER	exchange rate
FDI	foreign direct (or direct foreign) investment
FESC	Foreign Exchange Swap Centre
f.o.b.	free on board
FTC	foreign trade corporation
GATT	General Agreement on Tariffs and Trade
GDP	gross domestic product
HCDCS	Harmonized Commodity Description and Coding System
H–O	Heckscher–Ohlin (model)
IEDB	International Economic Data Bank
IPR	import performance ratio
IRR	internal rate of return
MAP	market-adjusted price
MKP	market procurement price
MOA	Ministry of Agriculture
MOFEC	Ministry of Foreign Trade and Economic Cooperation
MOFERT	Ministry of Foreign Economic Relations and Trade
MOFT	Ministry of Foreign Trade
NEPR	net export performance ratio
NGP	negotiated procurement price
NPV	net present value
NRP	nominal rate of protection
NSP	net social profitability
OLS	ordinary least squares
PPP	purchase power parity
R&D	research and development
RMB	Renminbi

SACP	State Administration of Commodity Prices
SCO	Special Commissioner's Offices
SEZ	Special Economic Zone
SGP	state-guide price
SITC	Standard International Trade Classification
SLP	state-list procurement price
SMP	social marginal productivity
SPC	State Planning Commission
SSB	State Statistical Bureau
SSTC	State Science and Technology Commission
UN	United Nations
UNCTAD	United Nations Conference on Trade and Development
UNIDO	United Nations Industrial Development Organization
WLS	weighted least squares
WTO	World Trade Organization

Abbreviations used in tables

-	negligible
..	not available
na	not applicable

1 Introduction

In the recent economic reforms, China has successfully transformed itself from a closed and centrally planned economy to a more open and market-oriented economy. Over the past two decades, China has also enjoyed unprecedented growth and is fast becoming a key player in the world economy. Understanding the changing nature of the Chinese economy and the dynamic elements behind China's recent ascendancy will be vital for the world's future.

This book seeks to explain the dynamic forces behind China's rapid expansion of foreign trade in recent years. Foreign trade has made a tremendous contribution to the overall performance of the Chinese economy and its transformation into one of the world's largest trading nations. To what extent have China's economic reforms in general, and its trade reforms in particular, impacted on its trade performance? How has this improved the efficiency of the domestic tradable goods-producing industries? This book links China's recent trade performance with the evolving comparative advantage of its domestic tradable goods producing industries to shed new light on the driving forces behind China's recent strong growth.

KEY QUESTIONS

China's economic reforms have been aimed at improving efficiency in resource allocation. 'Open-door' policies and the promotion of foreign trade have been seen as important ways to make the domestic economy efficient. The East Asian experience indicates that outward-oriented economic policies can contribute to rapid economic growth and development. Increasing numbers of developing countries, which had earlier followed inward-looking policies, have recognized the importance of openness and have either changed, or are changing, their trade policies accordingly. In the process of shifting from inward to outward-oriented policies, these countries have also altered their trade specializations according to their resource and factor endowments. The central policy issue here is the exploitation of each country's comparative advantage *vis-à-vis* the rest of the world.

China's foreign trade is being actively promoted and is growing at an unprecedented rate. However, the continuing success of the reforms requires more efficient trade mechanisms. In addition, the assessment of efficiency in trade and production in a transitional economy such as China's is often hindered by serious distortions in domestic goods and factor markets and

1

requires the use of more sophisticated methods of analysis to reveal the underlying economic values of various productive activities.

This book applies the notion of comparative advantage to the analysis of China's changing commodity patterns of trade and production in assessing the impact of economic reforms on resource allocation in the Chinese economy. It also examines the possible directions of resource reallocation in the process of economic restructuring. This study has three goals:

- to trace the evolving patterns of China's commodity trade and its performance in the world market in the context of the trade reforms over the past two decades
- to measure China's changing comparative advantage structure for the same period; in the context of the current situation of the Chinese economy, the domestic resource cost $(DRC)^1$ method is chosen to quantify China's changing structure of comparative advantage at the detailed commodity level
- to determine, once DRC is estimated for all tradable goods, whether the patterns of China's trade and production are consistent with its underlying comparative advantage, and whether, during the reform process, the patterns of trade and production have converged toward, or diverged from, comparative advantage

The results will not only shed new light on our understanding of the reforms' impact on the economy but also reveal the underlying forces that could bring about possible future changes in China's trade patterns.

OUTLINE OF THE BOOK

The book is organized in ten chapters. Chapter 2 describes the process and major reforms in China's foreign trade system since 1979 and their implications for resource allocation efficiency in the trading sector, and the analysis sets the background for the subsequent quantitative analysis.

Chapter 3 provides information about the characteristics of China's tradable goods to be analyzed in this study. It aggregates all tradable goods in China into 61 commodity groups. The empirical analysis of this study will be carried out at this level of aggregation. However, to facilitate discussion, the tradable goods will be further clustered into five broad categories according to their factor intensities: agricultural products, natural resource products, physical capital-intensive products, human capital-intensive products and unskilled labour-intensive products.

Foreign trade trends since 1950 are briefly analyzed in Chapter 4 and commodity patterns from 1978 to 1995 examined. The suitability of indices used in empirical work of this type are discussed and a synthetic measure, the net export performance ratio (NEPR), is compiled and used to quantify China's trade patterns.

A review of the Ricardo and the Heckscher–Ohlin versions of comparative advantage and their various expressions are presented in Chapter 5. The principle of comparative advantage is then linked to the measure of DRC, followed by an elaboration of the DRC method and its empirical applications. The computation of DRC requires three sets of data: the border–domestic price ratios for tradable commodities, the shadow price conversion factors for primary factors of production and the input–output coefficients. These are estimated in Chapters 6–9.

The relative price structure is estimated in Chapter 6. A direct price comparison is made for all tradables for the entire reform period, and the tradable goods price reforms and their quantitative impact on China's domestic relative price structure are examined in detail. The border–domestic price ratios for agricultural and non-agricultural products are estimated, and the chapter concludes with an overview of the impact of economic reforms, particularly price reforms, on China's domestic goods markets.

The issues concerning the shadow pricing for primary factors of production in the DRC measures are examined in Chapter 7. The shadow price is estimated for capital, skilled and unskilled labour, respectively; the results reflect the changes in the factor market's distortions.

The empirical results of the DRC for China's comparative advantage in tradable commodities in the period 1978–95 are presented and analyzed in Chapter 8. A brief outline of the data issues and estimates of Chinese input–output coefficients are presented. The DRC is computed for 61 tradable goods groups, followed by a multiple-commodity analysis of the changing structures of China's comparative advantage over this period.

Changes in the efficiency of resource allocation in Chinese trading and tradable goods-producing sectors are assessed in Chapter 9 by comparison of the NEPR measures of China's actual trade patterns with DRC estimates of its comparative advantage.

The study provides an integrated analysis of China's evolving trade and production structure and the interplay of trade and production over the recent reform period. The information and empirical results gathered in each chapter could also be used individually to reveal a specific aspect of the overall picture. For instance, the estimation in Chapter 6 of the relative price structure shows the impact of the price reform on the domestic market for tradable goods while the results of shadow prices in Chapter 7 demonstrate the impact of the reforms in China's domestic market for primary factors.

2 Reforming a Centrally Planned Foreign Trade System

China was one of the world's most isolated economies prior to 1978, trading only about 0.75 per cent of the world's total exports and imports. Since then, China's foreign trade has been growing at an average rate of 15.5 per cent a year in nominal terms, more than twice as fast as world trade. Between 1978 and 1997, the volume of total trade rose from US$21 billion to US$325 billion and the volume of exports had increased by 18.9 times in nominal terms. Significantly, more than 80 per cent of these exports are manufactured goods. By 1997, China had become the 10th largest trading nation in the world, up from the 37th less than two decades ago.

This spectacular expansion of China's domestic economy in general, and its foreign trade in particular, has largely resulted from the sweeping economic reforms adopted since the late 1970s. There have been two basic shifts in the Chinese economy. The first is the shift of resource-allocation mechanisms from central planning to market forces; the second is the shift of development strategies from an inward to an outward orientation. The conjunction of a burgeoning domestic economy and receptive conditions outside China has given foreign trade a leading role in facilitating and accelerating China's economic transition.

As in most socialist countries, China's pre-reform foreign trade was controlled by the state and transactions were conducted through a dozen national foreign trade corporations (FTCs) affiliated with the Ministry of Foreign Trade (MOFT).[1] Each FTC was assigned the task of exclusively handling the export and import of a particular category of commodities. The FTCs used their provincial subsidiaries to purchase domestic goods for export as well as to deliver imports to domestic end-users. The domestic purchasing prices of exports and the sale prices of imports were fixed and did not reflect world market prices.

Trade policies were also centrally directed through annual national plans that specified the quantities and values of each commodity to be traded as well as the foreign exchange required. Foreign exchange was in turn centrally controlled by the Bank of China. All profits were submitted to the central budget while any losses were fully subsidized by the government. Individual FTCs were thus not ultimately responsible for the financial consequences of their trade transactions and practices. The trade system was designed to

5

secure key imports with China's limited foreign exchange earnings, just as the fixed pricing served to insulate China's producers from world market fluctuations.

On the other hand, potential gains from trade in terms of social welfare or added value were largely ignored. The apparent physical benefits from trade were usually achieved at a high cost in the form of resource misallocation caused by trade specialization that ran against China's comparative advantage. Hidden costs grew as exports expanded to meet 'essential' import demands. If China was to move away from its self-reliant development strategy, this over-centralized trade system had to be thoroughly overhauled and reformed.

FOREIGN TRADE SYSTEM REFORM: AN OVERVIEW

The initial goal of China's economic reforms was modest – the development of a 'planned commodity economy' (Chinese Communist Party 1984:VII). As the benefits of market-oriented reforms have become increasingly obvious, a consensus has been gradually reached among not only leaders but also general population. At the 14th National Congress of the Chinese Communist Party (CCP) in 1992, the goal of the reforms was revised to establishing a 'socialist market economy' (Jiang Zemin 1992). This can be interpreted to mean that eventually the market will become the principal mechanism of resource allocation, while the state becomes an indirect regulator of market activities.

Foreign trade reforms have been introduced to transform the trading corporations and tradable goods producers into independent market operators and improve their efficiency. This is no easy task, however: foreign trade was at the junction of two conflicting markets types – an internal and heavily controlled market and an external, largely free, market. Given the presence of serious distortions in the domestic economy, a simple decentralization of trade decision-making procedures itself was not enough to improve resource allocation. For example, if domestic price remained distorted, the decentralized FTCs would respond only to these distorted market signals: the outcome of such reforms would be merely a replacement of one type of inefficiency by another. The success of trade reforms therefore relies not only on the measures taken in the trade sector itself but also on changes in other related areas such as domestic pricing, tax and enterprise reform. However, as the foreign trade sector deals directly with the world market, it is much better positioned than any other sector of the economy to embrace the new free and open market-oriented policies and measures.

A Chronology of the Trade Reforms since 1978

China's foreign trade reforms have evolved through four consecutive phases.

The First Phase of Reforms, 1979–84

A series of measures was introduced in 1979 to promote exports and boost foreign exchange earnings to revitalize an economy which had yet to recover from the disastrous Cultural Revolution. Major measures introduced included the decentralization of foreign trade administration, devaluation of domestic currency via the introduction of a higher internal settlement rate for exports and imports, implementation of foreign exchange retention schemes for exporters, and the establishment of Special Economic Zones (SEZs) to encourage foreign investment.

These changes meant that provincial and departmental authorities were allowed to establish their own FTCs to promote exports. The central export and import plans were simplified and direct control over trade was partially replaced by indirect measures, including a licensing system for exports and imports and 'guidance plans' which focused more on profits rather than quotas. This initial period saw a rapid increase in the number of decentralized FTCs and a substantial rise in the volume of trade.

The Second Phase of Reforms, 1985–87

In September 1984, the State Council approved a proposal by the Ministry of Foreign Economic Relations and Trade (MOFERT) on further reforms. The new package re-emphasized the importance of separating government functions from FTC management, further simplifying the central plan for exports and imports and reducing the number of commodities subject to central planning.

To tackle the problems associated with the centralized financial system in trade, an agent system was introduced into the state FTC aimed at changing FTCs from quasi-government bodies to independent operators. FTCs were to operate on a commission basis, leaving trade decisions to their clients. The new system was designed to transfer financial responsibility for foreign trade transactions from the FTCs to domestic export producers or import users.

The official exchange rate was devalued several times during this period. The gap between the official rate and the average domestic costs of exporting narrowed. The internal settlement rate was therefore brought to an end in 1985 when the official rate was raised to its level. A more important development was the establishment of foreign exchange swap markets in the SEZs and a number of major cities. For the first time, foreign exchange was allowed to flow in part through non-centrally controlled channels.

This phase also witnessed an institutionalizing of the reform measures adopted in the early years. The rigid central controls over foreign trade were replaced by an array of indirect or regulatory instruments, which enabled domestic producers to adjust faster to the changing conditions in both internal and external markets.

The Third Phase of Reforms, 1988–93

In late 1987, the government announced an even more ambitious outward-oriented development strategy for China's coastal areas, setting the stage for a new round of trade reforms. The focus of these reforms shifted from decentralizing the administrative and managerial structures of the foreign trade system to further improving the operational efficiency of FTCs.

A major policy initiative was the introduction in the beginning of 1988 of a foreign trade contract responsibility system (CRS) to all FTCs to reshape the trade-related financial relationships between the central and provincial governments, on the one hand, and between provincial governments and individual FTCs on the other. All the subsidiaries of national FTCs were transferred to the provincial authorities to become provincial FTCs while the national FTCs that remained under central government control handled only central government-related business. Three-year contracts were signed between all provincial authorities or national FTCs and the central government requiring the fulfilment of three targets: foreign exchange earnings from exports, foreign exchange submission to the central budget and cost ceilings for exports. The last target froze the central government's fiscal assistance for exports; above-target losses, if any, had to be borne solely by provincial governments or national FTCs themselves. As a reward, FTCs could retain up to 80 per cent of foreign exchange earnings from above-quota exports. To encourage FTCs to finance the increased exports by themselves, the restrictions on spending the retained foreign exchange were relaxed and the foreign exchange swap markets were further liberalized.

Fixing financial assistance through the CRS was another major step towards abolishing the trade subsidies that had burdened the central government since 1980. Fiscal subsidies for exports were finally removed in 1991 and a comprehensive export tax rebate system was introduced (Li Lanqing 1991).

The successes in export reforms were encouraging. To establish a 'managed open trading system', the export and import quota and licence systems were overhauled and made more transparent in 1993. These measures were also part of the government's efforts to re-enter the General Agreement on Tariffs and Trade (GATT) or the World Trade Organization (WTO).

The Fourth Phase of Reforms, 1994–98

A number of bold fiscal and financial reforms were introduced in 1994, of which the most important was in the foreign exchange regime. At the beginning of 1994, the two-tier exchange rate system was abolished when official and swap exchange rates were finally unified. A nationwide inter-bank exchange market was established to determine the rate and the allocation of foreign currencies. Trading companies and producers were no longer required to sell part of their foreign exchange earnings at a low price to the government. The foreign exchange retention system was also abolished. Exporters and importers could now buy and sell foreign exchange freely from the Bank of China and the Renminbi (RMB) was made virtually convertible on the current account.

The CRS was replaced by a new system emphasizing assets management similar to that of corporate structures in market economies. The aim was to induce the state FTCs to target asset preservation and growth. These reforms have been a great success – China's exports have grown dramatically in recent years, which has in turn contributed to the overall growth of the Chinese economy.

MAJOR TRADE REFORM MEASURES, 1978–97

The state monopoly over foreign trade was conducted through controlling trading corporations, tradable goods, pricing and foreign exchange. The reforms in this sector since 1979 can therefore be seen as a gradual process of lessening, shifting and finally removing the state's control.

Decentralizing Foreign Trade Corporations

While the MOFT controlled foreign trade through its 15 affiliated national FTCs (each of which specialized in a group of commodities), actual transactions were conducted by FTC provincial subsidiaries supervised by local MOFT branches. Goods to be exported were purchased from domestic producers; imports were also purchased from abroad and delivered to domestic trading companies through FTCs. Even domestic trading companies were not allowed to deal directly with foreign firms, let alone domestic producers and consumers.

In 1979, when the foreign trade administration began to be decentralized, two southern provinces, Guangdong and Fujian, were authorized to carry out their own external trade transactions. They immediately established their own trading corporations to handle local exports and imports. Other provincial governments, departments and large export enterprises were soon granted similar privileges. Decentralized FTCs were established nationwide and the exports of non-centrally controlled items shifted from national to regional FTCs.

Foreign trade was no longer administered solely by the central government. Responsibility was now divided between MOFERT-affiliated or other central department FTCs that were still controlled by the national government and linked to the central budget and provincial FTCs that were either linked to provincial budgets or financially independent. The foreign trade CRS finally delinked the subsidiaries of MOFERT's FTCs from the central government and turned them into provincial foreign trade organizations.

Table 2.1   Number of FTCs in China, 1978–94

1978	1984	1985	1986	1987	1988	1989	1991	1994
170	600	800	1 200	2 000	5 000	5 300	4 000	8 300

Sources: Wang Shouchun and Li Kanghua (1986:83); Qiu Deming (1988:14); Xu Feiqing (1988:338); Lu Yunchang (1985:109) Editorial Board of the Almanac of China's Foreign Economic Relations and Trade (1987:45, 1992/93:39); Wang Linshen (1990:34); Li Yushi (1991:99). Li Lanqing *et al.* (1995:353).

MOFERT has largely redefined itself as policy-maker, coordinator and monitor of the trade practices of all FTCs and enterprises with specially granted direct trading rights. In the early 1980s, the establishment of new FTCs was subject to approval by MOFERT. Since 1988, however, provincial governments have been authorized to establish their own FTCs without further MOFERT's approval.

These measures have led to a dramatic increase in the number of FTCs (Table 2.1). In 1978, there were only 15 national FTCs with about 170 provincial subsidiaries. By 1987, the number had increased to about 2000, among which 250 were established by enterprises (Editorial Board of Almanac of China's Foreign Economic Relations and Trade 1988:44). After the partial transfer of the authority for examining and approving FTCs from central government to the provincial authorities in 1988, nearly 2000 FTCs were approved and set up across the country in just a few months. The number of FTCs further increased to about 5300 in 1989, some of which lacked the necessary experiences and qualification for handling foreign trade. This led to the State Council's call for a rectification of existing FTCs. After three years of cleaning up, the number of FTCs was cut back to about 4000 in 1991, among which 450 were export producers (Editorial Board of Almanac of China's Foreign Economic Relations and Trade 1992–3:39). By 1994, the number of FTCs and productive enterprises with self-trading rights had increased to 8300. In addition, all 100 000 foreign-invested firms also had self-trading rights. The monopoly of the state in foreign trade has well and truly been replaced by competition among various FTCs and domestic enterprises.

The MOFERT's and other central department's FTCs handle the trade of a few commodities which remain under central government control. The trade in other commodities is left to the provincial FTCs and enterprises. Regional FTCs can now operate outside their provincial boundaries to compete with other FTCs, facilitating the development of nationwide markets for most export goods.

The over-centralization in the trade system has fundamentally changed: in 1980, national FTCs dominated about 96.4 per cent of total trade (Table 2.2).

Table 2.2   Share of foreign trade by type of corporation, 1980 and 1991 (%)

FTCs	Total trade		Exports		Imports	
	1980	*1991*	*1980*	*1991*	*1980*	*1991*
MOFERT	96.4	10.6	96.6	1.5	96.2	20.8
Departmental	1.8	5.3	2.6	2.9	1.1	8
Provincial	1.3	83.4	0.4	95.2	2.3	70.1
Other	0.4	0.7	0.4	0.4	0.4	1.1

Sources: Customs General Administration (1981 and 1992).

By 1991, this figure had dropped to 16 per cent. This shift can be seen most clearly on the export side: by 1990, exports were almost exclusively handled by decentralized FTCs and export producers.

These developments, combined with the opening up of markets for export, stimulated competition. As various FTCs had different financial backgrounds, the competition was by no means fair and 'commodity wars' were frequently reported by the media.[2] To coordinate import and export activities in such a decentralized environment, China set up six 'Chambers of Commerce' along the lines of those of Japan, South Korea and Taiwan.[3] These semi-governmental organizations are supervised by MOFERT. It is compulsory for trading companies and export producers to join one of such chambers and comply with its advice regarding the prices, quantities and destinations of exports.

In addition, one of the goals of the trade reforms to date has been to make the state FTCs financially independent. The CRS allowed the government to freeze export subsidies to FTCs at the 1987 level for three years. The FTCs in light industries such as handicrafts and clothing were chosen to undergo an experiment in financial independence, in which all export subsidies were removed and the FTCs could retain all foreign exchange revenues. These measures proved to be successful: export subsidies declined substantially. This success enabled the central government to finally abolish all export subsidies in 1991 when the existing contracts with FTCs were due to be renewed.

Although the CRS improved the performance of FTCs, it was not as successful in tightening the FTCs' budgets. When the government stopped subsidizing the FTCs, the losses of some of these companies were instead financed by state bank loans. The government accelerated the process of introducing a tax rebate system to tackle this problem; exporters were now entitled to claim a return of the domestic value-added taxes they had paid during the production of exported goods. The tax rebate is regarded as being more in line with internationally accepted practice, and by 1994, the export tax rebate had been extended to all exported goods and finally replaced fiscal subsidies altogether as the principal export promotion policy.

One of the major weaknesses of the foreign trade CRS was that it encouraged short-term behaviour, with some FTCs seeking short-term profits at the expense of long-term gains. To accelerate the corporatization of state FTCs the foreign trade CRS was replaced in 1995 by a new system, based on capital assets preservation and growth. Under this system, state FTCs are required not only to fulfil annual export targets but also to make long-term investments to ensure a healthy growth in their capital assets.

Relaxing Tradable Commodity Control

Control over tradable goods was another important component in China's pre-reform trade system under which exportable and importable commodities were grouped into ten broad categories.[4] Each FTC was confined to a specific group of commodities and no duplication could occur. Commodities were traded strictly according to the central plan, which specified in detail quantities and values of goods purchased for exporting or importing. The export plans listed about 3500 commodities (Chen Yiyun 1991:12) while the import plans covered all imported goods.

When the administration of trade was partially transferred to provincial authorities in 1979, the comprehensive and mandatory central trade plans became inadequate. A 'guidance plan' was introduced along with the existing but simplified mandatory plans. The guidance plan was not compulsory and consisted mainly of financial targets, such as profits and foreign exchange earnings. It gave FTCs a certain amount of freedom to select commodities to fulfil the compulsory targets.

In 1985, the number of exportables under the command plan was sharply reduced to 101 goods or groups of goods while the remainder was covered only by guidance plans, which implied that only foreign exchange earning targets had to be fulfilled when exporting those goods. The plan for export procurement was also abolished. The only remaining command plan target that had to be fulfilled by all FTCs was the total export value (State Council 1984b).

Similarly, the quantitative import plan was restricted to a few key imported commodities financed and distributed by the central government through plan channels at uniform domestic prices, including grains, chemical fertilizers, steel products, timber and plant equipment. The mandatory import plans for these products were assigned only to specialized national FTCs. For all other imports, the central government allocated foreign currency to end-users and allowed them to commission appropriate FTCs to import for them (State Council 1984b). In 1992, commodities imported under the command plan accounted for only 20 per cent of the value of total imports (Tong Zhiguang 1992).

As the importance of central plans diminished and trade began to be carried out increasingly by decentralized FTCs and producers themselves, it became difficult for the central government to monitor and control trade flows. A tradable goods classification scheme was then introduced to facilitate the management of a decentralized foreign trade system. This scheme was not entirely new; in the pre-reform years, exportables were divided into two categories labelled as 'central' and 'local' commodities, respectively. The central government-controlled goods were exclusively handled by national FTCs affiliated to various central departments as well as the MOFT. In 1982, this system was replaced by a multi-tier export administration structure in which exportables were classified into three categories according to their importance to the national economy and placed under the administration of different authorities. Commodities in Category I were those staple exports or major foreign exchange earners, which were exclusively managed by the national FTCs. These included crude petroleum, refined petrol products, rice, coal and cotton yarn. Commodities in Category II fell into the business field of provincial FTCs, but subject to coordination from the relevant national FTCs. This was because these goods were either facing strong competition in foreign markets – such as fresh and live agricultural products exported to Hong Kong and Macao – or subject to quota restrictions from importing countries – such as textiles, clothing, footwear and steel products. In 1982 Categories I and II accounted for 37 and 41 per cent of total exports, respectively. The remaining commodities, all classified as Category III, were allowed to be exported freely by all FTCs (State Council 1982).

The number of commodities in each category was frequently altered by MOFERT according to its perceptions of the internal and external market conditions. For instance, the number of commodities in Category I was increased from 23 in the early 1980s to 34 in 1983 when MOFERT attempted to regain control of export activities to mitigate over-competition among FTCs and the tendency to depress export prices and raise export losses. In 1984 when a new round of foreign trade reforms was announced, the number of Category I goods was reduced to 16 (State Council 1984b). In 1988, the number of Category I goods was 21 while that of Category II was 91 (Chen Yiyun 1991:4–5).

During the same period, the restricted imported goods were similarly classified into two categories. A number of importable goods, perceived as essential to the economy, were singled out and monopolized by special national FTCs, while the remainder were handled by decentralized FTCs or enterprises with self-trading rights. The number of restricted imports varied during the reform period according to the process of market liberalization, dropping from 15 in the early 1980s to seven in 1984, including only steel products, chemical fertilizers, natural rubber, timber, tobacco, synthetic fibres and grains (State Council 1984b). In 1988, tobacco was taken off and sugar and refined petrol products were added to the list of Category I imports. Category II imports composed of eight commodity groups, including wool, plywood, paper and some basic chemical materials

Table 2.3   Number of licensed import categories, 1980–95

1980	1984	1985	1986	1987	1988	1989	1990	1991	1992	1995
13	28	30	42	45	53	53	53	53	53	36

Sources: 1980: State Import and Export Commission and MFT 1980b, 1984–9 and 1995: Editorial Board of the Almanac of China's Foreign Economic Relations and Trade, various issues from 1984 to 1995–6; 1989: 1991 and 1992: Tong Zhiguang (1992:2).

(Chen Yiyun 1991). In 1989, cotton, pesticides, plastic materials for farm use and tobacco were added to the list.

As quantitative central planning for tradable commodities weakened, a number of new measures were introduced to monitor the trading activities of local government and departmental FTCs. These measures are all in the form of indirect leverages such as import and export licensing and trade-related taxes. The import and export licensing system was first introduced as a temporary measure in 1980 at the onset of trade decentralization (State Import and Export Commission 1980a) and was formalized as a state trade regulation measure in 1984 (State Council 1984a). Under the import licensing system, imports were classified as restricted or unrestricted. National and provincial FTCs were allowed to import unrestricted goods so long as those goods fell within their approved business boundaries; to import restricted goods, however, all FTCs needed to apply for licences. Unlike FTCs, licences are required for unauthorized importers no matter what goods are imported, restricted or unrestricted.

The coverage of the import licensing system used to be comprehensive. Although import plans still played a role in controlling imports, it was the licensing system that prohibited most unauthorized imports. Imports on the restricted list varied in accordance with policy priorities. From 1980 to 1992, the number of restricted importable goods increased from 13 to 53 (Table 2.3). This increase in the number of restricted imports does not necessarily mean a tightening of import restriction because, in the early years of the reform period, the main mechanism of control were the compulsory import plans, not import licences. In recent years, the number of restricted imports has declined.

By 1994, the import administration system had finally been formalized. All imports were divided into two groups: machinery[5] and non-machinery (ordinary) imports. The former was put under either quota or non-quota control. The quota-controlled imports were those deemed to affect the domestic established industries and hamper domestic economic restructuring. However, the domestic users of these goods, once approved, could choose their own FTCs for importing. The non-quota-controlled products were those regarded as needed by the domestic economy. To increase transparency, detailed lists for quota- and non-quota-controlled imports are published and revised regularly.

The import of some non-machinery or ordinary goods is also under quota control: in 1994, there were 26 commodities or groups of commodities on the list. In 1995, this was reduced to 16 (mostly staple farm products and raw industrial materials). The rights to import the 12 most important staple products were exclusively assigned to designated national or provincial FTCs. Products outside the quota lists were allowed to be imported by other FTCs. (Liu Xiandong 1994). The import of unlisted imports is less restrictive and requires only registration with the import authorities.

The export licensing system was designed to serve three objectives: to restrict the export of scarce domestic resources, to preserve favourable prices for some primary exports (especially to Hong Kong and Macao), and to manage the export quotas. The issuing of export licenses was also decentralized. MOFERT and its Special Commissioner's Offices (SCO) in various port cities were in charge of key commodities while provincial trade bureau concentrated on the remaining licensed goods. The number of commodities subject to export licensing has been reduced gradually in recent years (Table 2.4). In April 1985, there were 127 groups on the list. By February 1986, the number had increased to 235, of which about 200 items were mainly exported to Hong Kong and Macao. This was a central government response to the rush in 1985 of 'illicit exports' of some commodities to Hong Kong and Macao markets as a result of trade decentralization. By 1995, the licensed exports had been reduced to 142.

In addition to licences, quotas have also been imposed on some staple, fresh and live goods whose prices are unstable in the world market. In the late 1980s, the licensed and quota-licensed exports amounted to roughly half of total export values, or about a quarter if crude petroleum and refined petroleum products were excluded (World Bank 1988:163).

To accelerate the process of trade liberalization, MOFERT has implemented a new export administrative procedure since the beginning of 1993.

Table 2.4   Number of licensed exports under the administration of different authorities, 1985–95

	1985	*1986*	*1987*	*1988*	*1989*	*1990*	*1991*	*1992*	*1993*	*1994*	*1995*
MOFERT	15	32	30	35	22	22	29	29	22	22	21
SCO	40	42	42	56	62	75	121	121	47	47	59
Provincial	72	161	140	166	81	88	84	85	74	74	62
Total	127	235	212	257	165	185	234	235	143	143	142

Sources: Editorial Board of the Almanac of China's Foreign Economic Relations and Trade, various issues from 1984–5 to 1996–7.

The number of licensed exports was more than halved, from 258 to 114.[6] The new system further categorizes licensed exports into two types: voluntary and passive quota-controlled exports. The former are the quantitative restrictions imposed by China itself while the latter are those imposed by importing countries. Among the total of 114 licensed exported goods, 92 were subject to voluntary quota restrictions while the remaining 22 were subject to passive quota restrictions. In the voluntary quota exports, 38 were 'plan quota' products, mainly energy and natural resource goods or key industrial raw materials. 16 of these, including crude oil, refined petroleum products, cotton and coal, remained under the control of the national FTCs. The remaining 54 voluntary quota products included those in which China had a dominant position in foreign markets, such as fresh farm products exported to Hong Kong and Macao. The passive quota restrictions were imposed on to the remaining 22 licensed exportables. The products under passive quota control include such products as textiles, steel products and some chemical materials (MOFERT 1992).

Export quotas are set by the MOFERT in consultation with the relevant export and import chambers of commerce and allocated to FTCs every year. To improve efficiency and to encourage competition, an increasing number of quotas have in recent years been distributed through auction.

As shown in Table 2.4, licensed exports have dropped from 66 to 30.5 per cent of total exports in recent years (*International Business*, 5 January 1993). The government intends to gradually reduce this number and further liberalize markets for exportable goods.

Linking Tradable Commodity Prices to the World Market

Tradable goods had to be priced independently in the domestic market to maintain the pre-reform separation of internal and external markets. Most analysts seem to have overlooked this crucial feature of the centrally planned trade system.[7] The tradable goods pricing policies served to insulate the domestic economy and this, combined with the long-running policy of price stabilization, resulted in a domestic price structure substantially diverged from international market prices. This serious price divergence, in turn, reinforced the need for the separate pricing for tradable goods in order to maintain stability in the domestic economy.

Domestic Pricing for Exportables

Prior to 1979, all exports were procured by a few FTCs and the domestic procurement prices of exports could be set at the same level as the domestic producer prices unless specific requirements for modifications were attached.[8] Even those products produced exclusively for export were priced on the basis of their domestic costs and a normal profit margin (State Council 1965, 1979b). Producers were ignorant of world demand for their products.

This situation ended in 1984 with the introduction of the agent-pricing scheme which shifted financial responsibility onto individual export producers and import users. It was believed that this would facilitate the linking of domestic export prices to world markets. In 1984, however, the domestic prices for most tradables remained seriously distorted. The drastic shift of financial responsibility from FTCs to domestic producers required a shift of fiscal subsidies from FTCs to export producers as well; otherwise it would have led to a loss of export markets and a sharp fall in export revenues. A multiple exchange rate system was proposed, but it soon proved to be too complicated and impractical. In April 1985 the nationwide implementation of the export agent system was postponed and export subsidies to FTCs were resumed (Fang Xiangdong 1992:55).

This setback did not mean that export pricing reforms stopped. In fact, the process of linking domestic prices with the world market continued for two reasons. First, the domestic market for exportables was rapidly liberalized and more and more goods were priced according to supply and demand. Second, the regional FTCs were permitted, after 1985, to operate outside their geographic boundaries and could purchase export items from across the country. The resulting competition among various FTCs narrowed their profit margins and closed the gap between domestic and international prices for most uncontrolled exports. International price signals were eventually passed onto domestic producers.

Since the introduction of the foreign trade CRS in 1988, export agent pricing has expanded rapidly, and the implementation of export tax rebates further facilitated agent pricing. Exporting FTCs can now act as sole trading agents and rely on the quality and efficiency of their services to attract customers; it is estimated that by 1995, 80 per cent of exports were based on agent pricing. As domestic markets are liberalized, exportable goods no longer need a separate pricing policy.

Domestic Pricing of Imported Goods

China adopted a uniform import pricing policy in 1964 to insulate its domestic economy (State Council 1963). The price of an imported good was, in principle, required to be pegged to the price of a comparable domestically produced good. Commodities not available domestically were marked up by a margin after the c.i.f. price was converted into domestic currency at the official exchange rate. The mark-up rate was equal to the difference between the official exchange rate and the average cost of earning foreign exchange through exports. If most exports were unprofitable at the official exchange rate, this practice could raise the under-valued foreign exchange to a level sufficient to cover the export costs and balance the budget. The mark-up prices for imported capital goods were also set at a level high enough to protect domestic industries. It was estimated that, between 1964 and 1980,

Table 2.5   Number of imported goods subject to domestic comparable pricing and
their shares in total import value, 1978–91

	No. of imports	*Import share* (%)
1978	..	80
1983	..	70
1984	..	57
1985	..	30
1986	31	..
1987	31	..
1988	28	20
1989	14	..
1990	8	..
1991	7	10

Sources: Wang Zhengzhi and Qiao Rongzhang (1988:202); Hu Bangding *et al.*
(1989:226, 230) Foreign Affair Prices Department (SACP) and Research Team
for Foreign Affair Prices at the People's University of China (1991:5).

imports priced through reference to comparable domestic commodities
accounted for 80 per cent of total import values while those priced by the
mark-up method accounted for 20 per cent (Hu Bangding *et al.* 1989:226).

Reforms in import pricing after the early 1980s were characterized by a
gradual reduction in the use of domestic comparable pricing and the
expansion of agent pricing. Import pricing reforms were carried out in two
phases after the early 1980s. The first phase was from 1981 to 1984, during
which an internal settlement exchange rate was introduced in merchandise
trade. As the internal rate was set at the level above the average cost of
earning foreign exchange through exports, the import costs, converted at the
internal rate, should have been on average sufficient to cover export costs.
The government was hence eager to replace mark-up pricing with agent
pricing to pass on the import costs to domestic users. The mark-up pricing
practice was reduced to a small number of imported goods, particularly
mechanical and electrical equipment and instruments from socialist
countries.[9] The use of comparable pricing was restricted only to the planned
imports paid for from the central government's foreign currency funds. All
remaining imports were subject to agent pricing. The central government was
keen to transfer financial responsibility for decentralized imports to local
authorities; as the importance of comparable domestic pricing diminished,
agent pricing was expanded and had become the principal import pricing
policy by 1984 (State Council 1984b).

The second phase of import pricing reforms began with the abolition of
mark-up pricing in 1985 after the internal settlement rate was phased out
(State Administration of Commodity Price 1985). It followed that all

imported goods were required to be, in principle, priced at their c.i.f. costs, converted at the official exchange rate, plus agent fees. Since then, the number of imports subject to comparable domestic pricing has fallen consistently (Table 2.5). In 1991, they included only seven commodity groups such as grains and chemical fertilizers, accounting for about 10 per cent of the value of total imports. Later, the prices of even this group of imports were no longer rigidly fixed at the uniform domestic plan price of comparable commodities. Instead, the planned imports were often transferred to end users at so-called 'import transfer prices' (*Jinkou bojiao jia*) which were usually higher than uniform domestic plan prices and lower than domestic market prices. These transfer prices were subject to variation should substantial changes occur in the world market.

These price reforms are aimed at the eventual abolition of fiscal subsidies to the state FTCs; this objective cannot be accomplished if domestic prices remain distorted and do not reflect the scarcity of resources. Import subsidies were a heavy burden to the government in the first half of the 1980s. This was because, despite a dramatic increase in the import costs resulting from domestic currency devaluation, a large proportion of imports were still distributed at the fixed plan prices to domestic users. This situation did not change until the mid-1980s when the agent pricing for imports and a two-tier price system were introduced for most intermediate inputs and producer goods, enabling the government to transfer import costs to domestic users. By 1991 centrally controlled imports (funded by the central government's foreign exchange funds) accounted for less than 30 per cent of total import value. Only a third of them were distributed on the basis of domestic comparable prices. One important item in this group of imports was grains, which remained supplied to urban residents at subsidized prices until 1993. Since the urban food subsidies began to be removed in 1993, the remaining import subsidies have declined even further.

The situation is more complicated for exports. In the pre-reform system, exports were hampered by an over-valued domestic currency and irrationally fixed domestic prices. The usual way in which the government could achieve its foreign exchange earning targets through exports without disturbing domestic supplies was to subsidize FTCs to export whatever goods were exportable. In this arrangement, FTCs acted simply as government accounting units; the extent to which exports could expand was thus determined only by the central government's capacity to subsidize.

As already discussed, an important development in ending export subsidies was the gradual expansion of an export tax rebate scheme. The implementation of this tax rebate was seen as an important measure to make China's foreign trade practices compatible with the existing international conventions. However, implementation was complicated by China's domestic taxation system which was based on a differential turnover tax for most exportable goods. The tax levy on final goods depended on the size of the turnover, and it was difficult and time-consuming to figure out precisely what percentage of taxes were paid by looking at the price of an exported product. A comprehensive export tax rebate scheme was finally introduced in 1991 as a part of the new foreign trade reform package and coincided with the implementation of a value-added tax, both of which enabled the government to finally abolish all direct fiscal subsidies to FTCs. As the taxes are rebated directly to export producers, the FTCs can now operate as genuine trading agents.

The use of agent pricing has also significantly enhanced the role of customs tariffs in regulating the trade flows. During the pre-reform years, customs tariffs had little impact on domestic prices because almost all import prices were directly pegged to domestic prices; the only role of customs tariffs was to generate revenues. This role was so obvious that, to simplify the procedure of collecting and submitting tariff revenues, the General Customs Administration was reduced to a divisional office under the MOFT from 1964 to 1979. Tariff revenues were integrated into the Ministry's account and handed over as part of total trade income to the central budget.

It was not until 1980 that the General Customs Administration was restored as an independent state body. Since then, its main functions have been redefined as to examine and release traded goods upon verification of the required documents, such as import and export licences and quotas and commodity inspection certificates. In the 1980s when domestic markets remained distorted, customs tariffs were used to curb undesired exports or imports induced largely by the price disparities between domestic and international markets. Temporary surcharges, such as the 'regulatory tariff' on specified exports or imports, were implemented regularly. The extension of agent pricing has given the Customs additional leverage to influence trade flows. Agent pricing requires import users to pay their own tariffs or other charges for the goods they import; the import tariffs thus become an important component of the domestic prices, which must be taken into consideration by domestic firms.

Enhancing the role of the Customs is also important for China's success in shifting its trade controls from quantity- to value-based instruments. Tariffs are more transparent than quantitative measures and therefore compatible with international standards. The government has recognized the importance of the Customs and has increasingly used tariffs as a major trade policy instrument. Such recognition, in recent years, has been reflected in its intensive efforts to rejoin the GATT or the WTO. As a major step towards full membership, China has been liberalizing its trade system by unilaterally reducing nominal tariff rates. During the pre-reform period, the nominal tariff rates were as high as 52.9 per cent.[10] Since 1980, when the General Customs Administration was restored, China reduced its import tariff rates for many commodities. In 1985, when a new customs regulation was passed by the National People's Congress, the Export and Import Tariff Schedule was thoroughly amended, and the nominal tariff rates were reduced in many categories.

Immediately after this, the average nominal tariff rate for imports was lowered to 38.4 per cent. After submitting its application for the GATT membership in 1986, China accelerated the process of domestic market liberalization. From March 1986 to 1991, tariffs were cut in 83 commodity lines of the tariff schedule. In 1992, China converted its customs commodity classification to the Harmonized Commodity Description and Coding System (HCDCS) to be more in line with GATT standards. In the new schedule, the tariff rates for 225 items were reduced. By the end of 1992, the import tariff rates for another 3371 import categories had been reduced; this covered 53.6 per cent of total tariff lines in the tariff schedule. The average nominal tariff rate was 39.9 per cent.[11] The trade-weighted average of nominal tariff protection was also reduced by 7.3 per cent. In 1993, the tariff rates for 2898 items in the tariff schedule were reduced; this lowered the average tariff rate to 36.4 per cent and the trade-weighted average rate of import tariffs to between 22.5 per cent (Ju and Wu 1993; Editorial Board 1993) and 28 per cent (Chen *et al.* 1993).

Despite the repeated reductions in tariff barriers, however, the average nominal tariff rate was still too high to justify a full GATT membership for China. Since the establishment of the GATT 50 years ago, after seven rounds of tariff negotiations, the average rate of import tariffs in GATT's developed country members has been reduced from 36 to about 5 per cent. The average tariff protection in the developing country members is about 13 per cent (Ju and Wu 1993). With the successful completion of the Uruguay Round, the tariff rates of the GATT/WTO member countries are expected to fall even further. To gain membership, China needed to contemplate even more drastic cuts in its import tariffs; the target would be to reduce the average tariff rate to at least 13 per cent.

The Chinese government expressed its readiness to meet this requirement. During its negotiation with the GATT contract parties in September 1994, the government made the commitment to a target tariff rate of 19.2 per cent and abolition of two-thirds of the existing import licences in three years (a decline of 56.9 per cent from 1993). This promise was fulfilled by two rounds of large-scale tariff reductions in the following three years. In April 1996, the tariff rates for 4944 items on the import tariff schedule were reduced significantly, which lowered the average tariff rate from 36.4 per cent to 23.2 per cent. The trade-weighted rate was estimated to have been reduced to 18 per cent.[12] A second round of tariff cuts was implemented in October 1997. This time, the tariff rates for 4874 out of a total 6633 items on the current tariff schedule were reduced, which brought down the average import tariff rate to 17 per cent, an average rate of reduction of 26 per cent.[13] These two large-scale tariff cuts more than halved China's average tariff rate in less than two years. It is expected that, as the nominal tariff protection rates are lowered, the quantitative restrictions on exports and imports will soon be reduced and removed.

It should be pointed out, however, that the nominal tariff rates might not accurately reflect the true openness of the Chinese economy. Although China still has relatively high nominal tariff rates for many tradable goods, the actual import tariffs, relative to total imports, have declined constantly in recent years. In 1985, the ratio of tariffs to imports was 16.3 per cent while, in 1995, it dropped to 2.6 per cent (State Statistical Bureau 1997). If illegal imports were included, the ratio could be even lower. This implies that the competition between domestic and foreign firms in China's domestic markets may actually be much fiercer than the nominal tariff rates suggest. The realignment of domestic prices with the world prices may have been more rapid than commonly believed.

Building a Foreign Exchange Market

The last important trade control instrument in China's traditional trade system was foreign exchange controls. In a market environment, the allocation and the rate of foreign exchange are inter-related: the market-determined rate directs the allocation of foreign exchange among its potential users. In a centrally planned economy, however, this link is broken: the two processes are separately determined by the planners. The aim of reforming China's foreign exchange system was therefore to rebuild the missing links. Reform in the foreign exchange system has been carried out on two fronts. First, a decentralized exchange reallocation system was created through the introduction of a foreign exchange retention scheme and a secondary market for retained foreign exchange. Second, the domestic currency was gradually devalued to narrow the gap between the official exchange rate and the secondary market rate. The final goal of the reform is to make the domestic currency, the Renminbi (RMB), internationally convertible.

Foreign Exchange Allocation

Foreign exchange control played a central part in China's old trade system. As the RMB was over-valued and the demand for imports was insatiable, the control over the allocation of foreign exchange had to be rigid. All foreign exchange-related transactions were conducted under the close supervision of the State Administration of Exchange Control. Earning and using foreign exchange were carefully separated. Domestic exporters were required to put all their foreign exchange earnings in the Bank of China while domestic importers had to comply with foreign exchange quotas in the import plans. The foreign exchange quota entitled its user to buy a certain amount of foreign currency from the Bank of China for an approved transaction. The holding of convertible foreign currencies by domestic firms was strictly forbidden.

The first change in this system occurred in 1979 with the introduction of a foreign exchange retention scheme. Departmental authorities, provincial governments, FTCs and export producers were henceforth entitled to retain a portion of the foreign exchange earnings from their exports, except for about 10 centrally controlled exports (State Council 1979b). The retained foreign exchange could be used to upgrade export production facilities or buy imports for local use.

In 1979, the retained exchange was set on the basis of FTC's above-quota export procurements in the previous year (State Council 1979b). It was modified in 1982 to be based on actual foreign exchange earnings in order to encourage exports and not export procurements (State Council 1982). The retention rate was later used by the government to pursue diverse objectives such as targeting certain industries or promoting regional development. For instance, to encourage machinery exports in the early 1980s, the retained foreign exchange earnings from machinery exports were set at 50 per cent (State Council 1982). For much of the 1980s, foreign exchange retention promoted development in the coastal areas in general, and the SEZs in Guangdong and Fujian provinces in particular. This bias stimulated unequal competition for exportable goods between the coastal and inland FTCs. In response to this problem, a new retention scheme set along industry lines or commodity groups instead of geographic locations was introduced in 1991. Differential retention rates were used to improve the commodity pattern of exports.

Foreign exchange retention rates were increased gradually to give more autonomy to FTCs and export producers. In the early 1980s, the retention rate was about 10 per cent of the annual foreign exchange earnings (State Council 1982). In 1985, it rose to 25 per cent for uncontrolled exportables (State Council 1985b). In 1988, the amount of foreign exchange submitted to the central budget was fixed by the foreign trade contract between the central and provincial governments. The above-target foreign exchange earnings could be shared by the central and local governments at a ratio of 2:8 (Wang Linshen 1990:44). After the removal of export subsidies in 1991, the favourable treatment for coastal areas in the retention system was terminated. The general retention rate was increased to 80 per cent for most exportable goods. Of the retained foreign exchange, 20 per cent could be shared equally between the local authorities and export producers while the remaining 60 per cent was retained by trading companies. 20 per cent of exchange earnings had to be submitted to the central government at the official exchange rate; the central government also had the right to purchase another 20 per cent of retained foreign exchange from FTCs at the swap market rate if needed (Zhang Guanghua 1991:40).

The rapid expansion of retained foreign exchange created a new category in China's foreign exchange system. Unlike the centrally controlled foreign exchange, the disposal of the retained foreign exchange was normally at the discretion of its holders. According to the regulations, the retained foreign exchange was to be used to buy new technologies or key equipment for improving export production. However, these self-funded imports were subject to various restrictions. The restrictions on the use of retained exchange were even tighter when serious trade deficits occurred–in 1985, for instance, after a sharp fall in the foreign exchange reserves, compulsory quotas were imposed on all holders of retained foreign exchange to curtail their self-funded imports (State Council 1985b). These quotas remained in place until 1988.

The other option for the holders of retained foreign exchange was to sell it to the bank. However, as the domestic currency was over-valued, to sell foreign exchange at the official rate was equivalent to paying an extra tax; there was little incentive for export producers and trading companies to follow that course. To encourage more effective use of retained foreign exchange, therefore, the Bank of China introduced a service for FTCs and export producers to swap their foreign exchange quotas.[14] The service was first provided on an experimental basis in October 1980 in 12 large and medium-sized cities (State Administration of Exchange Control and the Bank of China 1980). It was soon expanded to all the major provincial capitals. For the first time, the domestic firms and FTCs could sell their excess foreign exchange quotas to those in need at a slightly flexible rate. The ceiling rate was first set at 10 per cent above the official rate (State Administration of Exchange Control and the Bank of China 1980, and 1981). This represented a breakthrough in the highly centralized exchange allocation system and marked the beginning of a move toward the establishment of a fully functioning foreign exchange market. During the early period from 1980 to 1985, however, the role of the exchange swap service was limited by various restrictions such as entry permits, administrative approval of transactions and a low ceiling rate. Most importantly, it was limited by the small size of retained foreign exchange.

The first real functioning exchange market emerged in December 1985 when the Shenzhen SEZ set up a Foreign Exchange Swap Centre (FESC) as an experiment. In the centre, administrative restrictions were largely relaxed so that sellers and buyers could negotiate directly. Three other SEZs soon followed suit. Initially, there was a ceiling rate of 5 yuan per US dollar or 2.1 yuan above the official rate but this was lifted in November 1986.

Encouraged by the Shenzhen experiment, the three largest cities set up their own FESCs: Shanghai and Beijing in November 1986 and Tianjing in March 1987 (Sun Shanqing 1989:199). Toward the end of 1988, 20 centres were operating nationwide. The rapid expansion in the number of FESCs across the country was also inspired by the relaxation in 1986 of restrictions on foreign-invested firm's participation in foreign exchange trading (Editorial Board of ACFERT 1987:97). Foreign-invested firms were actually encouraged to trade in FESCs to balance their own foreign exchange accounts. By the end of 1992, over 100 FESCs were in operation; each province, autonomous region and centrally administered city had at least one centre of its own.

As the number of participants increased, the FESCs became an important player in the allocation of foreign exchange rates. The volume of foreign exchange traded through FESCs rose rapidly after 1986. In 1987, the volume of FESCs trading across the country was US$4.7 billion, approximately 12 per cent of total import value or 11 per cent of export earnings. In 1988, the foreign exchange retention rate was increased and firms were permitted to dispose freely of their retained foreign exchange under the foreign trade CRS. To encourage trade, the ceiling rate was also lifted in all FESCs. These reforms led to a boom in the trading of retained foreign exchange in FESCs; the volume of foreign exchange traded jumped from US$6.25 billion in 1988 to US$25.1 billion in 1992. It accounted for 31 per cent of import expenditures and 30 per cent of export revenues in that year (Table 2.6). To curtail black market trading, individual residents were also allowed to sell and, to some extent, buy foreign currencies through swap centres in December 1991. It was reported that, in 1992, US$ 0.19 and 0.16 billion was sold and bought by residents through swap centres (*People's Daily* [overseas edition], 16 February 1993). By the end of 1993, on the eve of exchange rate unification, a large proportion of China's foreign exchange had already been traded at market rates.

Foreign Exchange Rates

Changes in the domestic currency rates of foreign exchange have a strong impact on the relative price of tradable goods and therefore on the current account balance. In China's traditional centrally planned system, however, the current account balance was largely maintained through centralized trade plans rather than exchange rate adjustments. This control mechanism allowed the government to maintain an over-valued domestic currency for a prolonged period of time.

Table 2.6   Transactions of foreign exchange in the Foreign Exchange Swap Centres, 1987–92

| | Volume | As % of | |
	(*US$ billion*)	*Exports*	*Imports*
1987	4.7	11.9	10.8
1988	6.3	13.2	11.3
1989	8.5	16.4	14.6
1990	13.1	21.4	25.0
1991	20.5	28.5	32.1
1992	25.1	29.5	31.1

Sources: Economic Daily (2 February, 1992), International Monetary Fund (1992), *People's Daily* [overseas edition] (10 January 1992; 16 February 1993).

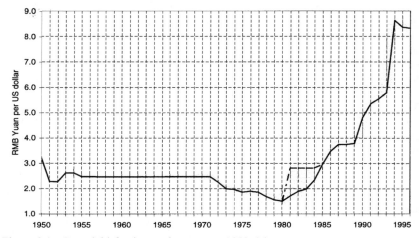

Figure 2.1   Renminbi foreign exchange rate, 1950–96

Sources: Statistical Department of Trade and Materials (SSB) (1990:513); State
Statistical Bureau (1997:588)

The official exchange rate was virtually fixed at RMB 2.46 yuan per US
dollar prior to the 1970s. In the 1970s, the domestic currency gradually
appreciated with worldwide inflation and the depreciation of the US dollar.
By the time China began economic reforms in the late 1970s, the RMB was at
its highest value since 1949 (Figure 2.1), seriously undermining China's
export efforts. After 1980 the government repeatedly devalued the RMB
against all major foreign currencies in an attempt to bring the over-valued
domestic currency down to a more realistic level. Three major rounds of the
RMB devaluation can be identified between 1980 and 1993.

The first round of devaluation began in 1980 with the introduction of an
internal settlement rate of 2.8 yuan per US dollar, which marked the
beginning of a four-year dual exchange rate system. The internal settlement
rate was determined on the basis of the average cost of earning foreign
exchange through exports in 1979 plus a 15 per cent margin. It was applicable
to merchandise trade only; the official exchange rate remained applicable to
all non-merchandise trade transactions. At the same time as the internal
settlement rate was instituted, the RMB began to be gradually devalued. The
official exchange rate had reached 2.8 yuan per US dollar by the end of 1984;
the internal settlement rate was thus made redundant and abolished in the
early 1985.

The second round of devaluation occurred between 1985 and 1986. The
RMB yuan – US dollar exchange rate slipped from 2.8 to 3.2 between
January 1985 and July 1986. In July 1986 the government announced a major
RMB devaluation by 15.8 per cent from 3.2 to 3.7 yuan per US dollar. It then
stabilized at 3.72 yuan through 1987 and 1988 (Table 2.7).

Table 2.7   Major devaluation of the Renminbi, 1981–92 (RMB yuan per US dollar)

Date	%	From	To
1 Jan. 1981	86.67	1.50	2.80
21 Aug. 1985	3.57	2.80	2.90
3 Oct. 1985	3.45	2.90	3.00
23 Oct. 1985	3.33	3.00	3.10
30 Oct. 1985	3.23	3.10	3.20
5 Jul. 1986	15.8	3.20	3.70
16 Dec. 1989	21.2	3.72	4.72
17 Nov. 1990	9.57	4.72	5.22
Apr. 1991–Mar. 1992	9.58	5.22	5.72

Sources: Wu Nianlu and Chen Quangeng (1987); Zhou Xiaochuan and Yang Zhigang (1996).

The stabilization of the official exchange rate combined with rising inflation led to a real appreciation of the yuan in 1987 and 1988. The third wave of devaluation began at the end of 1989 when the value of the RMB fell by 21.2 per cent against all other currencies, to 4.71 yuan per US dollar; 10 months later, on 17 November 1990, it was further reduced by 9.57 per cent to 5.22 yuan. Between April 1991 and March 1992, the RMB was drifted further down by another 9.58 per cent to reach 5.72 yuan per US dollar and then stayed there until the 1994 unification of the dual exchange rates.

In the most years of the reform period, Chinese foreign exchange rates were pegged to a basket of foreign currencies among which the US dollar was dominant. After 10 years of consistent devaluation, the problem of RMB over-valuation largely eased. In April 1991, the government began to adopt a more flexible policy to allow the RMB exchange rate to be adjusted more frequently at a smaller scale. The adjustments were mainly based on developments in the balance of payments, in external and internal foreign currency markets and domestic costs of exports. By March 1992, the official exchange rate was gradually depreciated to 5.73 yuan per US dollar. The variations in the average annual RMB rate of the US dollar are shown in Table 2.8.

At the same time as the RMB was being devalued, the gap between the official exchange rate and the secondary market rate in the FESCs narrowed. In the first half of the 1980s, the swap rate was regulated by the Bank of China to vary within a range of 10 per cent higher than the internal settlement or official rate. This implied a ceiling price of 3.08 yuan per US dollar for 1981–4 and 3.23 yuan in 1985. After the FESCs were established in 1986, the ceiling price restrictions eased. However, the regulation of the FESCs was in the hands of local authorities and foreign exchange transactions were localized and mainly made between local enterprises. There had been large

Table 2.8   China's foreign exchange rates, 1978–95 (RMB yuan per US dollar)[a]

Year	Official	FESC[b]	FESC/Official
1978	1.68	-	-
1979	1.55	n.a	n.a
1980	1.50	n.a	n.a
1981	1.71	3.08	1.10
1982	1.89	3.08	1.10
1983	1.98	3.08	1.10
1984	2.33	3.08	1.10
1985	2.94	3.23	1.10
1986	3.45	5.00	1.45
1987	3.72	5.70	1.53
1988	3.72	6.32	1.70
1989	3.77	6.38	1.69
1990	4.78	5.80	1.21
1991	5.32	5.90	1.11
1992	5.51	6.80	1.19
1993	5.76	8.50	1.48
1994	8.61	-	-
1995	8.35	-	-

Notes
[a] An internal settlement rate of 2.8 yuan per US dollar was used for merchandise trade in 1981–4.
[b] FESC = Foreign Exchange Swap Centre.
Sources: Official and internal settlement rates: International Monetary Fund, (1996), FESC rates: 1981–5: Economic Daily, (2 February, 1992), Wang Zhengzhi and Qiao Rongzhang (1988: 197); 1986: Rate in Shenzhen, Sun Shangqing (1989:197); 1987: Average rate of Shenzhen and Shanghai centres, Sun Shangqing (1989:198–9); 1988: Average rate of five major municipal swap centres from May to December, Editorial Board of the Almanac of China's Finance and Banking (1989:148); 1989–92 Yang Fan, (1993:3).

disparities and fluctuations in the swap rates between these local markets; for instance, in September 1987 the swap rate was 6.1 yuan per US dollar in Shenzhen and about 5.0–5.4 yuan in Shanghai. Cross-regional transactions were not permitted until 1991. The government tried to link regional FESCs into a nationwide exchange market in order to monitor the general trend of foreign exchange rate variations because the swap rates had become the most valuable reference for the government to judge its own official exchange rate policy.

Despite the diversity of regional swap rates, a general trend can nonetheless be identified. In 1988, when the ceiling rate was lifted, the swap rate surged to above 6.32 yuan per US dollar, 70 per cent higher than the official rate. By 1991, after the RMB was further devalued and more retained foreign exchange entered the FESCs, the swap rate dropped to below 6.0

yuan per US dollar–less than 10 per cent higher than the official rate. This indicates that the successive devaluations since 1980, combined with the opening up of foreign exchange markets, had substantially eased the problem of the over-valued RMB. The convergence between the two exchange rates also paved the way for further reforms in the exchange rate system.

In 1992, China emerged from three years of austerity measures and the economy rebounded strongly after Deng Xiaoping's much publicized tour to the south. From mid-1992, the swap rates in most FESCs started to rise and the narrowed gap between the swap and official rates began widening again. This rise in swap rates was driven by the rapid increase in the demand for foreign currencies for imports. It was also fuelled by renewed inflation expectations brought about by the extraordinarily high growth rate. By February 1993 the swap rates had climbed to 9 yuan per US dollar, 40 per cent higher than the official rate of 5.72. The government was forced to act by imposing a ceiling rate of 8 yuan with the hope of controlling the falling value of the RMB; this measure was unsuccessful because it soon dried out the trading in the FESCs and drove many potential traders to the black market. The ceiling rate was lifted in June, and within a few weeks, the swap rates had jumped to above 10 yuan per US dollar. This time the central bank, the People's Bank of China, intervened by selling about US$20 million in the Shanghai Swap Centre and successfully engineered the yuan's dramatic recovery nationwide. This was the first time that China's central bank had used policy-driven sales to rescue the RMB. The swap rate stabilized at about 8 yuan per US dollar, a rise of 22 per cent from its mid-June low of 10.92 yuan per US dollar (*Asian Wall Street Journal*, 12 July 1993).

The fluctuation of the yuan in late 1992 and early 1993 was a result of many factors: the relaxation of import controls and reduction of import quotas and tariffs, speculation over further devaluation of the RMB owing to the GATT negotiations, and unpredictably rapid expansion of domestic demand. However, it should be pointed out that the volatile yuan also reflected the defects of a partially reformed foreign exchange system. With a yearly turnover of about half of the nation's foreign exchange earnings, the FESCs had already become a major player in China's foreign exchange allocation system. However, the old quota control mechanisms remaining in place enabled enterprises to hold large amounts of foreign currencies at very low cost and encouraged speculative activities. It was urgent and also feasible for China to accelerate foreign exchange reform.

This is what occurred in 1994 when the dual exchange rates were unified. The swap markets were replaced by a nationwide inter-bank foreign exchange market which determined the official exchange rate and the foreign exchange retention system was abolished. Foreign exchange earnings could now be fully retained by FTCs or export producers. The planned allocation of foreign exchange was also abolished; the FTCs and domestic enterprises could buy and sell foreign currencies at the official rate in the Bank of China.

The restrictions on selling and buying foreign exchange for export and import trade were largely lifted. In July 1996, foreign-invested firms were also included in this new foreign exchange regime. The requirement for foreign-invested firms to balance their own foreign exchange account became virtually invalid, and by the end of 1996, China had formally completed the transition to the convertibility of the RMB on the current account.

The foreign exchange reform has been a success in the sense that it facilitates exports and foreign direct investment. Since 1994, the RMB exchange rate has been rather stable and even slightly appreciated. This is also attributable to a constant increase in the trade surplus and foreign capital inflows, indicates a considerable easing of the pressure of currency overvaluation and paves the way to full RMB convertibility.

IMPACT OF TRADE REFORMS

How successful have China's foreign trade-related reforms been? It is evident that a significant shift from the old to a new system has taken place in all the major areas of China's foreign trade:

• State monopoly of foreign trade has been abolished and replaced by competition among a large number of decentralized FTCs and enterprises.
• Direct control through the central plan on exports and imports has been replaced by a number of administrative and indirect regulatory measures, including licensing, taxation and tariffs.
• Domestic prices of tradable commodities have increasingly been determined by market forces and gradually linked to the world market. World market signals have begun to impact upon the domestic producers and consumers.
• The foreign exchange regime has completed its transition from rigid centralization to the partial convertibility of the RMB on the current account.

Although these changes indicate a significant departure of foreign trade management from central planning to a free and open market they still fall short of the requirements for a fully fledged market economy. For example, the intricate financial relationship between the decentralized state FTCs and the central or local governments have not yet been clearly defined; this has been the basic cause of the excessive competition frequently seen in domestic markets for certain exportable commodities. Such problems will undoubtedly impair the functioning of the newly established market. However, it seems unlikely that these problems will be severe enough to preclude the newly emerging market from exerting its influence. Moreover, China's economic reforms are far from over; many problems may disappear as the reforms proceed.

The impact of trade reforms can be seen in the tremendous growth of China's trade over the past two decades. As mentioned at the beginning of this chapter, the trade reforms have successfully opened the Chinese economy and transformed it into one of the world's largest trading nations. The emergence of domestic markets for tradable goods and the decentralization of trading companies has led to a boom in foreign trade activities at all levels.

It is not immediately clear, however, whether such a rapid expansion of trade has been associated with an improvement in the efficiency of foreign trade as well as in the tradable goods-producing industries. Trade theory suggests that a country's commodity trade and production should be conducted according to its comparative advantage if the potential gains from trade are to be fully exploited. To answer this question, we need to investigate the impact of the economic reforms on China's trade patterns and its underlying comparative advantage structure – and, more importantly, to what extent China's trade has been following its underlying comparative advantage over the reform period. The remainder of this book will comprehensively investigate these important issues.

3 Factor Intensity of Chinese Tradable Commodities

The analysis of trade patterns and comparative advantage should be conducted at a commodity level. In this chapter, the defined commodities or groups of commodities are classified into different categories according to their factor intensities. Alternative methods of estimating factor intensity are discussed in the context of their applicability to the Chinese economy; the purpose of this classification is to indicate the factor contents of Chinese tradable commodities and so facilitate the following discussion of China's trade patterns and comparative advantage.

AGGREGATION OF TRADABLE COMMODITIES AND THEIR DESCRIPTION

An empirical analysis of comparative advantage should be disaggregated at industry or commodity levels if it is to be used for policy purposes. However, a balance needs to be reached between comprehensiveness and manageability when the level of disaggregation for tradable commodities is considered. The number of commodities must be large enough to allow a meaningful portrait of China's trade patterns and comparative advantage structure, but it has to be confined within a manageable scale so that the data requirements will not go beyond what is available.

In this study, we group China's tradable commodities into 61 categories. They include 13 agricultural products, 6 industrial primary commodities and 42 manufactured product groups. The definitions of the commodities are largely in accordance with the Chinese Industrial Classification of the National Economy (1985) because the data used in the study are drawn largely from Chinese sources. The descriptions and the contents of individual groups are provided in Table 3.1. The concordance between the 61 commodities and the corresponding items in the Chinese Industrial Classification of the National Economy are in Table 3A.1 in the Appendix (p.47).

COMMODITY CLASSIFICATION CRITERIA

The way in which commodities are classified depends on the objective of a study. To relate the patterns of trade and production to comparative

Table 3.1   Tradable goods classification and description

Code	Description	Content
	Agricultural products (13)	
1.	Paddy rice	
2.	Wheat	
3.	Other grains	Maize, sorghum, millet, etc.
4.	Oil-bearing crops	Groundnuts, rape seed, sunflower seed, etc.
5.	Cotton	
6.	Other industrial crops	Hemp, jute, sugarcane and beet, silkworm cocoon, tobacco leaf, tea, etc.
7.	Vegetables	
8.	Fruits	Fresh and dried
9.	Forest products	Lacquer, tung oil, walnuts, natural rubber, etc.
10.	Wool and hides	
11.	Meat, eggs and milk	Inc. poultry, eggs, dairy products
12.	Fish	Freshwater and sea
13.	Other agricultural products	Sideline products, e.g. medicinal herbs
	Minerals and timber (6)	
14.	Coal	
15.	Crude petroleum	Inc. natural gas
16.	Ferrous minerals	
17.	Non-ferrous minerals	
18.	Non-metallic minerals	
19.	Timber	Inc. bamboo
	Manufactured products (42)	
20.	Sugar, tobacco and alcohol	
21.	Other processed food	
22.	Cotton textiles	
23.	Wool textiles	
24.	Hemp textiles	
25.	Silk textiles	
26.	Knitted goods	
27.	Other textiles	Inc. textile raw material preliminary treatment
28.	Clothing and leather goods	
29.	Furniture	Inc. plywood, etc.
30.	Paper	Inc. paperboard, etc.
31.	Cultural and sporting goods	Inc. articles for education, sports, arts and crafts
32.	Petroleum products	Gasoline, kerosene, diesel, etc.
33.	Coal products	Inc. coke and carbonized products
34.	Inorganic chemicals	Inorganic acids, soda, etc.
35.	Chemical fertilizers	Inc. agricultural chemicals
36.	Organic chemicals	Inc. dye, paint, etc.
37.	Household chemicals	
38.	Other chemicals	Plastic and synthetic materials
39.	Medicines	

Table 3.1   (Continued)

Code	Description	Content
40.	Chemical fibres	
41.	Rubber manufactures	
42.	Plastic articles	
43.	Cement	
44.	Glass	
45.	Ceramic products	Inc. refractory materials
46.	Other building materials	
47.	Iron	Inc. iron alloy
48.	Steel	
49.	Non-ferrous metals	
50.	Metal products	Inc. structures, wire, cutlery, etc.
51.	Agricultural machinery	
52.	Industrial equipment	Machine tools, general and special equipment
53.	Power station equipment	Inc. generators, boilers, etc.
54.	Household mechanical and electrical goods	Bicycles, sewing machines, refrigerators, watches, washing machines, etc.
55.	Railway equipment	
56.	Motor vehicles	
57.	Ships	
58.	Other transport equipment	Inc. aircraft, motorcycles, etc.
59.	Other engineering products	Electric machinery, instruments, etc.
60.	Electronic products	Inc. equipment and parts
61.	Household electronics	TV sets, videos, radio, etc.

Note: Contents are given only for those commodity groups whose descriptions are not self-evident.

advantage, the relative intensity of primary factors used in production–the factor intensity–should be identified.

In trade theory, commodities are usually distinguished in terms of the relative intensities of primary factors used in their production. This classification is based on the Heckscher–Ohlin theorem. In a simple Heckscher–Ohlin model with two factors of production, labour and capital, commodities are conveniently divided as labour- and capital-intensive, respectively. As agricultural and natural-resource goods comprise an important part of international trade, natural resources have since the 1970s been widely incorporated as an additional factor in the theoretical and empirical studies of international trade (Krueger 1977).

The present classification of tradable goods is based on a three-factor trade model–that is, natural resources, capital and labour. The natural resource-intensive goods are primary products and can be further divided into two groups: agricultural products and other natural resource goods (minerals and timber). Capital- and labour-intensive goods are manufactured goods. Capital-intensive goods can be divided into physical and human capital-intensive products. The latter may also be called technology- or skilled labour-intensive goods. The labour-intensive goods are hence reduced to include only unskilled labour-intensive goods. As a result, all Chinese tradable commodities can be classified into five groups: agricultural products, natural resource products, physical and human capital-intensive products, and unskilled labour-intensive products.

METHODS OF MEASURING FACTOR INTENSITY

Factor intensity can be measured in several ways. The empirical methods fall into two main competing approaches: stock measurement. vs. flow measurement, and the industry approach vs. the commodity approach.

Stock vs. Flow Measurement of Factor Intensity

The relative intensity of a factor embodied in a commodity can be measured either in physical unit terms, as a stock of that factor, or in value terms, as a flow of that factor's returns.

The stock measure of capital intensity has been adopted in a number of studies (Kenen 1965; Kenen and Yudin 1965; Branson and Junz 1971; Balassa 1979). Both physical and human capital are measured. A distinctive feature of this method is that it capitalizes wage differentials between skilled and unskilled labour at the estimated rate of return to arrive at the stock measure of human capital. The stock of capital per worker in industry i, k_i^s, can be formally expressed as

$$k_i^s = p_i^s + h_i^s = p_i^s + \frac{w_i - w_i^u}{r^h} \qquad (3.1)$$

where p_i^s and h_i^s denote the stock of physical and human capital per worker, respectively; w_i is the average wage rate, w_i^u the wage of unskilled labour, and r^h is the discount rate used in calculating the stock of human capital.

The flow measures of capital intensity have also had wide application in empirical work (Lary 1968; Roskamp and McKeekin 1968; Yahr 1968 and Balassa 1979). This method, working with the value-added of primary factors, regards the wage part of total value-added as the return to, and thus the flow measure of, human capital. The flow measure can be expressed as follows:

$$k_i^f = p_i^f + h_i^f \qquad (3.2)$$

where k_i^f is value-added per person in industry i, p_i^f and h_i^f are the non-wage and wage parts of the value-added, respectively.

In a perfectly competitive and risk-free equilibrium, the two measures would give the same result for physical capital intensity. However, this is not a realistic assumption to make. The possible inclusion in the non-wage value-added of items other than capital gains, such as risk premiums, may over-state capital intensity. In this regard, the stock measure seems to be preferable. The deficiency of the flow measure of human capital intensity is even more explicit when it includes unskilled wages in human capital, regarded as equal to the wage part of the value-added. This will certainly over-estimate human capital intensity. Although the stock measure correctly estimates human capital intensity by capitalizing the difference between the sectoral average wage rate and the unskilled wage rate, the measure relies, to a great extent, on the nature of the labour market because it is based on value rather than physical unit terms. In an imperfect labour market, as is the case for most countries, wage rates are influenced by government legislation or trade union bargaining powers. Even in a perfect labour market, wage rates are still unlikely to be solely determined by workers' skills. Many other elements–such as risk and working conditions–are also important determinants. The wage difference between the average and the unskilled levels may well include items other than skills; measures based on value terms are thus possibly misleading. To avoid this problem, it seems preferable to use, whenever possible, those measures based on physical rather than value terms.

Industry vs. Commodity Approach

The stock and flow measures are all based on the direct requirements for primary factors in the industry which produces a commodity as a final product. Alternatively, factor intensity can be measured by total factor requirements which include, in addition, the indirect use of factors in producing intermediate inputs into the production of that commodity. The former may be referred to as the 'industry approach' to factor intensity measurement because it reveals the factor intensity of a particular industry, while the latter may be called the 'commodity approach' because it shows the total amount of a factor's service embodied in the whole process of production of a commodity.

The industry approach to factor intensity measurement is relatively easy to apply because it requires only information on sectoral factor utilization, which is normally available from general statistical publications. For this reason, the industry approach has been widely used by the majority of empirical researchers. The stock and the flow measures discussed above are examples of the industry approach.

The commodity approach to factor intensity measurement is more data-demanding. In addition to information on sectoral factor utilization, it requires a detailed input–output table to derive a Leontief inverse matrix, so that the total requirements of factor inputs for individual commodities can be generated. The basic concepts of input–output analysis required for the factor intensity of trade patterns were initially, and later extensively, developed by

Leontief's studies of the factor contents of US foreign trade (Leontief 1953, 1956). This approach can also be employed in measuring the factor intensity of commodities.

Net output–that is, the part of gross output in excess of that used as intermediate inputs–may be consumed or exported. The underlying assumptions are that in the production of each good, intermediate goods are employed in fixed proportions and that no output involves joint products. Under these assumptions, the inter-industry transaction of commodities can be represented by the following commodity balance equation:

$$\mathbf{x} = \mathbf{Ax} + \mathbf{c} \tag{3.3}$$

where $\mathbf{x}$ denotes the column vector of sectoral gross outputs; $\mathbf{A}$ is the input coefficient matrix with element a_{ij} as the amount of commodity i employed as an intermediate good to produce one unit of commodity j; $\mathbf{c}$ is the column vector of sectoral final consumption of commodities. The domestic commodity balance equation can be transformed as follows

$$\mathbf{x} = [\mathbf{I} - \mathbf{A}]^{-1}\mathbf{c} \tag{3.4}$$

The inverse matrix $[\mathbf{I} - \mathbf{A}]^{-1}c$ can be expressed as

$$\mathbf{B} = [\mathbf{I} - \mathbf{A}]^{-1} = \mathbf{I} + \mathbf{A} + \mathbf{A}^2 + \ldots + \mathbf{A}^n \tag{3.5}$$

where the element b_{ij} is the amount of commodity i that is required directly and indirectly (through the successive employment of domestic intermediate goods) in the unit production of commodity j.

Since primary factors are assumed to be employed with fixed proportions to outputs, the matrix of total factor requirements for a certain bundle of unit gross output, $\mathbf{F}'$, can be estimated on the basis of the following relationship

$$\mathbf{F}' = \mathbf{F}[\mathbf{I} - \mathbf{A}]^{-1} \tag{3.6}$$

where $\mathbf{F}$ is the matrix of direct sectoral requirements of primary factors for the unit production of gross output with element f_{sj} the amount of primary factor s directly required in producing one unit of commodity j. The sectoral total requirements of primary factors, $\mathbf{d}$, can then be obtained by multiplying $\mathbf{F}'$ by the vector of sectoral gross output $\mathbf{x}$

$$\mathbf{d} = \mathbf{F}'\mathbf{x} \tag{3.7}$$

The total requirements of factors can either be estimated in physical terms as the stock of the factors or in value terms as the primary factors' returns–that is, the value-added.

The distinction between the two approaches has implications for different countries. The industry approach is more suitable for countries for which international trade or the international division of labour affects a large proportion of output. This allows them to import those intermediate inputs that use domestically scarce resources and concentrate on the final stage of the production that intensively uses domestically abundant factors. The commodity approach is more suitable for economies with limited import abilities which have to provide most intermediate inputs by themselves. They are therefore more likely to specialize in producing commodities that use domestically abundant factors in every–not just the final–stage of production. A commodity classification based on the commodity approach seems more likely to indicate the potential trade specialization for those countries.

The two approaches may give the same ranking of commodities in terms of their factor intensity if the factor intensities of all commodities are identical to those of their intermediate inputs. But it seems to be unusual that all capital-intensive industries would use only capital-intensive inputs and all labour-intensive industries only labour-intensive inputs. The following empirical results, however, indicate that the differences between the rankings of factor intensities for Chinese tradable commodities derived from the two approaches are not as large as expected.

APPLICABILITY TO CHINA

The experience of applying various methods to measuring factor intensity favours physical unit measures. This is particularly suitable for China. Since there were no properly functioning factor markets in China in many years of the period concerned, it would be unlikely for the returns to capital and labour to reflect the true degree of added value that would otherwise emerge in a free market situation. For this reason, the factor intensity measures, based on the observed value-added data such as wages and rents, could potentially distort the true picture of the factor contents of Chinese tradable commodities. In this regard, the physical unit measurement may be more appropriate than the value measurements in estimating the factor intensities of Chinese tradable commodities.

China's economy is still largely self-contained. Despite the increasing importance of economic links with the outside world, China still has a limited ability to import. The commodity approach to factor intensity measurement has hence been adopted. As China opens to the outside world, the production of some tradable goods is increasingly engaged in the international division of labour; the industry approach is hence becoming relevant. The factor intensities of Chinese commodities are thus estimated using both approaches. Where the two approaches give different results, the factor intensities for the goods involved are determined by the extent to which their production is related to imported inputs.

FACTOR INTENSITY OF CHINESE TRADABLE COMMODITIES

In the remainder of this chapter, 61 tradable commodities will be grouped into five categories, each of which represents a bundle of goods that intensively use a particular factor of production relative to others. These categories are land-intensive (agricultural), natural resource-intensive (minerals and timber), physical capital-intensive, human capital-intensive and unskilled labour-intensive goods. The first two groups are primary products and the last three are manufactures.

Classification Procedure

All commodities can be classified in principle by applying a suitable index to identify the relative intensity of usage of a particular factor of production. For some commodities, the intensively used primary factors are obvious. To reduce complexity, the commodity classification procedure is performed sequentially by initially categorizing the commodities whose factor intensities are most apparent–namely, land-intensive and other natural resource-intensive goods. The rest of the goods, all manufactured items, are then classified by using two indicators: sectoral physical capital stock and skill level.

The indicator for capital stock is relatively straightforward. It is the physical capital–labour ratio, defined as the net value of fixed capital assets (exclusive of depreciation) per worker.[1] The indicator for skill levels, however, needs to be estimated by proxy because data on labour skills are not readily available from Chinese statistics. The educational structure of sectoral employees is used as a proxy for the skill content of manufacturing industries.

'Skilled labour' is defined as those who have education above the high school level (over nine years of schooling). Those who have education below that level are considered as 'unskilled'. The educational structure of the labour force may or may not be consistent with the actual skills pattern which should be directly estimated from production data. To eliminate potential bias, the share of technical personnel in the sectoral labour force is also calculated and used. A skill index is constructed for each manufacturing industry. The skill index is defined as the product of the percentage share of skilled labour and the percentage share of technical personnel in the total labour force; this index is taken as a proxy for human capital utilization.

Manufactured goods are accordingly classified into three categories: physical capital-intensive, human capital-intensive and unskilled labour-intensive goods. The grouping procedure is illustrated in Figure 3.1. All unskilled labour-intensive goods are expected to have a low magnitude of both the physical capital–labour ratio and the skill index. They should therefore mainly be located in the bottom left corner of the diagram. The physical capital–intensive goods, by definition, are expected to have a higher capital–labour ratio and a moderate position on the skill index. They are most likely to be located along Ray I. Similarly, human capital-intensive goods with a high level on the skill index and modest capital–labour ratios,

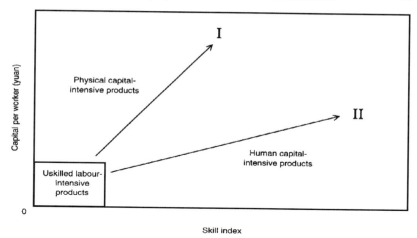

Figure 3.1   Factor intensity classification of manufactured goods

relative to physical capital-intensive goods, are expected to be found around Ray II. Figure 3.1 helps to set out a framework for identifying the relative factor intensities of individual manufactured goods.

The sectoral capital–labour ratios, and the percentage of skilled labour and technical personnel shares in the sectoral labour force are calculated from *Data on the 1985 Industrial Census of the People's Republic of China* (State Council, Office for the Leading Group of National Industrial Census, 1988). The indicators thus constructed reflect the direct requirements of primary factors in sectoral productive activities. The total requirements of primary factors can then be estimated using (3.7).[2] Hence, the physical capital–labour ratios and the skill index can be calculated from the total requirements of physical capital assets, the skilled and unskilled labour and the technical personnel derived from (3.7).

Commodity Classification and Estimated Results

Of the 61 tradable goods, 19 primary products are first categorized into two groups since their factor contents are most obvious.

Agricultural Goods

13 commodities or commodity groups are identified in this category: Paddy Rice (1), Wheat (2), Other Grains (3), Oil-bearing Crops (4), Cotton (5), Other Industrial Crops (6), Vegetables (7), Fruits (8), Forest Products (9), Wool and Hides (10), Meat, Eggs and Milk (11), Fish (12), and Other Agricultural Products (13).

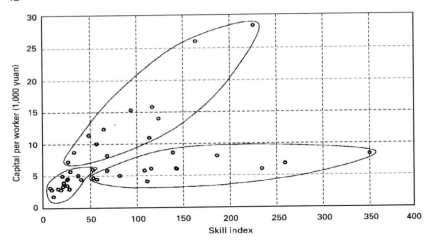

Figure 3.2　Factor intensity estimation of Chinese manufactured goods: industry approach
Sources: See Table 3A.2.

Natural Resource Goods

Included in this category are timber and five groups of mineral products: Coal (14), Crude Oil and Natural Gas (15), Ferrous Minerals (15), Non-Ferrous Minerals (16) and Non-Metal Minerals (17).

These two groups of goods are analogous to what the Chinese Industrial Classification specifies as 'agricultural products' and 'primary industrial products'.

The other tradable goods consist of 42 groups of manufactured products which can be classified into three categories by applying the physical capital–labour ratio and the skill index. The estimates calculated from the direct requirements of factors are reported in Appendix Table 3A.2 (p.49) and plotted in Figure 3.2. The results from the total requirements of factors are plotted in Figure 3.3. As expected, the two figures display a similar pattern and therefore it is fairly easy to group most commodities into three distinctive categories. A few exceptions will be singled out and discussed separately.

Physical Capital-intensive Goods

As shown in Figure 3.3, 15 goods or groups of goods can be identified as physical capital-intensive. The estimated physical capital–labour ratios and skill indexes for these goods are reported in Table 3.2. Compared with Figure 3.2, it can be seen that, for 11 of the total 15 goods, the two approaches give the same results. They are Petroleum Products (32), Steel (48), Non-Ferrous

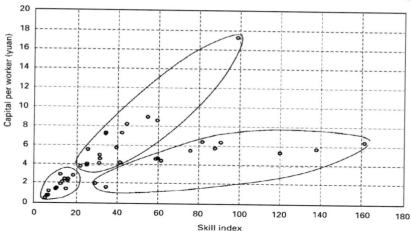

Figure 3.3 Factor intensity estimation of Chinese manufactured goods: commodity approach
Sources: See Tables 3.2–3.4

Metals (49), Chemical Fertilizers (35), Coal Products (33), Iron (47), Chemical Fibres (40), Inorganic Chemicals (34), Cement (43), Other Chemicals (38) and Organic Chemicals (36). Only the remaining four product groups need to be individually examined.

Table 3.2   Physical capital–intensive manufactured goods (15)

Commodities	Capital–labour ratio	Skill index
32. Petroleum products	17 274	98.15
48. Steel	9 048	54.51
49. Non-ferrous metals	8 690	59.24
35. Chemical fertilizers	8 298	44.26
33. Coal products	7 411	34.12
47. Iron	7 403	42.00
40. Chemical fibres	7 320	33.98
34. Inorganic chemicals	5 889	39.19
43. Cement	5 684	25.47
38. Other chemicals	5 107	31.19
44. Glass	4 716	31.32
50. Metal products	4 247	30.92
42. Plastic articles	4 178	25.16
36. Organic chemicals	4 029	24.96
45. Ceramic products	3 918	21.97

Note: The physical capital–labour ratios are in RMB yuan.
Source: State Council, Office for the Leading Group of National Industrial Census (1988).

According to the total requirements of capital and labour, the three remaining commodities, Glass (44), Metal Products (50) and Plastic Articles (42), are also physical capital-intensive because of their relatively high physical capital content. However, in the industry approach, they are included in the unskilled labour-intensive group because of their relatively low direct requirements of physical capital per worker. The difference between these two approaches is reflected more sharply in the fourth remaining commodity group–Sugar, Tobacco and Alcohol (20). This group as a manufacturing industry has a relatively high average physical capital intensity (RMB 8687 yuan per worker). However, the intermediate inputs they use in production are mainly from agriculture in which very little capital is used. If direct factor requirements are used as a classification benchmark, Sugar, etc. (20) is physical capital-intensive. When the factor contents of intermediate inputs are taken into account, however, it turns out to be very labour-intensive with the fourth lowest physical capital–labour ratio and skill index. In addition, none of these four groups uses imported inputs intensively in their production. For this reason, the results of the commodity approach are used for these four goods. Glass (44), Metal Products (50) and Plastic Articles (42) are classified as physical capital-intensive goods while Sugar, Tobacco and Alcohol (20) are classified as unskilled labour-intensive goods.

Human Capital-intensive Goods

This category of tradable goods can also be referred to as skilled labour-intensive goods. Figure 3.3 shows that 13 commodities or commodity groups

Table 3.3   Human capital–intensive manufactured goods (13)

Commodities	Capital–labour ratio	Skill index
58. Other transport equipment	6 517	160.35
60. Electronic equipment	5 812	136.76
61. Household electronics	5 448	119.00
55. Railway equipment	6 487	90.29
53. Power station equipment	5 876	87.47
57. Ships	6 528	81.31
52. Industrial equipment	5 621	75.52
59. Other engineering products	4 546	61.17
56. Motor vehicles	4 796	59.52
51. Agricultural machinery	4 729	58.57
54. Household mechanical/electrical goods	4 328	41.17
39. Medicines	1 675	34.19
37. Household chemicals	2 087	29.19

Note: The physical capital–labour ratios are in RMB yuan.
Source: As for Table 3.2.

fall into this category according to the commodity approach. They are Other Transport Equipment (58), Electronic Products (60), Household Electronics (61), Railway Equipment (55), Power Station Equipment (53), Ships (57), Industrial Equipment (52), Other Engineering Products (59), Motor Vehicles (56), Agricultural Machinery (51), Household Mechanical and Electrical Goods (54), Medicines (39) and Household Chemicals (37). Their physical capital–labour ratios and skill indexes are presented in Table 3.3.

The industry approach picks up 14 commodity groups as human capital-intensive among which 13 are included in Table 3.3. The only exception is Rubber Manufactures (41) located at the edge of the human capital-intensive group boundary close to the unskilled labour-intensive group in Figure 3.2. It seems rather arbitrary to put it in either group. This ambiguity could be removed when the factor contents of intermediate inputs are taken into account. Rubber Manufactures (41) are clearly identified by the commodity approach as a group of unskilled labour-intensive goods with the sixth lowest physical capital–labour ratio and the eleventh lowest skill index. It is obvious that Rubber Manufactures (41) should be included in the unskilled labour-intensive group below.

Unskilled Labour-intensive Goods

The remaining 14 manufactured goods, all scattered in the bottom left corner of Figure 3.3, are defined as unskilled labour-intensive because both their physical capital–labour ratios and skill indexes are low. They include all textiles (22–27), Other Building Materials (46), Furniture (29), Cultural and

Table 3.4   Unskilled labour–intensive manufactured goods (14)

Commodities	Capital–labour ratio	Skill index
29. Furniture	2 945	18.49
26. Knitted goods	2 537	16.06
31. Cultural and sporting goods	2 356	15.80
41. Rubber manufactures	1 471	15.01
25. Silk textiles	2 554	14.36
30. Paper	2 237	13.20
23. Wool textiles	2 005	12.44
46. Other building materials	3 046	12.31
28. Clothing and leather goods	1 573	10.48
22. Cotton textiles	1 468	10.08
20. Sugar, tobacco and alcohol	1 247	6.70
24. Hemp textiles	793	6.43
21. Other processed food	785	5.78
27. Other textiles	521	4.86

Note: The physical capital–labour ratios are in RMB yuan.
Source: See Table 3.2.

Sporting Goods (31), Paper (30), Clothing and Leather Goods (28), Rubber Manufactures (41), Sugar, etc. (20) and Other Processed Food (21) (Table 3.4).

CONCLUSION

Generally speaking, oil and coal products, metal products, chemical products, and main building materials such as cement and glass are physical capital-intensive. Machinery, transport equipment, electrical and electronic appliances, medicines and household chemicals are human capital-intensive. Textiles, clothing, furniture, cultural goods, processed food and other building materials are unskilled labour-intensive. The first two are composed largely of the products of heavy industries while the last consists mainly of products from light industries. The physical capital-intensive goods are mostly semi-finished or intermediate products while human capital and unskilled labour-intensive goods are generally manufactured final products.

It is difficult to compare the factor intensity classification of Chinese tradable commodities with those of other countries since the definitions of commodity groups and different methods of estimation usually vary. The technology divergences between China and other countries–particularly, industrial countries–will certainly result in different uses of primary factors of production and therefore different factor intensities for the same categories of goods. In addition, the quality of commodities under the same title may not be identical and comparable. This is particularly so in the case of more sophisticated manufactured products.

The above classification of Chinese tradable commodities, however, seems largely consistent with commodity classification systems based on other country's data. For example, Balassa (1977) uses US data to show that, among other things, textiles, clothing, footwear, furniture and leather goods are among the lowest value-added industries and machinery, aircraft and electronic equipment are among the highest value-added industries. The former are unskilled labour-intensive goods while the latter capital-intensive goods.

The information on the factor contents of China's tradable goods will be useful in examining China's trade patterns and comparative advantage structure. The following chapters discuss the extent to which China's trade patterns have been shaped by its recent economic reforms and how each of these tradable groups has been affected in the process.

APPENDIX

Table 3A.1 Concordance between 61 tradable categories used in this study and China's Industrial Classification of National Economic Activities (CICNEA)

Code description	CICNEA code
1. Paddy rice	11
2. Wheat	11
3. Other grains	11
4. Oil-bearing crops	11
5. Cotton	11
6. Other industrial crops	11
7. Vegetables	11
8. Fruits	11
9. Forest products	2
10. Wool and hides	31
11. Meat, eggs and milk	32, 33
12. Fish	4
13. Other agricultural products	12
14. Coal	8
15. Crude petroleum	9
16. Ferrous minerals	10
17. Non-ferrous minerals	11
18. Non-metallic minerals	12, 13, 14
19. Timber	15
20. Sugar, tobacco and alcohol	174, 191, 192, 20
21. Other processed food	17(-174), 19(-191, 192), 21
22. Cotton textiles	222
23. Wool textiles	224
24. Hemp textiles	226
25. Silk textiles	227
26. Knitted goods	228
27. Other textiles	221, 229
28. Clothing and leather goods	24, 25
29. Furniture	26, 27
30. Paper	28
31. Cultural and sporting goods	29, 30, 31
32. Petroleum products	34
33. Coal products	35
34. Inorganic chemicals	361
35. Chemical fertilizers	362, 363
36. Organic chemicals	365
37. Household chemicals	377
38. Other chemicals	372, 375, 376
39. Medicines	38
40. Chemical fibres	40
41. Rubber manufactures	41
42. Plastic articles	43
43. Cement	451, 452

Table 3A.1   (Continued)

Code description	CICNEA code
44. Glass	454
45. Ceramic products	456, 457
46. Other building materials	45(-451, 452, 454, 456, 457)
47. Iron	481, 488
48. Steel	482, 483
49. Non-ferrous metals	49
50. Metal products	51
51. Agricultural machinery	542
52. Industrial equipment	53 (-531, 562, 563, 568)
53. Power station equipment	531, 581
54. Household mechanical/electrical goods	548, 586, 662
55. Railway equipment	561
56. Motor vehicles	562
57. Ships	563
58. Other transport equipment	56(-561, 562, 563, 568)
59. Other engineering products	58(-581, 586, 588), 63(-638), 661
60. Electronic products	60(-616, 618)
61. Household electronics	616

Note: '-' = 'exclusive of'.
Source: *Industrial Classification and Codes for National Economic Activities* (Guomin jingji hangye fenlei yu daima), GB 4754-84.

Table 3A.2   Physical capital–labour ratio and skill index for Chinese tradable manufactures: industry approach

Code	Description	Capital–labour ratio	Skill index
20.	Sugar, tobacco and alcohol	8 687	31.94
21.	Other processed food	4 955	19.18
22.	Cotton textiles	4 424	39.29
23.	Wool textiles	5 968	51.79
24.	Hemp textiles	4 541	25.17
25.	Silk textiles	3 318	19.89
26.	Knitted goods	3 499	24.42
27.	Other textiles	3 116	6.28
28.	Clothing and leather goods	1 776	9.69
29.	Furniture	2 974	14.59
30.	Paper	5 671	27.93
31.	Cultural and sports goods	2 794	17.60
32.	Petroleum products	28 377	225.74
33.	Coal products	11 346	47.50
34.	Inorganic chemicals	8 134	67.55
35.	Chemical fertilizers	12 308	64.03
36.	Organic chemicals	10 916	113.22
37.	Household chemicals	5 758	67.42
38.	Other chemicals	15 779	116.62
39.	Medicines	6 068	141.90
40.	Chemical fibres	25 985	163.78
41.	Rubber manufactures	4 616	52.48
42.	Plastic articles	4 396	24.42
43.	Cement	7 178	25.53
44.	Glass	5 035	36.29
45.	Ceramic products	3 907	20.69
46.	Other building materials	2 822	7.86
47.	Iron	9 995	56.33
48.	Steel	15 260	93.63
49.	Non-ferrous metals	13 949	123.25
50.	Metal products	2 926	26.79
51.	Agricultural machinery	4 978	81.10
52.	Industrial equipment	6 060	114.94
53.	Power station equipment	5 976	142.79
54.	Household mechanical/electrical goods	4 425	56.45
55.	Railway equipment	7 988	185.93
56.	Motor vehicles	5 755	107.76
57.	Ships	8 552	138.76
58.	Other transport equipment	8 166	350.29
59.	Other engineering products	4 055	110.48
60.	Electronic products	6 741	259.06
61.	Household electronics	5 899	234.01

Source: See Table 3.2.

4 China's Foreign Trade Patterns and Performance

Foreign trade has always played an important role in China's economic development (Eckstein 1966; Chen 1975; Hsiao 1977, Hsu 1989). It has outstripped gross national output since 1950. From 1953 to 1996, gross domestic product (GDP) grew at 10.8 per cent per annum in nominal terms (State Statistical Bureau, Department of National Economic Accounting 1998:3–4). During the same period, the total value of China's foreign trade increased at an average annual rate of 11.8 per cent in nominal terms, with annual growth rates of exports and imports at 12.3 and 11.4 per cent respectively (State Statistical Bureau 1997:588).

However, the sharp rise in exports and imports since the late 1970s when the economic reforms began has been even more striking (Figure 4.1). If the last four decades are divided into the pre-reform period between 1953 and 1977 and the reform period of 1978 onward, the accelerated growth of China's foreign trade since 1978 has been remarkable. From 1953 to 1977, the total value of China's foreign trade increased at an average annual rate of 7.9 per cent with exports and imports growing, respectively, at 8.7 and 7.2 per cent annually. Between 1978 and 1996, however, the total value of China's trade rose sharply at a 15.8 per cent per annum and exports and imports

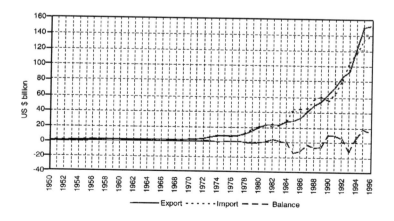

Figure 4.1   China's exports, imports and trade balance, 1950-96
Source: State Statistical Bureau (1986, 1997).

51

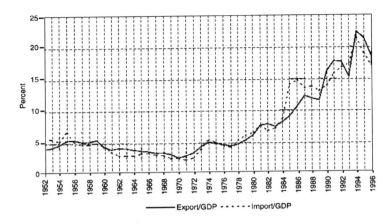

Figure 4.2   Export and import shares in China's gross domestic product, 1952–96
Source: State Statistical Bureau (1985, 1997); Department of National Economic Accounting (SSB) (1998).

grew, respectively, at 16.4 and 15.2 per cent per annum (State Statistical Bureau 1997:588).

The reform period also witnessed a dramatic rise in the significance of foreign trade to the national economy. In 1977, exports and imports accounted, respectively, for about 4 per cent of GDP (Figure 4.2). Since then, these ratios have grown steadily. The shares of exports and imports in GDP reached a peak of 22.3 and 21.3 per cent in 1994 while in 1996, they remained at a level above 18.5 and 17 per cent, respectively.

The changing composition of China's foreign trade has been equally remarkable. China used to be an exporter of primary products. Figure 4.3 shows that in the early 1950s agricultural commodities comprised about 80 per cent of China's total exports. It was not until 1973, when China normalized its relations with the western world, that this ratio began to decline. However, this process was halted by the turbulent domestic political situation of the 1970s. In the 20 years prior to 1977, the share of non-agricultural or industrial products (minerals and manufactured goods) in total exports hovered between one-quarter and one-third until it moved closer to 40 per cent in the mid-1970s. After the beginning of the economic reforms, non-agricultural exports began to increase, jumping from just below 40 per cent to above 60 per cent from 1978 to 1982, largely because of a rise in petroleum exports. In the mid-1980s, agricultural exports rebounded, thanks to the unprecedented increase in agricultural output after successful rural reforms. As domestic industrial output growth picked up, the trend of increasing industrial exports in general, and manufactured exports in particular, resumed. The share of manufactures in China's total exports has now reached over 90 per cent.

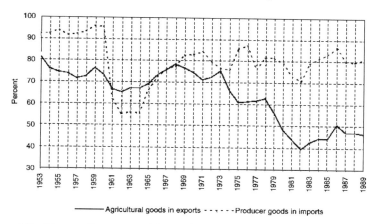

Figure 4.3   Commodity compositions of China's exports and imports, 1953–89
Source: Editorial Board of the ACFERT (1991:294, 298).

The commodity composition of China's imports has also changed over time, but at a slower pace. Producer goods dominated China's imports in the pre-reform years (Figure 4.3)–the only exception was during the famine of the early 1960s, when the government was forced to import substantial amounts of food after widespread harvest failure. The domination of producer goods in imports has remained even after the economic reforms: to some extent, this also reflects the fact that state controls over imports were still largely in place, especially in the 1980s.

COMMODITY COMPOSITION OF CHINA'S FOREIGN TRADE

To discuss the changes in the composition of trade in terms of commodity groups classified according to their factor intensities, all merchandise trade items covered by the United Nation's Standard International Trade Classification (SITC) are grouped into the same five categories: agricultural products, natural resource products, physical capital-intensive, human capital-intensive and unskilled labour-intensive manufactured products.[1] Their concordance between the 61 Chinese tradable good groups and the SITC (Revised) items is presented in Appendix Table 4A.1 (p.67).

Figure 4.4 shows that China's annual export volumes of all five defined tradable groups grew rapidly over the reform period. Agricultural exports increased at an annual average rate of 7.8 per cent from US$1.9 to US$7.4 billion. Natural resource exports increased at an annual average rate of 9.1 per cent from US$1.2 to US$4.6 billion with a peak of US$6.4 billion in 1985. Manufactured exports have grown at a much faster rate than primary exports. Physical capital-intensive exports rose at an annual average rate of

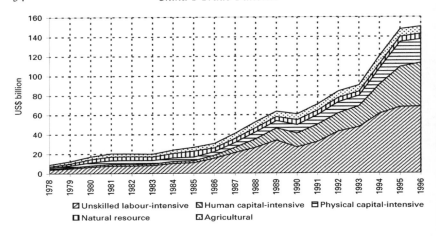

Figure 4.4   China's exports, 1978–96
Source: United Nations Statistical Office, New York.

18.4 per cent from US$1.2 to US$24.2 billion. Human capital-intensive exports grew at 24.6 per cent from US$0.9 to US$44.9 billion and the exports of unskilled labour-intensive manufactured goods grew at 17.3 per cent per annum from US$3.9 to US$68.2 billion.[2]

The rapid growth of exports was also associated with structural changes in the commodity composition of exports (Table 4.1). If the five groups are aggregated into two broad categories as primary and manufactured goods, it again becomes clear that between 1978 and 1996 the share of primary goods shrank while that of manufactured products increased. The share of agricultural products in total exports declined from 21 to just 4.3 per cent. The share of other natural resource-intensive goods in total exports increased between 1978 and 1985, largely because of a sharp rise in crude oil prices and the subsequent government push to increase oil exports. As crude oil prices declined after the mid-1980s, the share of natural resource-intensive goods in total exports declined markedly (Table 4.1). By 1996, manufactured goods were accounting for 92 per cent of China's total exports.

Within the export sector, the share of physical capital-intensive goods rose in the early 1980s and then fell back. This group of commodities includes resource-based metal products such as iron and steel which were then in short supply domestically. The high share of this group in the early 1980s was the result of large-scale domestic restructuring in which investments in heavy industries were sharply reduced and transferred to light industries. As China's domestic industry emerged from the structural adjustments and resumed its high growth rate in the mid-1980s, the rising demand for capital-intensive products such as iron and steel caused this group of exports to decline. However, manufactured goods as a whole continued to increase their share in

Table 4.1 Commodity composition of China's exports, 1978–96 (%)

Year	Agricultural goods	Natural resource	Physical capital	Human capital	Unskilled labour
1978	21.4	13.0	12.8	9.5	43.3
1979	19.3	15.0	15.7	8.7	41.3
1980	16.3	18.6	18.5	7.8	38.7
1981	16.0	17.7	19.2	7.9	38.2
1982	14.4	19.3	19.9	7.7	38.7
1983	14.6	18.2	17.7	8.2	41.3
1984	14.6	19.1	15.2	8.2	42.9
1985	14.6	23.0	13.9	7.6	40.9
1986	14.8	12.8	12.0	10.1	50.3
1987	12.8	10.0	12.2	13.0	51.9
1988	11.5	8.2	13.5	16.4	50.3
1989	8.7	6.5	11.9	19.4	53.4
1990	9.9	8.3	14.3	23.4	44.1
1991	9.2	6.4	13.8	24.9	45.6
1992	7.9	5.4	13.5	22.3	50.9
1993	7.1	4.7	12.1	23.7	52.4
1994	7.0	3.5	13.6	25.0	50.8
1995	5.3	3.6	17.3	27.9	46.0
1996	4.3	3.7	16.1	29.8	45.4

Source: See Figure 4.4 (p.54).

total exports, largely driven by the increase in exports of human capital intensive and unskilled labour-intensive goods (Table 4.1). Over the whole period, the share of the former tripled from below 10 to almost 30 per cent while the already large share of the latter continued to rise by 10 percentage points from 43 to 53 per cent between 1978 and 1989, falling back to 45 per cent thereafter in 1996.[3] The share of physical capital-intensive exports moved modestly in a range between 12 and 20 per cent over the same period, following China's domestic economic growth cycles.

These developments were facilitated by a number of significant reforms adopted during this period: the establishment of the SEZs, the opening up of coastal cities to foreign investment, the provision of incentives for foreign investment, foreign trade reforms and the adoption of the foreign exchange retention scheme for exporters. Foreign trade corporations, enterprises and local authorities all gained more autonomy in making export decisions and became eager to maximize exports for their own interests.

Firms from Hong Kong and Taiwan responded by moving their labour-intensive manufacturing industries to Southeast China, particularly to Guangdong and Fujian provinces, to take advantage of the abundant supplies of cheap labour. A large proportion of early Hong Kong investment went into township and village enterprises in the form of compensation

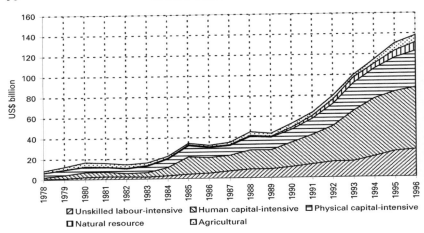

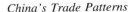

Figure 4.5   China's imports, 1978-96
Source: See Figure 4.4

trade or export-processing or assembling operations. In 1987, 7 per cent of Guangdong's exports came from township enterprises and 27 per cent from processing or assembling enterprises (State Statistical Bureau 1989b:181). By 1990, exports from processing or assembling operations accounted for 41 per cent of China's total exports, resulting in an upsurge of unskilled labour-intensive manufactures exports (Sung Yun-wing 1991b:1). In the 1990s, China's traditional labour-intensive manufactured exports such as textiles and clothing have been gradually replaced by new items such as household electrical appliances and electronic goods assembled in China with parts and components imported from overseas. In 1997, processed and assembled exports were worth US$99.6 billion, accounting for more than 54.5 per cent of China's total exports for the first time in history (*Monthly Customs Statistics* 1997(12):10).[4]

The commodity composition of China's exports can be compared with that of its imports (Figure 4.5). Although, unlike exports, the value of imports was characterized by some fluctuations, certain general trends can be identified. The imports of primary products were fairly stable and the rapid increase in total imports was mainly attributable to the rise in the imports of manufactured goods, especially human capital-intensive goods.

The commodity composition of China's imports is revealed in Table 4.2. The share of agricultural products in total imports dropped from 21 to just 5 per cent while that of natural resource-intensive goods increased from 2 to 6 per cent, occurring mostly in the 1990s. The share of physical capital-intensive goods decreased from above 50 to below 26 per cent of total imports while human capital-intensive goods and unskilled labour-intensive goods expanded their shares in total imports from 17.2 per cent and 9 per cent to

Table 4.2   Commodity composition of China's imports, 1978–96 (%)

Year	Agricultural goods	Natural resource	Physical capital	Human capital	Unskilled labour
1978	21.4	2.2	50.1	17.2	9.0
1979	22.1	1.7	41.8	26.0	8.5
1980	24.8	2.6	30.6	28.6	13.5
1981	24.2	2.0	27.8	28.6	17.4
1982	24.2	4.1	31.8	22.8	17.1
1983	16.7	3.8	39.1	26.6	13.7
1984	9.1	3.3	37.5	36.4	13.7
1985	4.2	2.7	31.3	49.3	12.5
1986	4.5	2.5	30.0	47.2	15.8
1987	6.8	2.2	27.1	43.7	20.3
1988	7.9	2.2	28.8	41.8	19.3
1989	6.8	2.1	28.0	43.2	20.0
1990	7.1	3.8	23.4	45.4	20.3
1991	5.0	4.3	24.6	45.3	20.7
1992	4.5	5.4	26.9	43.6	19.5
1993	2.6	5.4	27.1	48.9	16.0
1994	3.7	4.1	25.3	48.9	17.9
1995	5.6	5.1	25.3	44.4	19.6
1996	5.0	6.0	25.7	43.6	19.7

Source: See Figure 4.4 (p.54).

43.6 per cent and 19.7 per cent, respectively. The decline in the shares of agricultural products and physical capital-intensive goods in total imports reflected an improvement in the domestic supplies of these products, which seemed to be a clear result of the ongoing economic reforms. The rapid growth of the economy also increased the demand for the importation of natural resources that became increasingly in short supply domestically. For instance, in late 1979, crude oil imports were virtually zero while, in recent years, they increased steadily–in 1995 and 1996, China became a net importer of crude oil.

The impact of the reforms begun in 1978 on imports was not felt until 1982 when the economic adjustment program, implemented in the late 1970s and early 1980s, was completed. The adjustment was aimed at restoring balance to an economy that had been badly shaken by the chaotic decade of the Cultural Revolution. Several changes in the import structure during the reform period are evident. First, one of the most important achievements of economic reforms was a marked improvement in agricultural productivity following the implementation of the household contract responsibility system. With a substantial increase in agricultural production, the economy was able to reduce its agricultural imports; the value of agricultural imports, which consisted mainly of wheat and maize, dropped by more than 65 per cent from a peak of US$4.16 billion in 1980 to less than US$1.45 billion in

1985, lowering the share of agricultural products in total imports from 25 per cent in 1980 to a mere 4 per cent in 1985. Although agricultural production in the following years was not as high as earlier, agricultural imports and their share in total imports did not return to the high levels of the early 1980s.

Second, as the central government relaxed its control over small-scale investments and allowed large enterprises and local governments to participate in decision-making, investment booms occurred. These at first significantly increased the importation of capital goods and intermediate industrial inputs, mainly human capital-intensive goods such as machinery and transport equipment. However, the introduction of a two-tier price system in 1984 for producer goods greatly encouraged the domestic production of those goods, especially iron and steel products, and thus reduced their imports. Consequently, the share of human capital-intensive goods expanded while the share of physical capital-intensive goods contracted during this period.

Third, the rapid growth of unskilled labour-intensive exports (such as textiles) under the export promotion scheme strongly increased in the demand for textile yarn and fibres imports. This, in turn, increased the share of unskilled labour-intensive goods in total imports. Furthermore, along with the introduction of the foreign exchange retention scheme there was a considerable relaxation of restrictions on consumer goods imports which consisted of both human capital-intensive goods such as household electronics and unskilled labour-intensive goods such as foodstuffs and clothing. As a result, the share of these two groups of commodities in total imports increased substantially. In addition, the increase in the imports of parts and components for export processing and assembling activities since the late 1980s also contributed to the expansion of labour-intensive and human capital-intensive imports.

MEASURING TRADE PERFORMANCE

To provide a complete picture of China's overall trade performance, the foregoing analysis should be extended to include not only the changes in China's trade structure but also the changes in its trading position relative to the rest of the world.

Most indices about trade performance are associated with the so-called 'revealed' comparative advantage, which originated in Bela Balassa's work (1965). International trade theory suggests that a country's comparative advantage should be essentially related to the pre-trade relative prices of its products under competitive market conditions. However, these hypothetical pre-trade prices are not directly observable, and empirical research has to be based on the post-trade data on the prices or unit costs of products. Balassa's 'revealed' comparative advantage (Balassa 1965) is based on inferring a country's underlying comparative advantage from its actual trade performance.

To accurately reveal a country's comparative advantage from its trade patterns, a number of conditions must be met. First, there must be no distortions in domestic markets. Second, domestic producers must be independent decision-makers in production and trade. If these conditions are violated, the trade patterns will be distorted and it is, therefore, unlikely that those trade data will reveal anything about the country's underlying comparative advantage. In the case of China, these conditions are not likely to be satisfied, especially in the 1980s when foreign trade and the domestic markets were heavily regulated and world prices had little impact on China's domestic resource allocation. It is thus unlikely that China's comparative advantage will be revealed by its actual trade data. Nevertheless, it is the purpose of this study to test the existence of the link between China's foreign trade and its comparative advantage.

To deny the applicability of these indices in revealing China's comparative advantage, however, does not imply that they cannot be used at all in China's case. The indices of 'revealed' comparative advantage can still be useful in revealing China's actual trade patterns and the performance of Chinese products in the world market. A number of indices have been used in the literature in relation to the 'revealed' comparative advantage concept. Here, we select three of the most widely used ones to examine their suitability for analysing China's trade performance.

(1) Export Import Ratio (EIR)

This ratio, used in Balassa (1965), simply shows the net trade balance for a given commodity category, formally

$$EIR_j = \frac{X_j}{M_j} \tag{4.1}$$

where X_j and M_j denote the values of exports and imports of commodity j, respectively. It is expected that any improvement in trade performance will be reflected in a higher rate of growth in exports rather than imports. The measure is meaningful only when the exported and imported commodities described are close substitutes. They cannot be perfect substitutes, however, because, if they were, one would not normally expect the same commodity to be both imported and exported. The ratio would either be zero, when the commodity is exported only, or infinity when it is imported only. Changes in the ratio for individual commodity groups over time may also be of interest, but the observed differences in the EIRs across commodity groups may have more to do with the degree to which exports and imports are substitutes than with trade performance. More importantly, this ratio does not reveal anything about the position of the country's trade in that commodity relative to the world's trade as a whole. As a result, an important aspect of the overall trade performance is not captured.

(2) Export Performance Ratio (EPR)

The EPR, first used by Liesner (1958) and later adopted by Balassa (1965), is a country's share in the world exports of a given commodity relative to that country's overall share in total world exports—that is,

$$EPR_{ij} = \frac{X_{ij}/\sum_j X_{ij}}{\sum_i X_{ij}/\sum_i \sum_j X_{ij}} \tag{4.2}$$

where the subscripts i and j denote country and exported commodity, respectively. This index considers the share of a commodity the country exports in the world export market relative to the country's total exports in the world total exports. If EPR is greater than one, it implies that the country performs well in producing and exporting the commodity concerned. This is a clear advantage over the EIR.

The EPR is limited, however, because it restricts the investigation of a country's trade performance to exports alone. Imports are excluded by the argument that the observed import patterns are more likely than exports to be distorted by a country's protection policies. However, the exclusion of imports cannot be justified on the grounds of trade protection because exports are also subject to direct policy interventions. Furthermore, exports are also indirectly affected by the structure of import protection as well because the imported inputs are often used in export production.

(3) Net Export Ratio (NER)

Recognition of the potential bias involved in using export data alone in measuring a country's trade performance has led to the development of indices based on net exports such as the net export ratio (NER) (UNIDO 1982, 1986; Balassa 1986; Balassa and Bauwens 1988). This measure expresses the net exports of commodity j as a proportion of the total trade flows of commodity j—that is,

$$NER_j = \frac{X_j - M_j}{X_j + M_j} \tag{4.3}$$

This index overcomes some problems in the EPR, but it has similar problems to the EIR: it does not reveal the position of a country's trade in a given commodity relative to the rest of the world.

Given the limitations of the above indices, there is a need to construct an alternative trade performance measure, which should consider both a country's exports and imports of individual commodities as well as their relative position in the world market. Based on these considerations, we introduce a new measure, the net export performance ratio (NEPR), which can be expressed as

$$NEPR_{ij} = \frac{(X_{ij} - M_{ij})/\sum_i X_{ij}}{\sum_j X_{ij}/\sum_i \sum_j X_{ij}} = \frac{(X_{ij} - M_{ij})/\sum_j X_{ij}}{\sum_i X_{ij}/\sum_i \sum_j X_{ij}} \qquad (4.4)$$

The NEPR combines the merits of both EPR and NER. It differs from the EPR in its inclusion of competing imports and it also differs from the NER in its comparison of a given country's trade with the rest of the world. It may be helpful to interpret the NEPR index as being approximately equal to the difference between the export performance ratio (EPR) and the analogous import performance ratio (IPR), given by

$$D_{ij} = EPR_{ij} - IPR_{ij} = \frac{X_{ij}/\sum_i X_{ij}}{\sum_j X_{ij}/\sum_i \sum_j X_{ij}} - \frac{M_{ij}/\sum_i M_{ij}}{\sum_j M_{ij}/\sum_i \sum_j M_{ij}} \qquad (4.5)$$

In principle, the world imports of commodity j always equal the world exports of j and the world's total imports always equal its total exports. If a country's trade is balanced, as should be the case in the long run, then D_{ij} is exactly equal to the $NEPR_{ij}$ in (4.4). That is, the NEPR, given by (4.4), is equivalent to the difference between the export performance ratio and the import performance ratio, given by (4.5). It is easy to see that the NEPR measures for tradable goods vary in the following range,

$$\frac{1}{\sum_j X_{ij}/\sum_i \sum_j X_{ij}} \geq NEPR_{ij} \geq \frac{-1}{\sum_j M_{ij}/\sum_i \sum_j M_{ij}} \qquad (4.6)$$

The difference between the EPR and NEPR can be interpreted as the following. In the EPR, if the share of a commodity in its total world export volume is greater than the country's total exports in the world's total export volume, it then implies that the country has performed well in producing and exporting this commodity. In the NERP, however, one has to compare the EPR with the IPR. One can say only that the country has performed well in this commodity trade, unless the EPR is greater than the IPR–that is, the NEPR is greater than zero. In other words, to be a good performer in the world market for a given commodity, a country must be a net supplier instead of a net demander. That is, the NEPR must be greater than zero. To be an extremely good performer, moreover, the share of net exports in the world market for that commodity must exceed the share of the country in total world exports. That is, the NEPR must be greater than unity. The index shows the specialization of the country in the world production structure.

The variations in NEPR across commodities reflect only the structural changes in commodity patterns of trade. In other words, it reflects only the

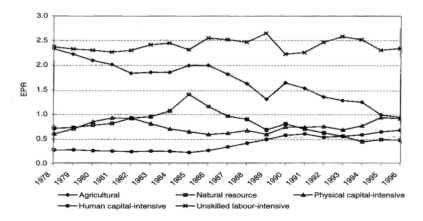

Figure 4.6   China's export performance ratio (EPR), 1978–96
Source: See Figure 4.4

relative changes across commodities and will not vary as a country's total trade grows relative to the rest of the world. If a country's trade specialization remains unchanged, as its share in total world exports grows, the NEPR estimates for all commodities will remain constant.

Now we apply the above three indices to China's trade data to see which one provides a better indication for China's overall trade performance. Figures 4.6–4.8 show the estimates of the EPR, NER and NEPR for China for the period between 1978 and 1996. As usual, we cluster all tradables into five groups and present the aggregated results.

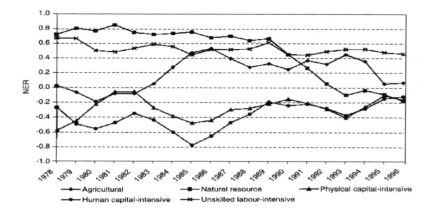

Figure 4.7   China's net export ratio (NER), 1978–96
Source: See Figure 4.4

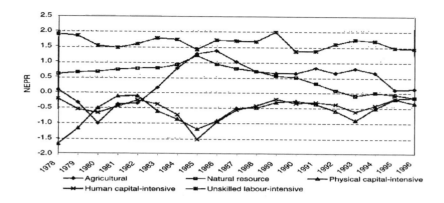

Figure 4.8   China's net export performance ratio (NEPR), 1978–96
Source: See Figure 4.4

According to the ranking results, the EPR estimates for unskilled labour-intensive goods and agricultural products are higher than unity for the whole period while those for physical and human capital-intensive goods are below unity. The EPR for natural resource-intensive goods first rose above, and then dropped below, unity (Figure 4.6). An EPR measure higher than unity means that a country's market share in the world for a given good is higher than the country's total export share in the world. This is regarded as an indication of good export performance. By this criteria, unskilled labour-intensive and agricultural goods can be seen as having performed well. By the same measure, the performances of physical and human capital-intensive goods as well as natural resource-intensive goods were less impressive.

By definition, the EPR describes China's position only as an exporter in the world market (Figure 4.6). As an indicator of overall trade performance, the EPR has serious shortcomings. In the case of agricultural products, for instance, the EPR measures suggest that China did very well in exporting in the late 1970s and the early 1980s. This is misleading, as China actually imported an even larger amount of agricultural products in the early 1980s and was a net importer of these products. Take grains as an example. China had been a net importer of grains from the early 1960s up to 1983. The government adopted a trade policy that was intended to supplement the domestic supply of grains by exporting rice in exchange for wheat because the international price of rice was higher than that of wheat. A given quantity of rice could be exchanged for a greater volume of wheat in the world market. China is the world's largest producer of rice. By exporting a large quantity of rice and importing even more wheat, the domestic food supply could be increased. China had been a large exporter of rice and, at the same time, a large importer of wheat until very recently; if one uses only China's exports as an indication for its trade performance, the result therefore could be misleading.

The NER overcomes the shortcomings associated with the EPR. Figure 4.7 indicates that China was indeed a net importer of agricultural products between 1979 and 1982 and a net exporter of these products in the following years owing to the increase in domestic agricultural production. However, the NER measures do not indicate China's trade performance in relation with the rest of the world because they compare only the net exports of a given commodity with China's own total trade of that commodity. The NER commodity ranking, again, does not reflect the true picture of China's overall trade performance.

Compared with the EPR and NER measures, the NEPR is a better indicator for China's overall trade performance because it removes the limitations and combines the advantages of the EPR and NER. It takes account of not only China's own exports and imports but also its trade position in the world market. A high value of this index for a commodity implies that China's contribution to that particular world market is greater than its average share in the world total trade. This reflects China's concentration on the export of that commodity and also its specialization in the world production structure. We now use the NEPR measures to reveal the changing patterns of China's foreign trade over the past two decades.

CHINA'S FOREIGN TRADE PERFORMANCE, 1978–96

General trends in China's trade performance during the period 1978–96 can be seen in Figure 4.8.[5] Five sub-periods can be identified in terms of relative changes in the NEPR measures for tradables.

1978–80

The NEPR for agricultural products dropped to a low point in 1980 and then started to rise concomitantly with increasing domestic agricultural output and declining imports. The NEPR measures for natural resource products increased marginally. As for manufactured goods, the NEPR for unskilled labour-intensive manufactures declined while that for physical capital-intensive manufactures increased sharply.

The NEPR measures for manufactured goods exhibited some unusual trends here, possibly for two reasons. First, an economic readjustment programme was implemented in the early 1980s, which was intended to eliminate the adverse impacts of the ambitious Four Modernizations programme introduced in 1977 and restore the balance in the macroeconomy.

Under the programme, investment priorities were shifted away from heavy to light industries and imports of producer goods were restricted in an attempt to reduce the trade deficit. As a result of these policies, heavy industrial enterprises were encouraged to export their capital-intensive products. Second, despite the announcement of economic reforms in 1978, foreign trade continued to be dominated by a system in which all losses were subsidized by the central government. As a result, capital-intensive producer goods were exported and unskilled labour-intensive goods, especially consumer goods, were not exported owing to high domestic demands. To transform the heavy industry-biased economic structure, the government encouraged the production of consumer goods by increasing the imports of intermediate inputs that were needed to produce these goods, such as textile raw materials. This also increased the share of unskilled labour-intensive goods in total imports.

1981–85

Trade reforms began to take shape during this period. They focused, to a large extent, on the decentralization of foreign trade management. As domestic price reforms lagged behind trade reforms, the decentralization of foreign trade resulted in a surge of imports of raw materials and capital goods because the world market prices for these goods were relatively lower than their domestic prices. Figure 4.8 shows that the NEPR for all manufactured goods declined, which indicated some competition from the world market. Exports of petroleum and coal continued to rise. The most remarkable improvement in trade performance during this time occurred in agricultural products, in which China moved from a net importer to a net exporter.

1985–89

A new trend emerged in China's foreign trade. It is apparent from Figure 4.8 that the NEPR measures for primary products, agricultural and natural resource-intensive goods declined and the NEPR measures for manufactured goods increased. The decline in the NEPR for primary goods seems to be the result of a combination of several factors. First, China was by no means a natural resource-rich country in terms of *per capita* endowments. The rapid growth of the domestic economy raised the demand for primary products and, accordingly, reduced exports and increased the imports of these goods despite the rise in domestic supplies. Second, the decrease in agricultural production after 1985 also contributed to the decline in net exports of agricultural products. Third, the decline in the trade performance of natural resource goods was also, to a great extent, attributable to the drop in world petroleum prices and the consequent decline in China's petroleum exports, a major product in this group.

1990–92

Austerity measures were implemented to bring down high inflation and structural imbalances caused by the high growth of the late 1980s; the growth of the domestic economy slowed dramatically. However, this period saw a rapid growth of China's exports and a build-up of trade surplus. It can be seen in Figure 4.8 that the NEPR measures for natural resource products showed a continuous downward trend. The NEPR measures for agricultural products, human and physical capital-intensive goods maintained their positions in the world market; the NEPR measures for unskilled labour-intensive products even increased slightly. The fall in domestic demand actually drove domestic producers to seek foreign markets for their products. Foreign investments, especially from Hong Kong and Taiwan, further accelerated the growth of trade during this period. In terms of overall trade performance, however, China hardly improved its position *vis-à-vis* the world market.

1993–96

In 1993, China renewed its double-digit economic growth rate. The sudden relaxation of financial and fiscal policies saw a rapid expansion of the domestic economy; demand for industrial raw materials and capital goods skyrocketed so that exports declined and imports increased and in 1993, China reported the largest trade deficit since 1985. For fear of returning to high inflation, the government responded quickly by reintroducing tight monetary policies in 1994. Exports renewed their momentum as domestic demand tightened. A unique feature of this period was that the NEPR measures for human and physical capital-intensive goods rose strongly after 1993 while the NEPR measures for other groups fell. The NEPR measures for agricultural products declined most rapidly and stabilized only after 1995. The NEPR for natural resource-intensive products maintained its level. The NEPR for unskilled labour-intensive products also fell slightly.

While primary exports declined, manufactured exports demonstrated steady growth. The improvement can be seen as the result of the further opening up of the domestic economy and the introduction of foreign investment and technologies that increased the productivity and competitiveness of China's manufacturing industries. In addition, the trends that have emerged since 1993 possibly indicate the directions of important changes that are most likely to occur in China's trade patterns in the years to come.

CONCLUSIONS

Foreign trade is no longer a residual of the central economic plans and its growth is no longer limited by the shortages or surpluses inherent in the economic plans (Hsu 1989). This change has been most obviously reflected in the changes in the commodity patterns of trade. The abolition of the centrally controlled trade system, combined with other reform measures, has created an environment in which enterprises are able to respond vigorously to market signals and various incentive schemes; export and import decisions can now be made at the lower levels and profit-making has become a more important motive for trading.

All these changes do not necessarily mean that China has already established an efficient system of foreign trade. The foreign trade system is still only partially reformed; more importantly, the ultimate success of the foreign trade reforms depends largely on reforms of the economy as a whole. For instance, the mismatch of the domestic price structure with that in the international market makes it very difficult, if not impossible, for independent enterprises to operate efficiently across the boundaries of the two systems without causing large disturbances to the structure of the domestic economy. This is the dilemma that has constantly confronted trading companies and tradable goods producers during the reform period.

How should we assess the impact of various reform policies on the performance of trading companies and tradable goods producers in a partially reformed economy? Is it true that all the changes in China's commodity patterns of trade have been driven by the goal of improving production and making more efficient use of available resources? To answer these questions, we need to find a criterion to quantitatively assess the changes that have occurred in China's foreign trade over the past two decades.

APPENDIX

Table 4A.1   Concordance between the 61 Chinese tradables and the UN's Standard International Trade Classification (revised)

Commodities	SITC (revised)
Agricultural goods (13)	
1. Paddy rice	421
2. Wheat	410
3. Other grains	043, 044, 045, 08111, 2214
4. Oil-bearing crops	2211, 2216, 2218
5. Cotton	2631, 2633
6. Other industrial crops	05482, 1210, 2611, 2612, 2640, 265
7. Vegetables	0541, 0542, 0544, 0545, 0546, 05481, 05483, 05484, 05489, 08112, 08119
8. Fruits	0511, 0512, 0513, 0514, 0515, 0519, 52

Table 4A.1   (Continued)

Commodities	SITC (revised)
9. Forest products	0517, 0711, 0721, 075, 2212, 2213, 2215, 2217, 2219, 2311, 2921, 2925, 2926, 2927, 29291, 29294, 29299
10. Wool and hides	211, 212, 2621, 2623, 2625, 29111, 29113, 29191, 29195, 29199
11. Meat, eggs and milk	00, 011, 0250, 0223, 29192, 29193, 29196, 41131, 41132, 41139, 9410
12. Fish	0311, 0313, 29112, 29114, 29115, 29194, 29197, 4111
13. Other agricultural products	29198, 2922, 2924

Natural resource intensive-goods (6)

14. Coal	3214, 3215, 3216, 3217
15. Crude petroleum	3310, 3411
16. Ferrous minerals	281, 282
17. Non-ferrous minerals	283, 284, 285, 286
18. Non-metallic minerals	2712, 2713, 2714, 273, 274, 275, 276, 667
19. Timber	24, 2923, 29292, 29293

Physical capital-intensive goods (15)

32. Petroleum refining	332, 5211
33. Coal products	3218, 3412, 5214
34. Inorganic chemicals	511, 513, 514, 515
35. Chemical fertilizers	2711, 5213, 561, 5992
36. Organic chemicals	512, 53, 5997, 5999
38. Other chemicals	2312, 2313, 2314, 571, 581, 5996
40. Chemical fibres	266
42. Plastic articles	893
43. Cement	6612, 66183
44. Glass	664, 665
45. Ceramic products	6623, 6624, 6637, 6639, 666
47. Iron	6711, 6712, 6713, 6714, 6715
48. Steel	672, 673, 674, 675, 676, 677, 678, 679
49. Non-ferrous metals	68
50. Metal products	69

Human capital-intensive goods (13)

37. Household chemicals	41133, 41134, 41135, 431, 55, 59953, 59954, 59955, 59956, 59957, 59959, 8623, 8624.
39. Medicines	541
51. Agricultural machinery	712
52. Industrial equipment	7141, 7149, 715, 716, 7171, 7172, 718, 71911, 71913, 71914, 71915, 71919, 7192, 7193, 7195, 7196, 7197, 7198, 7199, 721, 726, 8121
53. Power station equipment	711, 7221

Table 4A.1 (Continued)

Commodities	SITC (revised)
54. Household mechanical/electrical goods	7173, 71912, 7194, 7250, 7331, 8614, 8615, 8616, 864
55. Railway equipment	731
56. Motor vehicles	732
57. Ships	735
58. Other transport equipment	7333, 7334, 734, 95101
59. Other engineering products	7222, 723, 7291, 7292, 7294, 7295, 7296, 7297, 72992, 72993, 72994, 72998, 72999, 8123, 8124, 8613, 8617, 8618, 8619, 899, 95102, 95103, 95104, 95105, 95106
60. Electronic products	7142, 7143, 72491, 72492, 72499, 7293, 72991, 72995
61. Household electronics	7241, 7242, 8911, 8912

Unskilled labour-intensive goods (14)

20. Sugar, tobacco and alcohol	0611, 0612, 0615, 0619, 112, 122
21. Other processed food	012, 013, 0221, 0222, 023, 024, 0312, 032, 0422, 046, 047, 048, 053, 055, 0616, 0620, 0713, 0722, 0723, 073, 074, 0812, 0813, 0814, 0819, 09, 111, 42, 59951, 59952
22. Cotton textiles	6513, 6514, 6516, 6517, 652, 6535, 6536, 6540, 6555, 6558, 6559, 6562, 65662
23. Wool textiles	2628, 6512, 6532, 65392, 65393, 6551, 35661, 6575, 6576, 6577
24. Hemp textiles	6515, 6519, 6533, 6534, 65391, 65394, 65395, 65396, 6554, 6556, 6561, 65669, 6569, 6574, 6578
25. Silk textiles	6511, 6531
26. Knitted goods	6537, 84141, 84142, 84143
27. Other textiles	2613, 2622, 2626, 2627, 2629, 2632, 2634, 267
28. Clothing and leather goods	61, 6557, 831, 8411, 8412, 8413, 84144, 84145, 8415, 8416, 8420, 851,
29. Furniture	63, 821
30. Paper	251, 641, 6421
31. Cultural and sporting goods	6422, 6423, 6429, 863, 8914, 8918, 8919, 892, 894, 895, 896, 897, 9610
41. Rubber manufactures	62
46. Other building materials	6518, 6538, 6611, 6613, 66181, 66182, 6631, 6632, 6634, 6635, 6636, 6638, 72996, 8122, 8611, 8612

Source: United Nations (1960).

Table 4A.2 China's net export performance ratio (NEPR), 1978–95

Product/Year	1978	1979	1980	1981	1982	1983
1. Paddy rice	13.96	13.17	7.45	1.47	3.83	0.65
2. Wheat	-10.94	-10.82	-13.24	-11.60	-10.95	-8.86
3. Other grain	-0.84	-1.70	-1.48	-0.58	-0.97	-0.39
4. Oil-bearing crops	2.82	3.29	5.62	14.93	5.75	7.53
5. Cotton	-12.34	-14.84	-16.73	-11.70	-6.54	-2.13
6. Other industrial crops	1.41	2.11	1.07	-0.09	0.68	1.19
7. Vegetables	3.41	3.62	4.31	3.99	3.00	2.87
8. Fruits	1.61	1.43	1.21	1.12	1.04	1.02
9. Forest products	-0.55	-0.59	-0.72	0.11	0.36	0.16
10. Wool and hides	2.71	2.11	2.15	2.27	0.61	2.50
11. Meat, etc.	4.47	3.44	3.55	2.82	3.04	2.80
12. Fish	3.88	3.87	3.72	3.21	2.49	1.88
13. Other agri. products	24.01	22.78	22.43	17.91	15.6	15.33
14. Coal	0.66	1.10	1.06	1.34	1.48	1.61
15. Crude petroleum	0.75	0.76	0.77	0.78	0.92	0.97
16. Ferrous metal ore	-1.70	-1.08	-0.83	-0.16	-0.19	-0.51
17. Non-ferr. minerals	0.77	0.67	0.80	1.08	0.15	-0.09
18. Non-metal minerals	0.51	0.59	0.68	1.01	1.03	1.01
19. Wood products	0.09	0.03	-0.55	-0.71	-1.76	-1.86
20. Sugar, tobacco and alcohol	-1.72	-1.09	-0.56	-0.61	-1.34	-0.81
21. Other processed food	2.32	1.81	1.68	1.60	1.47	1.66
22. Cotton textiles	3.51	3.44	1.89	0.68	1.59	2.42
23. Wool textiles	2.40	2.60	1.66	1.39	0.92	1.00
24. Hemp textiles	7.51	7.51	7.57	7.25	6.34	6.17
25. Silk textiles	32.09	29.75	31.60	28.53	23.10	23.55
26. Knitted goods	2.19	2.35	2.33	1.95	3.02	3.58
27. Other textiles	15.40	14.91	9.17	5.40	7.56	7.90
28. Clothing	2.52	2.91	3.36	3.54	3.77	4.04
29. Furniture	0.97	0.84	0.71	0.80	0.95	0.71
30. Paper	-0.41	-0.71	-1.44	-0.90	-0.61	-0.90
31. Cultural goods	1.06	0.99	0.83	0.87	0.78	0.59
32. Petroleum products	0.63	1.02	1.43	1.41	1.39	1.31
33. Coal products	0.19	0.08	0.20	0.15	0.27	0.20
34. Inorganic chemicals	-0.46	-0.23	0.34	0.86	0.79	0.32
35. Chem. fertilizers	-4.95	-5.20	-5.36	-4.41	-3.59	-4.77
36. Organic chemicals	-0.76	-0.30	-0.30	-0.19	-0.36	-0.19
37. Household chemicals	0.72	0.60	0.60	0.41	0.27	0.19
38. Other chemicals	-0.23	0.15	-0.37	-0.65	-1.22	-0.92
39. Medicine	0.95	1.07	1.25	1.04	0.95	0.97
40. Chemical fibres	-8.10	-5.25	-12.53	-15.37	-7.30	-4.49
41. Rubber manufactures	0.15	0.15	0.17	0.26	0.20	0.21
42. Plastic articles	0.15	0.12	0.07	0.10	0.13	0.03
43. Cement	1.94	1.26	2.30	1.28	0.70	-0.76
44. Glass	0.88	0.85	0.52	0.41	0.22	0.05
45. Ceramic products	2.66	2.28	2.04	1.77	2.26	2.21
46. Other building materials	0.57	0.48	0.39	0.32	0.22	0.17

Table 4A.2 (Continued)

1984	1985	1986	1987	1988	1989	1990	1991	1992	1993	1994	1995
1.52	3.70	2.90	3.37	0.14	0.01	-0.01	-0.03	0.08	0.63	1.04	-0.14
-6.05	-3.59	-3.31	-5.47	-6.81	-5.21	-7.51	-4.91	-3.77	-2.17	-2.31	-3.74
0.71	2.16	1.77	0.48	1.17	0.81	1.37	2.55	2.47	2.32	1.74	-1.43
5.49	5.24	6.06	4.64	3.56	3.07	4.45	5.47	3.51	4.04	2.94	2.59
2.43	3.73	5.66	6.41	3.72	-0.37	-2.52	-1.52	-1.33	1.28	-2.89	-4.26
1.48	1.11	0.85	0.81	0.68	0.72	1.12	1.26	0.78	1.08	0.91	0.42
2.15	2.27	3.08	2.34	2.29	1.71	1.99	2.05	1.96	1.96	2.07	1.65
0.78	0.56	0.45	0.50	0.43	0.30	0.38	0.25	0.27	0.30	0.29	0.28
0.30	0.30	0.37	-0.07	-0.35	0.39	0.02	-0.03	0.02	0.12	0.07	0.01
3.12	2.39	0.90	0.93	0.77	1.32	1.29	-0.13	-1.52	-2.22	-1.66	-2.41
2.65	1.97	1.76	1.48	1.13	1.02	1.62	1.32	0.96	0.84	0.91	1.02
1.95	1.79	2.35	2.27	2.74	2.31	2.35	1.56	1.42	1.10	1.07	1.11
11.35	7.88	10.01	9.10	8.96	8.80	10.10	6.72	5.34	4.77	6.73	6.40
1.29	0.98	1.06	1.34	1.26	1.08	1.70	1.74	1.62	1.50	1.46	1.53
1.15	1.62	1.35	1.06	1.00	0.64	0.69	0.44	0.19	-0.01	0.02	-0.08
-0.78	-1.35	-1.61	-1.15	0.05	-0.25	-1.68	-2.07	-3.09	-3.89	-3.09	-2.64
0.03	0.21	0.29	0.62	0.63	0.41	-0.43	-0.89	-1.22	-1.11	-0.89	-1.53
0.94	0.87	0.82	0.66	0.56	0.59	0.68	0.60	0.49	0.40	0.48	0.67
-1.91	-1.97	-0.86	-0.7	-1.03	-0.17	-0.79	-0.70	-0.64	-0.5	-0.32	-0.19
-0.76	-1.09	-0.47	-0.68	-0.89	-0.49	-0.10	-0.01	0.61	0.83	0.40	-0.02
1.33	1.19	1.09	0.84	0.80	0.75	0.74	0.69	0.62	0.71	0.41	0.23
2.58	0.91	1.66	1.77	1.16	0.74	-0.52	-0.88	-0.29	-0.27	-0.02	0.10
0.65	0.28	0.30	0.81	1.10	1.03	1.06	0.92	0.43	0.39	0.50	0.17
5.78	4.40	4.85	4.48	3.44	2.71	3.61	2.74	1.45	1.74	2.02	1.98
19.92	20.26	20.29	16.51	16.38	13.57	14.67	11.75	8.27	6.95	9.15	8.78
3.51	2.97	3.27	2.86	3.14	3.01	3.59	3.33	2.81	2.60	2.65	2.65
5.27	4.36	0.68	1.07	-2.06	4.56	5.89	4.82	2.46	2.87	3.10	1.21
4.00	3.75	4.43	4.33	4.54	5.19	4.06	4.26	4.81	5.10	5.08	4.54
0.58	0.32	0.27	-0.07	0.03	0.31	-0.02	0.18	0.35	0.42	0.57	0.75
-0.69	-0.90	-0.81	-0.86	-0.69	-0.48	-0.57	-0.77	-0.93	-0.86	-0.82	-0.63
0.84	1.12	1.45	1.97	2.43	2.96	1.01	1.12	1.96	2.08	2.17	2.14
1.18	1.08	0.57	0.45	0.29	0.00	0.23	0.03	-0.21	0.05	-0.51	-0.44
0.07	0.09	0.10	0.32	1.08	1.76	2.31	1.81	1.51	2.41	2.84	4.95
0.32	0.30	0.55	0.63	1.02	0.87	0.86	0.97	1.00	0.99	0.85	1.41
-4.70	-2.29	-1.56	-1.96	-2.43	-2.51	-6.13	-7.28	-6.12	-3.03	-2.71	-3.91
-0.31	-0.51	-0.28	-0.37	-0.48	-0.28	-0.18	-0.53	-0.43	-0.36	-0.25	-0.26
0.07	-0.29	-0.34	-0.60	-0.47	-0.38	0.13	-0.05	-0.08	-0.05	-0.08	-0.02
-1.88	-1.94	-1.21	-1.23	-2.05	-1.07	-0.69	-1.24	-2.09	-2.02	-1.78	-1.75
0.77	0.65	0.47	0.26	0.11	0.24	0.32	0.29	0.36	0.37	0.44	0.52
-7.93	-8.85	-5.16	-6.11	-5.26	-3.15	-7.78	-9.28	-6.03	-4.92	-5.30	-5.28
0.09	0.01	0.06	0.00	-0.04	-0.03	0.31	0.29	0.15	0.16	0.22	0.37
-0.10	-0.32	-0.08	0.17	0.54	0.98	0.40	0.42	0.86	1.03	1.20	1.23
-0.75	-0.61	-0.43	-0.32	-0.29	-0.12	3.85	5.90	2.71	0.26	0.66	1.89
-0.13	-0.82	-0.17	-0.14	-0.19	-0.17	0.11	0.07	-0.05	-0.16	-0.13	0.11
1.88	1.25	1.19	1.53	1.60	1.53	1.73	1.87	1.72	1.51	1.97	1.81
0.09	-0.25	-0.23	-0.21	-0.02	0.15	0.3	0.48	0.52	0.53	0.58	0.78

Table 4A.2 (Continued)

Product/Year	1978	1979	1980	1981	1982	1983
47. Pig iron	-4.79	-2.96	0.56	4.14	4.01	-2.32
48. Steel	-6.70	-5.70	-2.93	-1.26	-1.89	-4.33
49. Non-ferrous metals	-1.01	-0.91	-0.28	0.19	-0.47	-1.00
50. Metal products	0.41	0.27	-0.06	0.23	0.87	0.79
51. Agri. machinery	-0.35	-0.23	-0.16	0.03	-0.01	-0.07
52. Industrial equipment	-0.50	-1.40	-1.59	-1.22	-0.46	-0.72
53. Power station equipment	-0.33	-0.39	-0.68	-0.54	-0.74	-0.61
54. Household mech./elect. goods	0.25	0.20	-0.12	-0.24	-0.04	-0.23
55. Railway equipment	0.12	-0.01	-0.06	-0.02	-0.20	-0.02
56. Motor vehicles	-0.48	-0.49	-0.25	-0.17	-0.13	-0.21
57. Ships and boats	-1.18	-2.74	-3.31	-0.29	-1.66	-1.00
58. Transport equipment	-0.31	-0.21	-0.64	-0.03	-0.11	-0.77
59. Other engineering products	0.71	0.32	0.01	-0.02	0.26	-0.07
60. Electronic products	-0.19	-0.31	-0.47	-0.51	-0.47	-0.53
61. Household electronics	0.03	-0.84	-1.20	-1.28	-0.51	-0.53

Source: International Economic Data Bank, International Trade System, compiled from United Nations' International Trade Statistics, The Australian National University.

Table 4A.2 Continued

1984	1985	1986	1987	1988	1989	1990	1991	1992	1993	1994	1995
-2.26	-4.19	-2.28	1.60	4.03	1.91	0.98	2.66	2.93	2.23	2.72	5.38
-4.46	-5.71	-4.26	-2.50	-1.88	-1.55	-0.90	-0.65	-1.42	-4.47	-2.37	-0.63
-0.99	-1.07	-0.62	0.08	0.22	-0.04	0.01	-0.17	-0.82	-0.63	-0.09	-0.22
0.58	0.00	-0.11	0.21	0.47	0.50	0.72	0.78	0.78	0.69	0.75	0.87
-0.26	-0.38	-0.43	-0.19	-0.12	-0.19	-0.19	-0.10	-0.43	-0.39	-0.23	-0.08
-1.16	-2.45	-2.25	-1.46	-1.20	-0.94	-1.03	-1.03	-1.31	-2.06	-1.63	-1.38
-0.33	-0.56	-0.77	-0.60	-0.53	-0.60	-0.89	-0.65	-0.60	-0.51	-0.51	-0.21
-0.73	-1.98	-0.28	-0.08	0.44	0.99	0.35	0.27	0.53	0.59	0.84	1.08
-3.85	-1.90	-2.96	-3.50	-2.96	0.21	-1.42	0.94	1.39	1.03	1.68	3.49
-0.55	-1.11	-0.44	-0.17	-0.20	-0.15	-0.13	-0.20	-0.38	-0.54	-0.37	-0.14
-0.93	-1.92	-0.81	-0.03	-0.16	-0.30	-0.50	-0.05	0.04	-0.75	-0.80	-0.19
-0.32	-1.69	-0.73	-0.89	-0.39	-0.59	-0.66	-0.63	-0.76	-1.09	-1.36	-0.44
-0.36	-0.95	-0.83	-0.24	-0.04	0.12	-0.07	-0.06	0.02	-0.04	0.13	0.20
-0.97	-1.49	-1.12	-0.91	-0.76	-0.45	-0.52	-0.49	-0.57	-0.71	-0.49	-0.28
-1.67	-3.47	0.00	0.59	0.51	1.70	0.98	1.04	1.29	1.09	1.15	1.24

5 Measuring Comparative Advantage

The principle of comparative advantage has significant implications for the efficiency of resource allocation and economic growth. The term 'comparative advantage' is often used interchangeably with 'comparative cost' which is closely associated with the term 'opportunity cost'. The opportunity cost of a commodity is the value of other commodities which must be forgone so that one extra unit of a commodity may be obtained. This is equivalent to what is expressed in the literature of comparative advantage as 'relative price'–that is, the quantity of some commodity that must be given up in exchange for one unit of another commodity. In the classical case, the comparative advantage in a commodity is defined by the divergence between its autarkic and free trade relative prices.

The classical definition of comparative advantage is useful for explaining the origins and patterns of trade, but this is not the only expression of comparative advantage. The same questions can also be posed, not in terms of a comparison between autarkic and free trade prices, but in the context of disturbances to an initial trading equilibrium (Jones and Neary 1984). For most, if not all, countries, autarky is non-existent and trade is a fact of life. For a majority of countries, on the other hand, trade is subject to various restrictions and does not flow freely. In such circumstances, a comparison between autarkic and free trade relative prices is not possible.

This is by no means to say that the basic principle of comparative advantage is not applicable. In the context of improving resource allocation efficiency and exploiting gains from trade, the comparative advantage in a commodity can generally be defined by a comparison between its domestic opportunity cost and its relative border price. As Chenery suggests (1961:19)

> the optimum pattern of production and trade for a country is determined from a comparison of the opportunity cost of producing a given commodity with the price at which the commodity can be imported or exported.

Under the conditions of full employment and perfect competition, the opportunity cost of a commodity is equal to its market price which can, therefore, be used to determine comparative advantage. When domestic market distortions prevail, the opportunity cost can be seen only in the implicit shadow price. Comparative advantage should then be determined by a comparison between the domestic shadow price and the border price.

Two aspects should be noted here. First, domestic opportunity costs are not equivalent to autarkic prices. Second, border prices are not necessarily free trade prices and could potentially be very distorted. However, if these are the prices that the country confronts and cannot alter (at least in the short and medium term), then they can be taken as given and treated as free trade prices (the small-country assumption). More importantly, if the domestic opportunity cost of producing a commodity, after being adjusted for all known domestic distortions, remains different from its border price, this price divergence can be seen as a source of comparative advantage. This also signals potential gains from trade and possible improvements in resource allocation. Price divergence leads to comparative advantage and comparative advantage in turn induces gains from trade. The greater the price divergence the greater the gains from trade (Samuelson 1962; Krueger and Sonnenschein 1967).

The concept of comparative advantage used in this study is based on its implications for rational resource allocation. It is defined, as described above, by comparing domestic opportunity costs with related border prices. This definition retains the essence of comparative advantage when applied to issues of resource allocation and can be applied empirically. In the following sections, various expressions of comparative advantage will first be reviewed and the empirical proxies of comparative advantage will then be explored.

EXPRESSIONS OF COMPARATIVE ADVANTAGE

The principle of comparative advantage has been expressed in two alternative ways, by Ricardo and by Heckscher–Ohlin. Before turning to empirical measurement, we will briefly examine in this section how each model presents the concept of comparative advantage.

Ricardo Version

In a simple two-good and two-country Ricardian trade model, a country, denoted as the home country, produces X_1 and X_2 units of two goods using L_1 and L_2 units of labour, the only factor of production. The total labour force is L and the prices for the two goods are p_1 and p_2, respectively. In autarkic equilibrium, the value of total output is

$$Y = p_1 X_1 + p_2 X_2 \tag{5.1}$$

In equilibrium, the commodity prices are determined by the labour costs–that is, $p_1 = w l_1$ and $p_2 = w l_2$ where w denotes the wage rate and l_1 and l_2 are the fixed labour input coefficients equal to L_1/X_1 and L_2/X_2, respectively.

Suppose that there is a free trade equilibrium in the rest of the world in which prices, wage rates and labour input coefficients differ from those in the home country under autarky. The corresponding free trade or world parameters are distinguished from their autarkic counterparts by an asterisk. When the home country opens to trade, it will have a comparative advantage in X_1 if the following inequality is observed

$$\frac{l_1}{l_2} < \frac{l_1^*}{l_2^*} \tag{5.2}$$

This condition implies that the home country has a comparative advantage in X_1 and a comparative disadvantage in X_2 because the opportunity costs of producing X_1 in terms of the labour input in X_2 is less in the home country than in the rest of the world. Alternatively, the comparative advantage condition can be expressed as

$$\frac{l_1}{l_1^*} < \frac{l_2}{l_2^*} \tag{5.3}$$

This condition indicates that the home country has a comparative advantage in X_1 and a comparative disadvantage in X_2 simply because it is more efficient in producing X_1 than X_2 relative to the world.

Since relative labour inputs equal relative prices under perfect competition, the above conditions can also be expressed in terms of commodity prices

$$\frac{p_1}{p_2} < \frac{p_1^*}{p_2^*}, \quad \text{or} \quad \frac{p_1}{p_1^*} < \frac{p_2}{p_2^*} \tag{5.4}$$

This is referred to as the price indication of comparative advantage while the previous expression (5.3) is referred to as the quantity indication. It should be noted that in the simple Ricardian model labour productivity is the main determinant of comparative advantage.

Heckscher–Ohlin Version

In a simple Heckscher–Ohlin (H–O) model, the home country produces two goods, X_1 and X_2, with two factors of production, labour and capital. In a competitive equilibrium, the price of each output must equal its marginal cost, which, under constant returns to scale, equals the average cost. Therefore the equations of production equilibrium are

$$p_1 = w\,l_1 + r\,k_1 \tag{5.5}$$

$$p_2 = w\,l_2 + r\,k_2 \tag{5.6}$$

where k_1 and k_2 denote capital inputs into one unit of X_1 and X_2, respectively. Production has neoclassical characteristics including flexible factor input coefficients, that is, the ls and ks are determined by the wage rate w and capital rental rate r, respectively. With given endowments of labour and capital, L and K, wage and rental rates are expected to be determined in the home country.

Suppose that, in the pre-trade equilibrium, the home country has low capital and high labour endowments compared with the rest of the world, $K/L < K^*/L^*$, and hence a lower wage–rental ratio, $w/r < w^*/r^*$. In such circumstances, firms in the home country will use more labour in their production of X_1 and X_2 while firms in the rest of the world will use more capital. Since X_1 is labour-intensive, the proportion of labour input will be greater in X_1 than in X_2 in the home country. As a result, the capital–labour ratio in the production of X_1 will be lower in the home country and capital-labour ratio in the production of X_2 will be higher in the home country than in the rest of the world, that is,

$$\frac{k_1/l_1}{k_1^*/l_1^*} < \frac{k_2/l_2}{k_2^*/l_2^*} \tag{5.7}$$

The home country will have a comparative advantage in X_1 because its production of X_1 is more efficient than that of X_2 in comparison with the rest of the world. The opposite can be said of the world. This is the same as saying that the relative factor requirements of X_1 in terms of the factor requirements of X_2 are less in the home country than in the world,

$$\frac{k_1/l_1}{k_2/l_2} < \frac{k_1^*/l_1^*}{k_2^*/l_2^*} \tag{5.8}$$

implying higher home country factor productivity and therefore a comparative advantage in X_1.

In contrast to the simple Ricardian model, however, in a multigood, multifactor world, it is difficult to identify a country's comparative advantage through consideration of factor input coefficients or factor productivity. The Heckscher–Ohlin theorem bypasses this difficulty and allows identification of a country's comparative advantage through consideration of the factor endowments of the countries and the factor contents of the goods concerned.

According to the Heckscher–Ohlin theorem, a country has a comparative advantage in producing goods which intensively use its relatively abundant factors. The labour-abundant home country will therefore have a comparative advantage in production of the labour-intensive good X_1. This is because, with a sufficient endowment of labour, the home country enjoys a lower wage–rental ratio and hence a lower production cost of the labour-intensive good, X_1, than the rest of the world. Unlike the Ricardian model, therefore, the quantity indication of comparative advantage in the H–O model requires measurement of the home country's factor endowments relative to the rest of the world and a ranking of industries in accordance with their use of the factor relatively abundant in that country.

The Heckscher–Ohlin theorem postulates that the labour-abundant country will export labour-intensive goods and import capital-intensive goods. A country's comparative advantage can be measured only in proxy terms by consideration of the factor contents of traded goods, but factor intensity can be measured only after trade has taken place. To distinguish it from a quantity indication based on the pre-trade industry factor contents, this is referred to as the 'trade indication of comparative advantage.'

The Stolper–Samuelson theorem postulates that the costs of goods are positively linked to factor prices. In the home country where the wage–rental ratio is lower in autarky, the relative price of the labour-intensive good must be lower, that is,

$$\frac{p_1}{p_2} < \frac{p_1^*}{p_2^*}, \quad \text{because of} \quad \frac{w}{r} < \frac{w^*}{r^*} \tag{5.9}$$

or, equivalently,

$$\frac{p_1}{p_1^*} < \frac{p_2}{p_2^*} \tag{5.10}$$

This expression captures the price indication of comparative advantage in the H–O model as it defines labour abundance to mean a low relative autarkic wage–rental ratio and a low relative price of labour-intensive good. This expression is similar to its counterpart in the Ricardian model.

It should be noted that comparative advantage may not be the sole determinant of trade patterns. Consumption may also influence trade. In addition, the theory of comparative advantage assumes constant returns to scale in production, whereas increasing returns to scale are characteristic of many industries. Imperfect competition is also important in the determination of trade. These factors have led to the modifications of trade theory in recent years (Krugman 1979; Helpman and Krugman 1985). This is particularly relevant, however, to trade flows in differentiated products among countries with similar factor endowments, especially to intra-industry trade among industrial countries. Like most developing countries, however, China is mainly involved in inter-industry trade in most markets. In such circumstances, comparative advantage could still be seen as the principal determinant of efficient trade specialization.

EMPIRICAL MEASUREMENT OF A COUNTRY'S COMPARATIVE ADVANTAGE

The empirical studies on measuring comparative advantage have used one of the three indications examined above. Here, we compare these indications in the context of their applicability to China.

Quantity Indication

The quantity indication of comparative advantage is based on the descriptive characteristics of tradable goods classified by their utilization of factors of production. The quantity measure requires two sets of information: the factor intensities of traded goods and the factor endowments of a country. A test of the Heckscher–Ohlin theorem requires three sets of information: factor endowments, factor intensities and trade flows. To measure comparative advantage for a particular country, however, only the first two are needed.

Factor intensities can be estimated for a standard H–O model with two factors and two goods. In a generalized H–O model involving more than two factors and commodities, however, the factor-intensity characteristics of commodities cannot be established consistently. It has been suggested by Deardorff (1982, 1984) that factor intensities can be defined by factor shares instead of factor ratios. Factor shares, though, require measurement of factor intensities in terms of a common unit, normally factor returns, and not physical employment. Such a measure would inevitably be sensitive to factor market imperfections because imperfections distort factor usage and factor returns and thus bias the measure of factor intensity.

A country's endowment of factors of production can be estimated. The relative endowment of a factor may be defined as the country's share in the total world supply of that factor. Difficulties, however, arise with regard to the extent that the country should be considered as abundant in that factor. Answering this question would require a comprehensive multicountry investigation. Matching the ranking of factor abundance with the ranking of factor intensities in order to identify those commodities with a comparative advantage could be a daunting exercise.[1]

Generalization of the quantitative version of the Heckscher–Ohlin theorem involves further problems concerning its reliance on the rigid assumptions of technology similarity, factor price equalization, identical patterns of consumption and the absence of trends toward factor-intensity reversals (Ethier 1983:534–5).

An even more fundamental problem arising from the underlying proposition of the Heckscher–Ohlin theorem is that only one inter-country difference (that is, factor endowments) is regarded to determine a country's comparative advantage. It is undoubtedly true that factor endowment is a key determinant. But other inter-country differences, known or unknown, may also help shape a country's pattern of comparative advantage. The factor abundance measure may, therefore, provide only a partial picture about a country's comparative advantage structure.

Trade Indication

Comparative advantage may be regarded as the outcome of a combination of various factors and the shifts in comparative advantage constitute an even more complex phenomenon. The concept of comparative advantage refers to a pre-trade equilibrium, whereas in the empirical studies only post-trade data are available. This has led to the development of the indices of the so-called 'revealed' comparative advantage, as discussed earlier.

The indices of 'revealed' comparative advantage are based on the assumption that the relative costs of production as well as differences in non-price factors are reflected in the patterns of commodity trade. For instance, the high value of exports of a given commodity, relative to its imports, may indicate that the country has a comparative advantage in producing the good. A number of indicators have been used in the literature to describe a country's trade patterns in order to 'reveal' the underlying comparative advantage. They include, among others, the export performance ratio (EPR) [2] which expresses the ratio of a country's share in world exports of a particular commodity to its share in world exports of all goods (Balassa 1977, 1979); the export specialization ratio (Balassa 1965); and the net export ratio (NER) (UNIDO 1982, 1986).[3]

It can be argued, however, that a country's particular pattern of trade may not just reflect comparative advantage. The observed patterns of trade and the domestic production structure are also affected by other factors as well. For instance, the relatively high value of exports of a particular product may be the result of biased relative prices caused by direct state subsidies or other indirect incentives. This is especially so in a transitional economy in which the trade in a particular commodity or group of commodities could be easily manipulated by the state through price- or non-price-related instruments. As a result, the above indices may reveal only a country's actual trade performance, which may or may not be determined by its true comparative advantage.

Price Indication

An attractive feature of price indication is that it takes account of inter-country differences not only in factor endowments but also in all other known or unknown potential determinants which may have contributed to the price differentials. All determinants of comparative advantage must impact on the relative costs and, in a competitive environment, on the relative prices of products. Relative price differentials between countries thus embody all the information about comparative advantage. The price indication of comparative advantage also avoids the possible biases generated from those single-factor explanations.

Unfortunately, the empirical application of the price indication is practically impossible because the autarkic relative prices are not observable. All countries are more or less involved in trade, and it is highly unlikely that the prevailing prices reflect the autarkic prices in any way. As shown above, however, from the viewpoint of resource reallocation efficiency, the comparative advantage in a commodity can be defined more readily by a comparison between its domestic opportunity costs and its world price. In this context, a country is said to have a comparative advantage in producing a given commodity if the domestic opportunity cost is lower than the given world price. To maximize social welfare, resources should be reallocated until an equilibrium is reached in which no commodity is produced at a higher cost than the cost of an import and the marginal revenue from exports equals their marginal cost of domestic production. The price indication in an n-good world can thus be used as an expression of comparative advantage

$$\frac{p_1}{p_1^*} < \frac{p_2}{p_2^*} < \ldots < \frac{p_n}{p_n^*} \qquad (5.11)$$

A country can increase its welfare by simply reallocating the existing resources from the industries with the highest relative price to those with the lowest relative prices, This also implies an increase in the imports of the former and an increase in the exports of the latter.[4]

This expression is based on the prices of final consumption goods and the intermediate inputs are assumed away. In reality, however, the costs of intermediate inputs are a significant component of the final good's prices. Intermediate inputs also constitute a large proportion of international trade. The relative prices of intermediate inputs have a considerable impact on the prices of final goods. Intermediate inputs must be incorporated in any measure of comparative advantage. In a country with multiple goods and factors, the domestic equilibrium price of good j, p_j^D, equals the sum of the costs of intermediate inputs and the returns of primary factors, that is,

$$p_j^D = \sum_i a_{ij}^D \, p_i^D + \sum_s a_{sj}^F \, p_s^F \qquad (5.12)$$

where a_{ij}^D and a_{sj}^F represent the unit requirements of intermediate and factor inputs, respectively; p_j^D and p_s^F are the domestic prices of good j and primary factor s, respectively. The world price, p_j^*, could be expressed in the same way. Comparison could then be made between the relative value-added (net of intermediate input costs) rather than between the relative prices. For good j, it may be expressed as

$$\frac{\sum_s a_{sj}^F \, p_s^F}{p_j^* - \sum_i a_{ij}^* \, p_i^*} \qquad (5.13)$$

The numerator is the domestic value-added in terms of factor returns measured at the domestic equilibrium prices while the denominator is the international value-added measured at the world price. The comparative advantage could be determined by ranking the ratios for individual goods in the same way as in a simple Ricardian model.

The concept of comparative advantage lies at the core of the emphasis on trade as a key issue for development policy. A number of allocation criteria have been devised to make this approach to economic development operational (Chenery 1961). The measure of domestic resource cost (DRC) has, over time, come to be the most widely used of these criteria.

DOMESTIC RESOURCE COST (DRC) METHOD

Domestic resource cost is a measure of the social cost of the resources required by a given industry to earn or save one unit of foreign exchange. The early version of the DRC measure was called 'the cost of the dollar earned' (in the case of exports) or 'saved' (in the case of import substitutes) (Bruno 1962:106). The concept has been used not only as an *ex ante* measure of comparative advantage but also as an *ex post* measure of the costs of a restrictive trade system–that is, as an alternative measure of effective protection.

Since Bruno, DRC measures have been used in evaluating development projects and trade policies in many countries in which the official exchange rate and commodity prices are believed to be distorted. The first application appeared in work on the Israeli economy by Baharal (1956), Barkai (1956) and Toren (1957). A systematic analytical treatment appeared in the 1960s in works by Bruno (1962, 1965). Since then, the DRC has been widely used in many country studies by various authors including Krueger (1966) for Turkey, Leith (1976) for Ghana, Behrman (1977) for Chile, Balassa *et al.* (1984) for Morocco, Greenaway and Milner (1990) for Madagascar and Warr (1991) for Indonesia, to name only a few.

In the original DRC estimation,[5] the world price of a tradable good, P, is decomposed into two parts–the domestic costs C_d and the import costs C_m. As P and C_m are expressed in terms of a foreign currency, they should be converted into the domestic currency using the exchange rate, ER (units of domestic currency per unit of the foreign exchange). Under the ideal conditions of competitive free trade where domestic market prices are identical to their corresponding world prices or social values, and technologies are generally accessible, the DRC for all commodities would equal an equilibrium exchange rate. This yields the expression $P \times ER = C_d + C_m \times ER$. In the real world, however, the DRC for individual goods may differ from the equilibrium exchange rate. Rearranging the above formula gives

$$DRC = \frac{C_d}{P - C_m} \qquad (5.14)$$

This is a measure of the domestic resource cost of foreign exchange earned or saved in producing a particular commodity. A DRC estimate below the equilibrium exchange rate indicates a comparative advantage for the country concerned and, otherwise, a disadvantage. For most countries, particularly for developing countries, the DRC estimates for various industries will not necessarily equal the exchange rate when the domestic and import cost components are estimated at the social values or border prices.

The DRC concept had its origin in some inter-related investment criteria, an example of which is the Net Social Profitability (NSP). Using the above notations, the NSP can be expressed as follows

$$NSP = P \times ER - C_d - C_m \times ER \qquad\qquad (5.15)$$

A project should be considered if the NSP estimate is positive. It is clear that $NSP = 0$ is equivalent to $DRC = 1$, $NSP > 0$ is equivalent to $DRC < 1$ and $NSP < 1$ is identical to $DRC > 1$ when ER is the shadow exchange rate. This general criterion is logically equivalent to the Social Marginal Productivity (SMP) criterion. The difference is that the unknown variable is not the rate of profit but the price of foreign exchange in terms of domestic resources.

Although the principle of DRC has remained the same since the 1950s, the practical methods for estimating DRC have developed considerably. Individual authors have usually followed their own versions of the DRC measure in empirical studies because of either theoretical considerations or data availability. Empirical estimations of DRC usually involve two types of data: survey data and input–output information. The former considers only direct inputs of intermediate goods and primary factors while the latter takes into account indirect inputs as well. If data are available, the input–output method is clearly preferred to the survey method because of its comprehensiveness and accuracy. The following discussion will concentrate only on the method using input–output data.

Two general types of empirical DRC estimations are identified by their different treatments of intermediate inputs. One focuses on the difference between domestically produced and imported inputs and attempts to calculate the actual costs of imported inputs. The other emphasizes the distinction between tradable and non-tradable inputs and therefore calculates the potential costs of tradable inputs. The earlier method relied on the breaking down of intermediate inputs into their domestic and import components. Bruno initially considered that the accuracy of DRC measures depended on the correct breakdown of cost components, otherwise, systematic bias would occur (1965:115). This claim was accepted by some authors (Pearson, Akrasanee and Nelson 1976). In fact, however, if an input–output table and shadow prices are used, no serious bias will occur even though some foreign exchange items are erroneously counted as primary factor costs. Using an input–output table, a missing item in the denominator will automatically be captured in the numerator. The item in the numerator will be measured at the shadow prices of primary factors which, in principle, are equivalent to the same item measured at the border price. An increase in foreign exchange revenue owing to a missing item, therefore, will be offset by an equivalent increase in domestic factor costs, leaving the estimated DRC unchanged. Bruno noted this point when he discussed the treatment of tradable but not actually traded (imported) goods (1972). He suggested that such goods could in principle be included in either the denominator or numerator. 'If the evaluation is made at opportunity cost, it would make no difference for the decision criterion' (1972:20 n. 10). If this is the case, a simplified version of the DRC measure can be readily formulated. It is based on the distinction of inputs between potentially tradable and non-tradable instead of actually traded and not traded. Assuming first that (5.12) holds, in the presence of domestic distortions, the border prices for tradable goods, p_j^B, and the shadow prices for the factors, p_s^S, should be used in the DRC formula. The DRC can be expressed in the net value (value-added) terms as [6]

$$DRC_j = \frac{\sum_s a_{sj}^F \, p_s^S}{p_j^B - \sum_i a_{ij}^D \, p_j^B} \tag{5.16}$$

This DRC expression is much simpler than the original version in which inputs were divided into the domestic and imported components. It also avoids the estimation of the shadow exchange rate. The basic principles remain the same but the interpretation is slightly different. The DRC estimates here compare two types of value-added, one measured at the shadow prices of domestic primary factors and the other at the border prices of tradables. The results indicate the domestic resource (primary factor) costs of a unit of the value-added measured at the border prices. This is a proxy for a country's comparative advantage.

The above equation ignores any non-tradable goods. In reality, tradables are produced using not only tradable inputs and primary factors, but also non-tradable goods and services as well. Using the above DRC method, non-tradable inputs can be readily incorporated into the formula.[7] When non-tradable goods are included, the domestic prices of tradable goods and non-tradable goods may be shown, respectively, as

$$p_j^T = \sum_i a_{ij}^{TT} \, p_i^T + \sum_k a_{kj}^{NT} \, p_k^N + \sum_s a_{sj}^{FT} \, p_s^F \tag{5.17}$$

$$p_j^N = \sum_i a_{ij}^{TN} \, p_i^T + \sum_k a_{kj}^{NN} \, p_k^N + \sum_s a_{sj}^{FN} \, p_s^F \tag{5.18}$$

where a_{ij}^{TT}, a_{kj}^{NT} and a_{sj}^{FT} denotes the tradable intermediate good i, the non-tradable intermediate good k and the primary factor s used in the production of tradable good j, respectively, and so on; p_k^N is the price of primary factor k. This expression indicates that the price of tradable good j is composed of the costs of tradable and non-tradable inputs as well as primary factors. Using input–output relationships, the requirement for non-tradable inputs in the production of tradable goods can be decomposed into the requirements for tradable goods, $\tilde{a}_{ij}^T$, and the primary factors, $\tilde{a}_{ij}^F$. The domestic price of tradable good j can then be shown as

$$p_j^T = \sum_i (a_{ij}^{TT} + \tilde{a}_{ij}^T) \, p_i^T + \sum_s (a_{sj}^{FT} + \tilde{a}_{ij}^F) \, p_s^F \tag{5.19}$$

The DRC for tradable good j is therefore

$$DRC_j = \frac{\sum\limits_{s}(a_{sj}^{FT} + \tilde{a}_{ij}^{F})\, p_s^S}{p_j^T - \sum\limits_{i}(a_{ij}^{TT} + \tilde{a}_{ij}^{T})\, p_i^T} \tag{5.20}$$

INTERPRETATION AND COMPARISON OF DRC RESULTS

The DRC estimates for various tradable goods are usually ranked and compared according to their actual magnitudes. In many circumstances, however, the DRC estimates cannot be compared in such a simple manner. It is surprising that no attention has been paid to possible problems involved in interpreting and comparing these estimates.

Magnitude of DRC Estimates and the Use of DRP

The DRC estimate for a given commodity is a ratio of two components–the primary factor returns measured at the shadow prices and the value-added measured at the border prices. The returns to the primary factors used in production, no matter how distorted the factor markets may be, should always be positive. The value-added for a given commodity may be positive, zero or negative, depending on which input coefficients are used: international a_{ij}^{*} or domestic a_{ij}^{D}. The former are supposed to be the ones under free trade conditions and the latter under distorted conditions. If a_{ij}^{*} are used, the estimates obtained will be the true international value-added for the commodity concerned. The magnitude of this value-added should always be positive. The DRC thus estimated would accurately compare domestic factor costs with the true international value-added.

In the real world, however, the international input coefficients a_{ij}^{*} are not readily available. In empirical studies, the domestic input coefficients a_{ij}^{D} are often adopted as an alternative under the strong assumption of technological similarity. In practice, this is not likely to be the case. Domestic input coefficients cannot be regarded as optimal given all the distortions in the domestic goods and factors markets. Therefore, the value-added estimated using the domestic coefficients a_{ij}^{D} and the border price p_i^{B} will certainly be different from the true international value-added. In the presence of high protection which usually causes sharp divergences between the domestic and international price levels, the value-added thus estimated could be zero or even negative. As a result, the DRC estimates for some tradables could be undefined.

This raises serious difficulties for ranking and comparing industries or commodities directly by their DRC estimates. One cannot rank, for instance, a DRC estimate of –10 ahead of a DRC estimate of –100 because the former might actually result from a larger negative value-added than the latter, which indicates a higher degree of comparative disadvantage. To overcome this problem, we use the inverse of the DRC in this study. The inverse DRC measure could be conversely defined as the amount of foreign exchange earned by one unit of combined domestic resources (primary factors). It measures the foreign exchange revenue potentially generated by employing a marginal unit of domestic currency worth of factors. It can be conveniently referred to as domestic resource productivity (DRP), which may be expressed as

$$DRP_j = \frac{p_j^B - \sum_i (a_{ij}^{TT} + \tilde{a}_{ij}^T) \, p_j^B}{\sum_s (a_{sj}^{FT} + \tilde{a}_{ij}^F) \, p_s^S} \tag{5.21}$$

This measure allows a consistent ranking of tradable commodities directly according to their estimated results. It is also literally consistent with the concept of comparative advantage itself. In general, the benchmark of unity can be used to distinguish tradable goods into two groups. A DRP estimate above unity is a sign of comparative advantage in the industry or commodity concerned. If the DRP estimate is below unity, the industry concerned is regarded as having a comparative disadvantage. A relatively high DRP estimate shows a stronger comparative advantage than a low DRP estimate. In the remainder of this study, we will use the DRP instead of the DRC in measuring comparative advantage.

Interpretation of DRP Estimates

The DRP is based on the concept of comparative advantage. As a proxy, however, it also differs from the original concept of comparative advantage. These differences can be seen from a comparison between the DRP expression in (5.21) and the expression for comparative advantage in (5.13). In (5.21), the border price and the shadow price replace the free trade prices for tradable goods and the autarkic prices for primary factors. This may be justified on the grounds that the country concerned is unlikely to influence the world prices. So, the border prices for the goods it trades can be taken as the given free trade prices. Given goods prices, the shadow prices for primary factors can also be derived. The other difference between (5.21) and (5.13) is the intermediate input coefficients. In the DRP expression, the domestic input coefficients are used to replace the world's input coefficients. Such a deviation warrants a careful interpretation of the DRP as a proxy for comparative advantage.

Unlike (5.13), comparison here is no longer made between two distinctive equilibrium situations: autarky and free trade. Instead, it is made between the factor shadow costs and the net revenue generated at the free trade prices by domestic producers with the existing technology and input–output structure. This description could be interpreted as to coincide with a situation in which the domestic markets have just been liberalized, but the firm's demands for factors and intermediate goods have not yet been changed (for example, when a country suddenly removes all its trade barriers). The domestic producers are suddenly exposed to free trade prices, but they have not yet adjusted their demands for factor and intermediate inputs.

The DRP ratio used in such a situation could indicate which domestic industries are likely to survive. The denominator of (5.21) shows the factor costs valued at free trade prices, for which domestic producers have to pay to the factor owners. The numerator measures the net revenue that domestic producers would get from selling their products under the same circumstance. The DRP as a whole, therefore, measures the net social benefit in terms of the foreign exchange equivalent that would be earned or saved by one unit of domestic resources through tradable goods production. If the denominator is smaller than the numerator, the industry concerned would not survive because the net revenue from the sales of its products would not be sufficient to reward the factor services used in production. In extreme cases, the value-added derived from domestic coefficients but valued at world prices could be zero or negative. For those industries whose input requirements are unusually high due probably to the low domestic prices of these intermediate goods relative to the rest of the world, the DRP measures could well be negative. It implies that the industry concerned is unlikely to survive the transition to a free trade situation.

In addition, unlike the classical concept of comparative advantage, the DRP is dynamic in the sense that it does not compare two well-established static equilibria. Instead, it measures the resource-allocation efficiency of a transitional economy. When the DRP is applied to two consequent periods, it measures the changes at the margin in the ratio of value-added. It can be expected that, as the economy moves away from distortion toward free trade, production adjustments will eventually be made so that the domestic input–output structure becomes similar to that of the world. The DRP estimates, if applied to a period of economic liberalization, will converge to unity for all industries over time. This distinctive feature of the DRP could provide valuable insight in detecting to what extent an economy moves away from distortion or how effective the reform policies have been.

The adoption of DRP as a proxy for comparative advantage can be justified on the grounds that it embodies the same information for optimal resource allocation. Reallocating domestic resources across industries in the ranking order of their DRP estimates will move the economy in the same direction as indicated by the theory of comparative advantage. The DRP ranking of industries should, therefore, be consistent with the underlying comparative advantage measures.

Comparison of DRP Estimates

The ratios of the DRP could be estimated and compared either across various commodities (industries) or for a commodity over consecutive time periods. The DRP estimates for tradable goods for a single period of time could be directly compared with each other. This cross-sectional comparison reveals in which commodity or group of commodities the country has comparative advantage and to what extent it has comparative advantage. A high DRP estimate is associated with a high degree of comparative advantage. The variations in DRP estimates show the differences between the domestic economy and the rest of the world, which are determined by differences in technical efficiency, shown in the input use coefficients, and the domestic–world relative price structure.

The DRP estimates for the same group of tradables over several periods of time could also be compared with each other. Unlike the comparison for a single period, the intertemporal comparison should be concerned only with the rankings, not the levels, of the DRP estimates. This is because, as domestic distortions are reduced, the DRP estimates for all tradables tend to converge to unity. Changes in the level of the DRP estimate for a tradable good over time may also include such a general trend. It is, therefore, the relative ranking positions in the DRP estimates that provide the most important information about a country's changing comparative advantage structure over time.

CONCLUSION

The DRP method has been discussed in detail as a proxy for comparative advantage. In the following chapters, the DRP method will be used to measure the changing structure of China's comparative advantage for the reform period 1978–95. The DRP will be estimated for all tradable goods produced in China. The results will enhance our understanding of the impact of the economic reforms and open-door policies on the resource allocation efficiency of the economy.

The application of the DRP method requires three sets of data: the international–domestic price ratios of tradable commodities, the shadow price conversion factors for primary factors of production and the input–output coefficients. Price ratios will be discussed in Chapter 6 which also provides a detailed account of China's price reforms and their impact on the domestic market for tradable goods. Shadow factor prices will be estimated in Chapter 7 which also reveals the impact of economic reforms on China's factors markets. Input–output coefficients will be derived from the published input–output tables and various Chinese sources, which will be discussed in Chapter 8.

6 Tradable Goods Price Structure in China, 1978–95

At the onset of economic reforms, China's domestic price structures had diverged substantially from that of the rest of the world owing to 30 years of central planning and isolation. These distortions had resulted in a huge loss of allocative efficiency for the Chinese economy and hindered the opening up of the domestic economy. It was clear that the domestic price system had to be reformed and realigned with the rest of the world. After nearly two decades of intensive economic reforms, by 1995, 89 per cent of consumer goods and 78 per cent of producer goods were being sold at market prices (Editorial Board of the *PYC* 1996). However, the impact of economic reform on China's domestic price structure has not been subject to rigorous empirical scrutiny. Although the magnitude of China's domestic price distortions can be indirectly measured using data on the sectoral profit rates of Chinese industries,[1] few attempts have been made to directly quantify the changes in the differentials between China's domestic prices and the world prices at a commodity level.[2]

This chapter compares domestic prices for all tradable goods in China against their border prices for every year between 1978 and 1995 to reveal the changing structure of the relative prices for tradables. These price changes indicate to what extent China's distorted domestic goods markets have been realigned with their international counterparts during the reform period. The results will be used later in calculating DRP. The relative prices for all tradables can also be interpreted as China's effective exchange rates,[3] which are instrumental in determining the purchasing power of China's domestic currency. With this information, China's GDP can be alternatively measured on the purchasing power parity (PPP) basis.

ESTIMATING RELATIVE PRICES

The differentials between domestic and border prices for tradable goods are normally estimated using the rates of nominal protection. The nominal rate of protection (NRP) for tradable good j may be expressed as the deviation of its domestic price p_j^d from its border price, p_j^w, that is,

$$NRP_j = \frac{p_j^d - ep_j^w}{ep_j^w} \tag{6.1}$$

where *e* is the exchange rate, defined as the domestic currency price of one unit of foreign currency. The most conventional way to estimate NRP is to use nominal border tax rates. This method, however, has a number of limitations. First, the import tariffs for exportables are redundant or even misleading, which could lead to an over-estimation of the domestic and border price differentials for goods that are never imported. Second, this method assumes that the observed domestic prices differ from border prices only by the nominal rates of border taxes (including tariffs and duties). In many countries, however, this may not be the case. Sometimes, border taxes may not actually be collected for various reasons. As a result, the ratio of border tax revenues to total imports may be lower than the nominal tariff rates may suggest.[4] Third, the most important assumption behind this method is that quantitative restrictions are not a dominant form of protection and can be ignored. It may be true that tariff rates and duty collection ratios are an acceptable proxy for nominal rates of protection in market economies where foreign trade is conducted by privately owned and profit-motivated firms. In a non-market economy such as China's, however, this link between domestic and world prices through border taxes is broken.

We will therefore adopt here the method of direct comparison of domestic and border prices. This method does not rely on any assumption about the relationship between nominal protection rates and international prices. It also avoids possible over-estimation of domestic prices for exports if only their import tariff rates are used. Most importantly, it can capture the impacts of all the price or quantitative restrictions or promotions on tradable prices. The problem with this method, however, is a practical one. It is usually difficult to obtain sufficient information on domestic and international prices. It may also be difficult to establish to what extent an imported good is identical to or substitutable for a domestically produced good. Price comparisons are particularly difficult for differentiated manufactures. Moreover, the transitional nature of the Chinese economy during the reform period makes price comparisons even more intricate because several domestic prices often coexisted for the same products.

These problems are by no means insoluble. There seems no reason to believe that the price comparison method will generate more biased estimates than the tariff-based methods under the current conditions of the Chinese economy.[5] Undoubtedly, the accuracy of the price comparison is dependent on the quality and accessability of price information. Chinese statistics are now increasingly being published. If all available information on domestic and international prices is thoroughly explored, the price comparison method should yield better estimates of the relative price structure for China than the other methods, even taking into account potential errors.

For the purpose of this study, the ratio of the domestic to the border price will be estimated for all Chinese tradable goods which are clustered into 61 categories. During the period concerned, the Chinese economy was undergoing a dramatic transition and domestic price structures were constantly changing. These reform-induced changes in the domestic prices of tradable goods contributed far more than border price variations to the patterns of China's relative prices during this period. Therefore, we need first to examine China's economic reforms and their impact on the domestic prices of tradable goods.

CHINA'S COMMODITY PRICE SYSTEM AND ITS REFORMS

Many economic reform policies have contributed to the reshaping of China's relative price structure. The focus here will be on the price reforms that have not received sufficient attention in the literature.[6]

Price reform has been a key component of China's market-oriented reform for the past two decades. In line with the other reforms, it aims at transforming China's erstwhile rigid price structure into a market-driven one. The way in which China conducts its price reforms has been described as 'gradualist' in comparison with the 'big bang' approach.[7] However, the term 'gradualist' does not accurately capture the essence of the reforms in China. Price reform in China combines both administrative adjustments of planned prices with gradual, sometimes drastic, relaxation or removal of price controls on a large number of commodities. A distinctive feature of the Chinese approach to price reforms is its adoption of an unprecedented two-tier price system. Under this system one product is allowed to have two, or more, prices. The old price is confined only to the portion of the output subject to central control and allocation. The above-quota output is allowed to be sold to the market at a price determined by supply and demand. Through such a unique and unorthodox system China has been able instantly to create a parallel free market for almost every product and, at the same time, maintain the continuity of the existing planned production and allocation. Over time, the planned production quota is cut back consistently to allow market production to expand. The two-tier price system thus provides leverage for the government to guide the process of marketization.

Agricultural Price System

China's price system is distinguished between agricultural and industrial products. Two broad types of domestic prices used to apply to agricultural products in China: procurement and market prices. The agricultural monopoly procurement system was implemented in the mid-1950s. It began with food grains and was soon extended to other products. By 1959, all major agricultural products were included in the state monopoly procurement system.

Under the system, all agricultural goods in China were divided into three broad categories on the basis of their importance to the economy. Category I goods, regarded as essential, were under the direct control of the central government. These goods were normally distributed across the whole country. They included major food grains, oil-bearing crops and major industrial crops such as cotton. These commodities were purchased at the state-list prices exclusively by the state commercial companies which sought to extract as much agricultural surplus as possible for industrialisation. Category II goods were also purchased by the government, but were regarded as less important than those in Category I and did not require nation-wide distribution; some were handled by provincial governments. After fulfilment of assigned targets, the excess produce could, in principle, be sold in free markets. However, very little was sold because market activities were tightly restricted at the time. The major goods in this category were pork, eggs, hemp and hides. The remaining agricultural commodities were all included in Category III. A large proportion of these goods was purchased by provincial governments for local distribution. All goods in Categories I and II and some in Category III were subject to state-list procurement prices while the remainder of Category III goods were subject to negotiable procurement prices. By 1978, Category I and II goods accounted for about 80 per cent of the total value of agricultural procurement in China (Wang Zhengzhi and Qiao Rongzhang 1988).

This system remained virtually unchanged until the late 1970s when the reforms began. The number of Category I and II commodities were gradually reduced and some less rigid types of procurement prices, such as above-quota prices and negotiated procurement prices, were introduced along with the state-list procurement prices. The agricultural monopoly procurement system was formally abolished in 1985 and replaced by a contract procurement system. Under the new system, a contract was signed by a household with the government in advance of the production season specifying a procurement quota for a particular commodity. The contracted procurement quota was limited to a small number of key agricultural commodities while the disposal of other commodities was at individual producers' discretion. After the 1985 reforms, there were three types of agricultural prices: the state-list procurement prices, the state-guidance prices and the market-adjustment prices. Included in state-list prices were the contract procurement price, a weighted average of previous state-list procurement prices and above-quota procurement prices, which was also called the 'proportional prices'. The overall procurement price levels could be altered through changing the shares of the commodities involved in calculating these prices as well as the procurement prices themselves. For relatively important commodities outside the contract procurement system, the state-guidance prices applied, which were regarded as non-compulsory planned prices. The remainder of agricultural goods was traded at market-adjustment prices which included negotiable procurement, market procurement and free market prices. By 1995, 78.6 per cent of agricultural procurement were made at market prices while only 17 per cent and 4.4 per cent were made at the state-list price and the state-guidance price, respectively (Editorial Board of the *PYC*, 1996:386).

Industrial Price System

For planning and controlling purposes, industrial products in China used to be classified into two broad groups: industrial producer goods and industrial consumer goods. The distribution of the former was handled by the Ministry of Materials and Equipment (*Wuzibu*) while that of the latter by the Ministry of Commerce (*Shangyebu*). Similar to agricultural products, all industrial products were also divided into three categories according to their importance to production and consumption. The prices of goods in each category were controlled by the State Administration of Commodity Prices or the State Planning Commission, the departments of the central government in charge of the production of those products and the provincial or local governments responsible for the local production of those goods.

This categorization of industrial products and the related administrative system remained unchanged at the beginning of economic reforms, but the composition of three categories changed rapidly in the 1980s, which reflected the early decentralization measures. The number of the centrally controlled industrial producer goods (Categories I and II) was reduced dramatically (Table 6.1). Goods in Category I under the direct control of the State Planning Commission were also reduced from 256 to 20 items between 1982 and 1986.

Table 6.1   Number of centrally controlled industrial producer goods in China, 1950–87

Year	State control	Department control	Total
1950	8	n.a.	8
1953	112	115	227
1957	231	301	532
1963	256	260	516
1965	370	222	592
1972	49	168	217
1978	53	636	689
1979	210	581	791
1981	256	581	837
1982	256	581	837
1985	23	n.a.	n.a.
1986	20	n.a.	n.a.
1987	n.a.	n.a.	27

Sources: Xu Feiqing (1988:203); Zhong Pengrong (1990:115); Zhou Taihe *et al.* (1984); Zhu Rongji *et al.* (1985).

The number of items in Categories I and II of industrial consumer goods dropped sharply during this period. In 1979, about 200 product groups were monopolistically purchased and distributed by the Ministry of Commerce, accounting for about 80 per cent of total commercial purchase value. In 1986, only 22 groups of products remained under the direct control of the Ministry (Guo Jinwu *et al.*, 1987:208–11; Xu Feiqing 1988:194), which amounted to about 30 per cent of the total value of commercial purchases. Among these products, 14 were industrial goods[8] and eight were agricultural products.

As an attempt to create markets for industrial products, control over the prices of industrial products was gradually lifted. The process of reforming industrial producer goods prices can be divided into three sub-periods. Between 1979 and 1984, the focus was on price adjustments in an attempt to correct or reduce the most serious distortions in plan prices. These included increases in the prices of key industrial raw materials and intermediate goods, such as coal, pig iron and basic steel products. A floating price was also introduced for some engineering and electrical products, which were in excess supply, to encourage competition among producers.

In the second sub-period from 1984 to 1992, a two-tier price system was established. Enterprises were allowed, for the first time, to sell some above-quota output to the market at flexible prices. Numerous so-called 'Transaction Centres for Means of Production' were established in parallel with the contraction of the central plan system. By 1986, a total number of 1254 transaction centres were operational nationwide. These markets played an increasingly important role in the trade of industrial producer goods. In 1986, for instance, the market sales of steel products, timber and cement accounted for 38, 46 and 61 per cent of total trade in these goods, respectively (Xu Feiqing 1988:204). More importantly, after the introduction of the two-tier price system in 1984, even those controlled products were allowed to be partially distributed outside the central plan system. In 1987, for instance, only 47 per cent of steel products, 47 per cent of coal, 16 per cent of cement and 26 per cent of timber were handled by the central government (Zhong Pengrong 1990:115).

In 1987 and 1988, domestic price levels began to rise. Market prices for industrial raw materials and intermediate inputs increased dramatically and widened the gap between plan and market prices. The government was forced to intervene by introducing price ceilings for key industrial products in 1988. Between 1989 and 1991, austerity measures implemented to bring inflation down led to a rapid fall in domestic demand and a slowdown in economic growth. Falling domestic demand created an opportunity for the government to raise plan prices for key industrial goods that were in short supply. By the end of the three year period, the gap between the plan and market prices had narrowed considerably; for some industrial products, market prices were even lower than their corresponding plan prices. At the beginning of a fresh surge of growth in 1992, the government introduced dramatic measures to liberalise the prices for most industrial products and phase out the two-tier price system in the industrial sector which marked the beginning of the third sub-period of industrial price reform. In 1992, the number of commodities under state control was sharply reduced from 737 to 89. By 1995, industrial producer goods sold through the market accounted for 77.9 per cent of total sales while those sold under state-list prices and state-guidance prices accounted for only 15.6 and 6.5 per cent, respectively (Editorial Board of the *PYC* 1996:387).

The pace of decontrolling industrial consumer goods prices was relatively slow at the beginning. The government feared the impact radical changes in consumer goods prices might have on inflation because many of these products had been in short supply for a long time. Nonetheless, there were some minor price adjustments in this area: between 1982 and 1984, the prices of the so-called 'minor' consumer goods in Category III were liberalized. Between 1985 and 1986, the prices of some key industrial consumer goods, many of which were over-supplied, were further decontrolled.[9] The relaxation of price control over these goods helped to lower their prices and stimulate the restructuring of the industries involved. Not until 1993 and 1994 were the prices of most industrial consumer goods liberalised. By 1995, only 8.8 per cent and 2.4 per cent of total retail goods were sold at the state-list and state-guidance prices, respectively, while the remaining 88.8 per cent were all sold at market prices (Editorial Board of the *PYC* 1996:385).

The transitional nature of the Chinese economy during this period adds complexity to our price comparisons because more than two types of domestic prices were usually associated with each tradable product. It is therefore necessary to identify the quantitative significance of plan and market prices before obtaining an adequate estimate of the average domestic price of a given tradable product.

CHANGES IN CHINA'S DOMESTIC PRICES FOR AGRICULTURAL PRODUCTS

In this section, the relative importance of the two major types of domestic agricultural prices–procurement prices and market prices–are discussed in detail in order to determine which should be taken to represent the domestic price for each of the 13 agricultural product categories.

Agricultural Procurement Price

Agricultural procurement prices nearly doubled over the first decade of reform (State Statistical Bureau 1988). This increase was mainly caused by two factors. The first was the large-scale adjustments of the state-list procurement prices. The adjustments for major agricultural commodities

Table 6.2 Adjustment of state-list agricultural procurement prices in China, 1979–87 (%)

Item	1979	1980	1981	1985	1986	1987
Food grains	+ 20.86					
Wheat		+ 21.09				
Paddy rice	+ 20.35					+ 5 5[d]
Corn		+ 21.82			+ 10.0[d]	+ 6.5[d]
Sorghum	+ 18.97					
Soybeans	+ 15.00		+ 50.0			
Vegetable oils	+ 24.97					
Peanut oil	+ 27.78					
Sesame oil	+ 18.94					
Cottonseed oil	+ 24.97					
Sunflower oil	+ 24.54					
Rapeseed oil	+ 26.27					
Soybean oil	+ 16.28			+ 12 0[d]		
Industrial crops						
Cotton	+ 15.20[a]	+ 10.0				+ 5.0
Tobacco	+ 4–35		+ 20.3			
Hemp	+ 20.10					
Ramie	+ 25.60					
Sugar-beet	+ 25.00					
Sugar-cane	+ 20.25					
Tea	+ 20.00					
Animal products						
Wool	+ 5.60			25.~44[e]		
Goat-hides	+ 10.00					
Cattle-hides	+ 44.10~50.0					
Silkworm cocoons	+ 20.30					+ 34.0
Pork	+ 26.40			+ 31.75		
Eggs	+ 30.00					
Beef	+ 36.40~70.0					
Mutton	+ 22.70~34.9					
Fish	+ 20.30					
Forest products						
Timber	+ 30.60[b]		+ 36.0[c]		+ 44.00	
Bamboo	+ 24.10		+ 20.00			

Notes:
[a] For North China, an additional 5 per cent margin was added above the price as a subsidy in 1979.
[b] Applicable only to South China in 1979.
[c] Applicable only to the collectively owned forests in South China in 1981.
[d] Applicable only to North China.
[e] State-guidance price.
Sources: Editorial Board of Price: Theory and Practice (1986); Guo Jinwu *et al.* (1987); Hu Bangding *et al.* (1989); *Price: Theory and Practice*, various issues; Wang Zhengzhi and Qiao Rongzhang, (1988); Xu Feiqing, (1988); Zhou Taihe *et al.*, (1984); Zhu Rongji *et al.* (1985).

during the first 10 years of the reform period can be seen in Table 6.2. The first general procurement price adjustment in this period was announced in 1979. It involved an average 24.8 per cent increase in the procurement prices of 18 major agricultural product groups, ranging from grains, oil-bearing crops, cotton, sugarcane and hemp to pig, fish, cattle-hides and timber.[10] In the following years, the state-list procurement price was continuously adjusted for some selective goods. For instance, the state-list procurement price for cotton was raised again by 10 per cent in 1980 and that of soybeans by 50 per cent in 1981.

The second factor contributing to the overall rise in agricultural prices was the decline in the share of total agricultural procurement purchased at the state-list price and the increase in the procurement under the above-quota procurement price or the negotiable procurement price. The above-quota price was introduced in 1979 for some short-supplied Category I and II commodities, such as food grains, cotton, edible vegetable oils and fish. Provincial governments also paid above-quota prices for the products under their control. These prices were all higher than state-list procurement prices by a specified margin. For instance, the above-quota prices for food grains, cotton and edible vegetable oils were 50 per cent higher than their state-list procurement prices in 1979. Prices were determined through negotiation between government agents and producers and, therefore, were influenced by the market. Such prices were originally applied only to Category III commodities and, after 1981, were gradually extended to some above-quota Category II and even Category I commodities. After the assigned procurement quantity was fulfilled, producers were encouraged to sell some Category I and II goods to the government at the negotiable prices, which were normally higher than the above-quota prices but lower than the market prices.

In 1985, after the abolition of the state monopoly agricultural procurement system, only a few major agricultural commodities were still purchased by the state at the newly introduced 'proportional price' while other products were either purchased by the government at negotiated prices through contracts or sold directly by the producers to the market.

As a consequence of the reforms in the agricultural procurement system, the share of procurement purchased at the state-list prices in total agricultural procurement shrank (Table 6.3). Between 1978 and 1984, the share of agricultural products purchased at the state-list prices declined from 85 to 34 per cent, and that at the above-quota prices jumped from 8 to 34 per cent. The share of the negotiated prices rose from 2 to 14 per cent and that of the market procurement prices from 6 to 18 per cent. By 1988, the share of procurement under the state-list prices fell to less than 25 per cent of the value of total state procurement and the share purchased at the market-adjusted prices accounted for more than 50 per cent of the value of total procurement. The state procurement concentrated mainly in grains, vegetable oils and a few key industrial raw

Table 6.3   Value shares of agricultural procurement, by type of procurement prices, 1978–95 (%)

Year	SLP	AQP	NGP	MKP
1978	84.7	7.9	1.8	5.6
1979	71.7	16.7	4.9	6.7
1980	64.4	17.9	9.5	8.2
1981	58.2	20.9	11.5	9.4
1982	57.5	20.8	11.5	10.2
1983	48.0	28.1	13.4	10.5
1984	33.9	33.6	14.4	18.1

Year	SLP	SGP	MAP
1985	37.0	23.0	40.0
1986	35.3	21.0	43.7
1987	29.4	16.8	53.8
1988	24.0	19.0	57.0
1989	35.3	24.3	40.4
1990	..	..	..
1991	22.2	20.0	57.8
1992	12.5	5.7	81.8
1993	..	..	..
1994	16.6	4.1	79.3
1995	17.0	4.4	78.6

Notes: SLP State-list procurement price
AQP Above-quota procurement price
NGP Negotiated procurement price
MKP Market procurement price
SGP State-guidance price
MAP Market-adjusted price.
Sources: Editorial Board of *PYC*, (1989:97, 351; 1992, 1994:19, 1995:386); Wang Zhengzhi and Qiao Rongzhang (1988:94).

materials, such as cotton and wool. In April 1994, the state-list price was reintroduced for the contracted grains procurements. Unlike the state-list price in the early years, this time it aimed at protecting grain producers from lost income when grain market prices fall in times of good harvest. The state-list price was also raised substantially. As a result, the contracted grain procurement increased by 44 per cent in that year (Ma Hong, Liu Zhongyi and Lu Baipu. 1997).

Agricultural Market Price

Agricultural markets have developed as a result of the reforms, but the government still dominated trade in staple agricultural commodities. To what extent market prices should be used in the price comparison depends on the quantitative significance of markets for individual commodities. Developments in individual commodity markets need to be examined in detail.

Food Grains and Vegetable Oils

Food grains are among the most controlled commodities in China. They include the basic staple crops such as wheat, paddy rice, corn and soybeans, which initially were all classified as Category I. In 1981, for some food grains, producers were permitted, for the first time since the 1950s, to sell their above-procurement quota output on the market. Private dealers were also permitted to transport these commodities across the country. Although the compulsory procurement of food grains was replaced by contract procurement after 1985, the bulk of food grains remained to be purchased by the government because of continuing food subsidization for the urban population. As the procurement prices went up, urban retail prices of food grains became lower than the purchase prices. It is therefore almost impossible for private dealers to compete with the state retail companies in the trade of major food grains. Table 6.4 indicates that the government continued to dominate the food grains trade. The food grain market was very thin in terms of volume traded in the 1980s and hence market prices for food grains are not a reliable indicator of their domestic price level at that time.

Edible vegetable oils were also highly controlled and subsidized. Even after the elimination of the state monopoly procurement system, edible vegetable oils remained one of the handful of commodities still handled by the government. Only a negligible proportion of edible vegetable oils was traded in the market in 1985 (Table 6.4).

Table 6.4   Urban market transactions of agricultural products in China, 1979–85 (as % of sales of the state commercial system)

Commodity	1979	1980	1981	1982	1983	1984	1985
Food grains	1.5	2.4	2.0	2.5	2.3	2.8	3.6
Vegetable oils	1.3	2.1	1.9	1.1	1.2	1.8	1.8
Vegetables	6.7	10.9	9.8	16.3	23.6	35.3	94.8
Pork	2.9	4.8	6.5	6.5	9.4	10.2	25.6
Beef, mutton	11.5	29.1	37.7	32.0	30.5	20.9	60.1
Eggs	3.5	8.5	24.5	31.1	31.1	33.3	80.7
Poultry	18.9	53.4	72.5	67.9	71.2	88.8	162.5
Fish	10.4	20.9	24.5	24.0	29.7	44.0	67.2

Source: Planning Office (MOA) (1989:432–3).

This situation changed in the 1990s when price control was lifted for most agricultural products. The remaining state-list prices for a few staple goods are also adjusted frequently to reflect supply and demand. Thus for the second half of the reform period (1988–95) we can reliably use the procurement price indices published in the statistical yearbooks to represent the domestic price trend for agricultural products.

Industrial Crops and Animal Products

Industrial crops include, among others, cotton, jute, hemp, tobacco, sugarcane and silkworm cocoons. The government used to be the exclusive buyer of these crops. These products were regarded as essential raw materials for the manufacturing industry and hence were normally prevented from market transactions. This restriction was relaxed only gradually after 1979; in 1984, permission was given for sub-standard cotton to be handled by the producers themselves. This was the first time since 1954 that cotton had entered the market. In 1985, the government attempted to further liberalize the cotton trade by allowing output outside contracted purchase quotas to be sold on the market. However, this attempt failed due to the sharp fall of 34 per cent in cotton production in 1985. Cotton is still one of the few commodities whose price remains under government regulation.

The situation for animal products such as wool and hides was slightly different. These products were classified as Category II goods. After the 1985 reform of the agricultural procurement system, a small proportion of the output of these goods (above the state procurement quota) was allowed into the market. As all these goods were in short supply, provincial governments often implemented control measures of their own to secure raw material supplies for local manufacturing enterprises. Data on the market shares for these products are not available, though it is evident that the markets for these products were very thin in the 1980s.

Non-staple Foodstuffs

Non-staple foodstuffs include meat, poultry, eggs, dairy products, fish, vegetables and fruits. These products used to be included in Category II. Control over these goods was relaxed and their retail prices were liberalized after 1985. Unlike food grains and edible oils, the removal of retail price control created a boom for these commodities. Although still actively involved in the trade of these commodities, state commercial companies have only been a participant rather than a monopolizer in the market (Table 6.4).

Forest Products

The major commodities in this market are natural rubber, resin, raw lacquer, tung oil and walnuts. Before the introduction of reforms, most of these products were categorized as essential industrial raw materials and were under direct central government control. Except for natural rubber, markets have been progressively created for all these products. For instance, tung oil was downgraded in 1984 from a Category II to a Category III good and, as a result, its price became negotiable and subject to market conditions. In 1985, resin was assigned the state-guidance or adjusted price. Since then, most forest products have been freely available in the markets; state commercial corporations also purchase these products from the market for the government.

Sideline Products

'Sideline products' are mainly those collected or hunted in the wild. An important part of this group are the herbs and animal parts used in making traditional Chinese medicines. Producing or collecting medicinal materials is a traditional sideline activity for farm households in China while medicinal materials are also important exports.

Under the pre-reform system, medicinal materials were handled by the Ministry of Health on behalf of the central government. Important medicinal materials were classified as Category II, compulsory procurement, goods and the remainder were included in Category III. After 1979, the number of medicinal materials in Category II was reduced considerably. In 1984, only 24 varieties remained in this category. Apart from four rare medicinal materials under central government control, mainly for conservation, other medicinal materials in Category II could be sold to the market if the assigned quota of planned procurement was fulfilled. Controls over other medicinal materials were lifted in the early 1980s. Specialized markets for medicinal materials have since been established across the country and are actively involved in trade.

The quantitative importance of markets for agricultural products can be seen in the divergences between market and state-procurement prices (Table 6.5). Large differences occurred in the prices of products over which the market had little influence (food grains, oil-bearing crops). The market prices of meat, vegetables, fish and fruits were much higher than their state-list prices during 1978–84. After 1985, they came closer due to the removal of the monopoly procurement system and price controls. For medicinal materials, the price differentials were small, indicating that the market was functioning well.

Agricultural price liberalization accelerated at the end of the 1980s. Since the mid-1990s, the government has controlled only the procurement of major food grains, cotton, flue-cured tobacco and silkworm cocoons. The prices of other agricultural products are all determined by their supply and demand.

Domestic Price Trends for Agriculture Products

It is apparent that although the government remained the major purchaser and distributor of most agricultural products over the 1978–95 period, the government's purchase of agricultural goods was increasingly conducted at

Table 6.5 Ratio of market to state prices for agricultural products, 1979–87

Product	1979	1981	1983	1985	1987
1. Paddy rice	3.61	3.32	2.75	2.13	2.40
2. Wheat	3.09	2.98	2.55	2.03	2.51
3. Other grains	4.49	3.98	3.09	2.26	2.71
4. Oil-bearing crops	2.71	2.00	2.10	2.13	2.25
5. Cotton	n.a.	n.a.	n.a.	n.a.	n.a.
6. Other industrial crops	n.a.	n.a.	n.a.	n.a.	n.a.
7. Vegetables	1.88	1.74	2.00	1.31	1.18
8. Fruits	1.62	1.40	1.42	1.02	1.05
9. Forest products	..	..	..	..	..
10. Wool and hides	n.a.	n.a.	n.a.	n.a.	n.a.
11. Meat, eggs and milk	1.35	1.20	0.94	1.09	1.16
12. Fish	1.85	1.62	1.68	1.17	1.02
13. Other agricultural products	0.99	1.03	0.96	0.83	1.87

Sources: Economic Information, various issues (1985–7); *Specialized Farm Household Business Newspapers*, various issues (1987); State Statistical Bureau, 1981–9; Urban Social and Economic Survey Team (SSB) (1988).

flexible instead of fixed procurement prices. The proportion of state procurement at the non-state-list prices increased as the reforms proceeded. The increasing market influence on agricultural prices was reflected in the state procurement price indices reported in China's statistical yearbooks. The domestic procurement prices can be seen as the closest approximation to domestic prices for most agricultural products during the period. As the role of the market increased for meat, vegetables, fish and fruits after 1985, market instead of procurement prices will to be used for the prices for these products for the period 1985–87. Since 1988, state control over the price of these products has been gradually removed and therefore, the published procurement price indices can actually capture the domestic price trends for these products. We will therefore use the procurement price indices for meat, vegetables, fish and fruit as well.

The domestic price trends for agricultural products, estimated as a combination of the state procurement and market prices, are presented in Table 6.6. Significant increases in the price of every group of agricultural products are evident between 1978 and 1995.

CHANGES IN CHINA'S DOMESTIC PRICES FOR INDUSTRIAL PRODUCTS

The frequent adjustments and gradual liberalization of state prices for industrial products complicate price comparisons for industrial products.

Since there were no readily available statistics on changes in the domestic prices of industrial products, data had to be collected and analyzed for each of the 48 tradable industrial good groups covered in this study. Basic data sources are the documents on state-list prices, the adjustments of state prices, the reports on market prices for industrial products from the transaction centres for the means of production materials and the information on consumer goods prices from the state commercial system. To facilitate the discussion, we will separate these industrial products into five groups, and highlight the most important price changes in each of the 48 industrial tradable goods over the recent reform period. The discussion will mainly focus on the years between 1978 and 1987 when most significant price reforms were introduced and the state and market prices interacted with each other under the so-called 'two-tier' price system. For this sub-period, there are few consistent statistics on price changes.[11] As already discussed, the two-tier price for most industrial products was phased out in the early 1990s. Beginning in 1990, the State Statistical Bureau compiled and published the ex-factory price index for 15 industries which, though too aggregate for this study, could be readily taken to represent the domestic price trends for industrial tradable goods.[12] Since 1987, the price deflators for China's 40 industries have also been available from various publications of the State Statistical Bureau.[13] These two sources of domestic prices will be used to represent domestic price trends for most industrial products over the sub-period 1988–95, if not otherwise indicated.

Natural Resource-based Industrial Goods (14–19)

The most serious distortion in the pre-reform industrial price structure was the low prices of most primary goods, including energy and minerals, relative to that of manufactured products. Price reform in the past two decades has therefore aimed at raising the prices of primary industrial commodities such as coal, crude oil and timber.

The price for *Coal (14)* had been so low for such a long time that 60 per cent of coal mines suffered losses in 1979 (Wang Zhengzhi and Qiao Rongzhang 1988:106). At the onset of the reforms, the state-list price of raw coal from the state-controlled coal mines was raised by almost 32 per cent. In 1983, the sale of the above-quota outputs was allowed to add a 20–50 per cent premium on the ex-factory price. In 1984, provincial coal mines were allowed to sell some of their output to the market at the free market price. The market price of raw coal surged to a level which was about double the state-list price. However, the coal sold by the mines was only 6.5 per cent of total coal sales in 1985 (State Council, Office for the Leading Group of National Industrial Census 1989b:126). This share did not increase much in the following two years. As the operational costs of coal mines increased in the late 1980s, however, the coal industry as a whole suffered losses from the fixed state price. In 1990 and 1992, the coal price for centrally controlled coal mines was

Table 6.6   China's domestic price trends for agricultural products (1–13), 1978–95

Product	1978	1979	1980	1981	1982	1983	1984
1. Paddy rice	100.0	117.7	117.7	117.7	124.2	139.2	158.2
2. Wheat	100.0	121.1	115.5	115.5	119.9	132.2	148.1
3. Other grains	100.0	119.2	119.5	122.3	138.3	153.0	167.2
4. Oil-bearing crops	100.0	131.8	138.1	144.2	146.0	146.9	148.2
5. Cotton	100.0	117.6	139.3	136.8	142.1	150.2	145.7
6. Other industrial crops	100.0	109.3	109.4	110.2	106.9	102.3	114.6
7. Vegetables	100.0	108.1	121.5	130.8	126.6	133.3	164.2
8. Fruits	100.0	99.5	118.3	128.0	137.1	154.5	201.0
9. Forest products	100.0	109.5	121.5	128.3	128.5	122.7	120.1
10. Wool and hides	100.0	104.2	110.7	100.0	123.2	134.6	178.7
11. Meat, etc.	100.0	135.8	151.4	159.6	164.6	218.4	222.2
12. Fish	100.0	117.1	129.7	135.7	142.9	164.1	178.4
13. Other agri. products	100.0	102.1	102.8	104.0	105.6	111.9	118.9

Sources: *Economic Information* (1985–7); Planning Office (MOA) (1989); *Specialized Farm Household Business Newspaper* (1987); State Statistical Bureau

raised twice by large margins (Editorial Board of the *PYC* 1991 and 1993). In 1993 and 1994 price control for the remaining centrally controlled coal mines was finally removed.

The pre-reform price of *Crude Petroleum (15)* was high relative to other energy resources such as coal, but incredibly low compared with world prices.[14] This posed a dilemma for price adjustment because raising the price would widen the gap between petroleum and other domestically produced energy products while lowering it would move it further away from world prices. The adjustments of domestic oil prices were unique. Between 1978 and 1987, the state-list prices of crude petroleum and natural gas remained unchanged. However, a so-called 'in-plan high price' was introduced in 1983 for two types of crude oil output: one was that originally planned for export but actually turned to domestic use, and the other was that saved through a scheme called 'substituting coal for petroleum' ('*Yimei daiyou*'). This 'in-plan high price' was set at international market levels. Although crude petroleum remained a monopolistically purchased good throughout the period, a two-tier price system was created within the plan distribution system and effectively raised crude oil prices.

The fixed state price for crude oil, however, continued to create enormous difficulties for the petroleum industry because its production costs increased rapidly as the prices of its inputs went up. The government began to raise the prices of crude oil and petroleum products in 1988–90. In 1992 and 1993, it also allowed a large quantity of 'in-plan' oil output to be sold at the higher market price. In 1994, the state price for crude oil was raised again in order to, finally, phase out the two-tier oil price system. In 1996, the government

(1978 = 100)

1985	1986	1987	1988	1989	1990	1991	1992	1993	1994	1995
163.7	182.6	206.7	247.7	323.7	299.7	287.4	280.0	348.8	537.2	649.0
150.8	168.1	173.8	200.2	244.1	224.5	211.5	232.9	245.5	373.6	497.3
188.0	204.5	210.7	222.9	288.5	282.2	257.1	286.3	344.2	482.6	646.9
153.4	158.5	168.4	198.9	237.2	234.4	228.5	216.9	262.0	384.1	395.4
141.3	141.2	156.4	169.9	208.4	269.1	274.7	261.0	291.0	466.8	613.8
124.5	132.2	145.8	193.9	213.5	223.2	232.0	229.2	244.1	296.7	374.8
204.9	219.2	265.0	352.5	378.4	354.3	341.1	366.0	420.6	548.2	676.1
257.1	283.6	303.2	423.3	381.8	372.3	397.6	368.9	370.8	444.6	503.3
122.1	125.6	131.7	182.7	192.2	162.4	166.3	178.5	198.3	221.7	233.0
256.2	433.2	450.1	605.8	665.8	598.4	582.8	599.2	671.1	886.5	989.3
225.5	233.6	266.1	396.8	434.9	404.9	394.3	423.1	485.3	739.7	859.5
248.5	268.6	328.4	427.8	448.6	437.5	447.7	471.0	537.8	593.3	616.2
145.9	113.7	127.1	206.0	145.6	139.0	161.1	184.9	188.6	201.9	204.6

(1981–9) Urban Social and Economic Survey Team (SSB) (1988).

further increased oil prices in an attempt to reduce the losses in the industry (Ma Hong, Liu Zhongyi and Lu Baipu 1997). Despite these efforts, however, China's domestic oil prices remain low relative to other industrial products, let alone to its world prices.

The most important commodity in *Ferrous Minerals (16)* is iron ore. As no domestic free market exists for iron ore, only the state-list price is considered here. The state price of iron ore was increased twice during 1978–87: by 49 per cent in 1980 and 47 per cent in 1984. Owing to the lack of information on the prices for *Non-ferrous Minerals (17)*, it is therefore assumed that the domestic price trends for these products followed that of non-ferrous metals, which will be discussed later.

Non-metal Minerals (18) covers a wide range of products, many of which are raw building materials such as chemical minerals, asbestos, gypsum, talc and china clay. Two major chemical minerals–sulphur iron pyrites and phosphatic minerals–made up a large proportion of the output value of this industry. Between 1978 and 1987, the state-list price was applicable only to the outputs of the centrally controlled mines while the provincial price was applicable to the outputs of regional mines. The centrally controlled mines were larger in size than the local mines which were owned by the provincial or local authorities, or even private individuals. As the outputs from the latter do not constitute a large proportion of total outputs, the state-list prices are taken to represent the domestic prices for this product group. As the pre-reform prices of chemical minerals were considered to be too low, the government increased their prices several times from the early 1980s onwards. In 1983, the price of sulphur iron pyrites was adjusted upwards by 22 per cent and the price of phosphate

Table 6.7   China's domestic price trends for industrial resources (14–19),

Product	1978	1979	1980	1981	1982	1983	1984	1985
14. Coal	100.0	125.8	141.2	138.7	139.6	144.7	147.7	162.8
15. Crude oil	100.0	100.0	100.0	100.0	100.0	128.6	155.9	182.4
16. Ferrous minerals	100.0	100.0	149.1	149.1	149.1	149.1	219.3	219.3
17. Non-ferrous minerals	100.0	100.7	101.3	100.1	101.8	101.8	109.2	113.5
18. Non-metal minerals	100.0	106.9	106.9	101.8	104.5	125.9	125.9	139.3
19. Timber	100.0	128.9	129.6	174.2	234.7	334.1	375.1	421.7

Sources: *Economic Information* (1984–7); Editorial Board of *Price: Theory and Practice* (1986); *Price: Theory and Practice* (1984–8); Editorial Board of *PYC*, (1989–95); Research Institute of Commodity Prices (SACP) (1985); State Council, Office for the Leading Group for the National Industrial Census, (1988, 1989b);

minerals was raised by 33 and 50 per cent in 1979 and 1983, respectively. As no adjustments were reported for the state-list prices of other non-metal minerals, it is assumed that they had remained unchanged for 1978–87. The state-list prices were chosen to represent domestic prices for these goods. For the sub-period since 1988, the ex-factory price index for the building material industry is used as a proxy.

Prior to the reforms, *Timber (19)* was categorized as an essential industrial raw material and came under the strict control of the central government. The free market was introduced only progressively after 1979. Before 1985, however, all timber produced in the state forests and 70–90 per cent of China's timber produced in collectively owned forests had to be sold to the government. Only sub-standard timber from collective forests could be made available in the market place. Since timber was in extremely short supply and only a small amount of output was allowed to be traded freely, the market price was so high that, in some areas, it was about six times the state procurement price. Following the abolition of the monopoly agricultural procurement in 1985, timber from collectively owned forests could either be sold to the government at a negotiable price or to the market at the market price. As more timber became available to the market, its market price started to fall. By 1986, the market price was only about 37 per cent higher than the state procurement price. However, timber from collectively owned forests constituted only a minor portion of total domestic output. Most timber was still purchased by the central or provincial governments although some reports indicated that the timber output distributed by the central government, as a proportion of total domestic timber resources (output and imports), dropped from 74.1 to 38.6 per cent between 1980 and 1986 (Wang Zhengzhi and Qiao Rongzhang 1988).[15] In 1990, the prices for logs and timber products from the state forests were increased by between 48 to 60 per cent (Editorial Board of the *PYC* 1991).

1978–95 (1978 = 100)

1986	1987	1988	1989	1990	1991	1992	1993	1994	1995
165.1	166.8	184.5	207.0	219.8	248.6	288.6	403.2	492.7	548.3
198.6	209.4	223.7	242.5	259.7	308.5	355.7	609.3	906.1	1097.3
219.3	219.3	255.6	312.4	348.0	401.4	463.0	737.4	795.4	847.5
130.1	131.3	151.5	183.3	202.2	230.9	263.6	415.8	444.0	468.5
139.3	139.3	158.0	195.3	194.5	206.3	229.2	327.4	352.2	374.8
483.5	580.8	855.0	989.3	1 150.5	1 294.3	1 444.6	1 732.2	2 630.1	3 197.9

State Planning Commission (1987, 1994); State Statistical Bureau (1981–8); Urban Social and Economic Survey Team (SSB) (1988); Wang Zhengzhi and Qiao Rongzhang (1988); Yang Songhao (1988).

The price trends for the six products of this group are reported in Table 6.7.

Light Industrial Products (20–31)

As *Sugar, Tobacco and Alcohol (20)* had been exclusively handled by the state in the 1980s, the changes in their domestic prices were mainly obtained from retail price statistics published by the state commercial system.[16] Similarly, state retail price indices for cereals and other processed foods were used in deriving the domestic price trend for *Other Processed Foods (21)* for the 1980s (Table 6.8). In the early 1990s, the prices of most of these products were liberalized. Thus, ex-factory price indices were used to derive their domestic price trends (Table 6.8).

The estimation of domestic price trends for textiles and clothing for the 1980s was based on state prices because of the domination of the state commercial system. The government was very sensitive to any rise in the prices of basic consumer goods such as textiles and the trade of these goods was therefore strictly controlled and monitored. Even the enterprise-self-marketing outputs had to be sold at the state-list prices. The price changes for *Cotton Textiles (22)* were estimated from the information on the state price adjustments. Cotton textiles were a basic consumer good and their prices had been kept stable throughout the pre-reform era. As the procurement price of cotton increased in the early 1980s, the costs of cotton textile production rose sharply, causing widespread losses in the industry.[17] As a counter measure, the state prices of cotton textiles were raised on average by 30 per cent in 1983. In the late 1980s and early 1990s, the price of cotton textiles was again increased with the adjustments of the cotton procurement prices.

The domestic price trends for *Wool Textiles (23)*, *Hemp Textiles (24)*, *Silk Textiles (25)* and *Knitted Goods (26)* were derived from the average retail prices. The prices of *Clothing and Leather Goods (28)* were estimated from the

Table 6.8 China's domestic price trends for light industrial products (21–31),

Product	1978	1979	1980	1981	1982	1983	1984
20. Sugar, tobacco, alcohol	100.0	100.1	100.6	108.9	117.8	125.2	111.5
21. Other processed food	100.0	104.4	108.8	111.6	114.5	117.5	120.1
22. Cotton textiles	100.0	100.0	100.0	100.0	100.0	130.0	130.0
23. Wool textiles	100.0	101.7	108.1	108.1	104.7	99.7	101.4
24. Hemp textiles	100.0	105.8	111.5	111.2	110.6	108.1	111.9
25. Silk textiles	100.0	97.1	100.0	100.0	100.0	102.9	105.7
26. Knitted goods	100.0	99.8	99.5	98.3	97.0	95.8	95.8
27. Other textiles	100.0	100.0	100.0	100.0	100.0	130.0	130.0
28. Clothing	100.0	99.8	99.5	98.3	97.0	95.8	95.8
29. Furniture	100.0	128.9	129.6	174.2	234.7	334.1	375.1
30. Paper	100.0	100.0	100.0	100.0	100.0	100.0	102.5
31. Cultural goods	100.0	98.6	97.2	96.0	94.8	90.8	90.6

Sources: See Table 6.7.

retail price index. Both were available from Chinese statistics. *Other Textiles (27)* includes the preliminary processing of textile raw materials, such as cotton ginning, and wool washing and degreasing, as well as some special textiles not elsewhere specified. As cotton composed more than 90 per cent of the value of total textile output, the domestic price trends for this group of textiles were assumed to have followed that of cotton textiles.

As *Furniture (29)* includes timber processing, the domestic price trends for this group were assumed to have followed that of Timber (19), a dominant input in its production. *Paper (30)* is another controlled product in China. The estimation of its domestic price trends was based on the state ex-factory prices of newsprint and machine-finished paper, which were increased gradually after 1984. The estimation of the domestic price trend for *Cultural and Sporting Goods (31)* was based on the retail price index reported by the state commercial system. The price trends for this group of goods are reported in Table 6.8.

Petroleum and Chemical Products (32–42)

Like crude oil, the prices for *Petroleum Products (32)* were quite low compared with their international counterparts over the period concerned. Relative to other industries, however, the petroleum refining industry used to enjoy high profits because of the low costs of crude oil. Like crude oil, therefore, the plan prices of refined petroleum products remained virtually unchanged in the first decade of the reforms. Low prices encouraged an inefficient use of resources: a large quantity of crude oil was used as fuel every year. A new scheme was therefore introduced in 1983 to encourage the use of

1978–95 (1978 = 100)

1985	1986	1987	1988	1989	1990	1991	1992	1993	1994	1995
119.9	125.7	135.4	247.8	293.2	295.9	293.4	306.6	341.1	385.3	439.1
136.1	146.6	158.8	183.5	212.3	242.4	246.8	267.2	299.9	353.2	413.9
130.0	130.0	130.0	154.3	191.7	206.0	220.6	232.4	262.3	375.7	457.0
109.0	115.5	133.4	152.2	181.8	187.9	175.8	197.2	214.0	269.1	314.7
122.5	144.3	144.3	163.0	163.9	167.7	155.4	151.3	154.8	183.5	212.5
120.0	127.6	142.2	157.4	182.3	182.8	166.0	158.3	158.7	184.4	209.2
96.7	99.8	103.3	123.8	155.2	168.5	165.6	171.0	185.6	233.3	286.5
130.0	130.0	130.0	154.3	191.7	206.0	220.6	232.4	262.3	375.7	457.0
96.7	99.8	103.3	120.0	142.7	155.7	169.7	171.1	201.7	234.2	272.8
421.7	483.5	580.8	855.0	989.3	1 150.5	1 294.3	1 444.6	1 732.2	2 630.1	3 197.9
126.8	154.2	181.6	223.2	274.5	280.8	289.0	296.8	323.2	344.5	497.8
92.0	92.9	95.2	106.7	118.5	127.1	134.5	137.6	152.2	166.0	184.9

coal as a substitute for crude oil in fuel consumption. The crude oil thus saved was refined and sold domestically at the 'in-plan high price'. From 1983 to 1987, the in-plan high price for gasoline, kerosene and diesel was about 50 per cent higher than the state-list ex-factory price. As the output of highly priced petroleum constituted only a small proportion of the total output of refined petroleum products, the average domestic prices of refined petroleum increased only marginally in the 1980s. In the 1990s, as the industry started making losses, the domestic price for oil products was increased steadily through either an increase in the state price or an increase in the sales at the in-plan high price.

Coal products (33) includes mainly coke and coal gas. Along with the price adjustments for raw coal, the state price of coke was also raised twice, by 23 per cent in 1980 and 33 per cent in 1984. It also followed the price adjustments for raw coal in the 1990s.

Five important chemicals are taken to represent *Inorganic Chemicals (34)* : sulphuric acid, nitric acid, hydrochloric acid, caustic soda and soda ash. These products made up 50–60 per cent of inorganic chemical production. In 1983, the state ex-factory prices of sulphuric acid, caustic soda and soda ash were adjusted upwards by 42, 22 and 50 per cent, respectively. State prices covered about 60 per cent of the total production of inorganic chemicals mainly from large and medium-sized state enterprises. The remainder came from small enterprises and their prices, which were normally higher than the state-list prices, were determined by local authorities. The two-tier price system after 1984 further increased the average price for these products. The price trend for this group therefore was estimated as the weighted average of the state and local prices for 1978–83 and the weighted average of the above two types of prices plus the market prices for 1984–7. The enterprise–self-marketing share in total output was used as the weight for market prices. The ex-factory price index was used for the years thereafter.

Chemical Fertilizers (35) also include pesticides. These are key agricultural inputs and subject to state control. In the late 1980s, however, an increasing proportion of chemical fertilizer output, either imported by regional authorities or produced outside the plans, was sold at a price above the state-list prices. Pesticide prices differed because of their quantities and varieties. State prices were applicable to only a few of them. The prices of most pesticides varied from region to region and were determined by local authorities. However, as chemical fertilizers constituted about 90 per cent of the value of total output in this category, we can rely on the fertilizer prices in deriving the price trend.

The prices of four major chemical fertilizers were used: ammonium sulphate, ammonium nitrate, urea and superphosphate. In 1983 and 1984, the state ex-factory prices of these products were raised by 14–22 per cent. At about the same time, the enterprises were granted the right to sell their above-quota outputs. The enterprise-marketed chemical fertilizers were estimated to be 38 per cent of total sales in 1984 and 1985. The market prices were reported to be about 30–50 per cent higher than the state-list prices. The price changes in the following years were estimated using the average annual growth rates derived from the ex-factory prices for 1985 and 1995 (Industrial Census data 1988 and 1996).

The prices of 32 organic chemicals and eight dyes were used to estimate the domestic price for *Organic Chemicals (36)*. Domestic pricing for this group was similar to that of other chemical products. As the pre-reform prices of these goods were high on average, there had been no significant increase in state ex-factory prices in the 1980s, though minor price adjustments were reported for some products. The weighted-average domestic price for this group decreased when their market prices were taken into account.

The state commercial retail prices of soap and matches were used to approximate the domestic price movements for *Household Chemicals (37)*. This is because these goods, together with synthetic detergents (whose price was closely related to that of soap), accounted for more than half the output value of the household chemical industry in China.

Included in *Other Chemicals (38)* are mainly various synthetic materials. As with organic chemicals, the state prices were fairly stable during this period. Following the introduction of the two-tier price system in 1984, the aggregate price level increased only moderately.

Two major price adjustments were made for *Medicines (39)* and related goods during 1978–87. In both cases, however, the price falls more than offset the price rises on average. The price for medicines fell by 10 per cent in 1980 and by another 4 per cent in 1985.

Chemical Fibres (40) refer to various man-made fibres. As chemical fibre prices were higher during the pre-reform period than natural fibre prices, the retail prices of various chemical fabrics were, on average, lowered by 13 per cent in 1981. The trend in the aggregate domestic price for chemical fibres was derived from the ex-factory price index for chemical fibre industry between 1984 and 1995 (State Council, Office for the Leading Group of National Industrial Census, 1988 and Editorial Board of the *PYC* 1995).

The domestic prices of *Rubber Manufactures (41)* changed little over the period 1978–87. It was assumed that the average price of rubber manufactures increased at a marginal rate of 0.8 per cent per annum (State Council, Office for the Leading Group of National Industrial Census, 1988). The domestic price trend for *Plastic Articles (42)* was derived from the average retail price of plastic shoes.

For some products, the above discussion focused only on the period 1978–87. For the following period, 1988–95, industrial output deflators which could be derived from China's statistical yearbooks and the 1995 industrial census data were used. As China's domestic prices are liberalized, these price deflators provide a better indicator for domestic price variations. The domestic price trends for this group of goods are reported in Table 6.9.

Building Materials and Metals (43–50)

As the price of *Cement (43)* was too low in the late 1970s, the ex-factory price of cement was raised by 11 per cent in 1980 and a further 60 per cent in 1986. However, the state-list price was applicable only to products from large and medium-sized enterprises which accounted for only 19 per cent of the total cement industry output in 1985 (State Council, Office for the Leading Group of National Industrial Census 1988). The price of cement from other enterprises was mainly controlled by provincial and local governments and was usually 20–30 per cent higher than the state-list ex-factory price (Yang Songhao 1988). During the two-tier price period in the 1980s, the market price for cement was between 1.5 and 2.5 times the state-list price. It was reported that over 20 per cent of cement was marketed directly by enterprises themselves during this period (State Council, Office for the Leading Group of National Industrial Census, 1988), which further increased the average price for cement. A rapid increase in cement output in the following years considerably eased the pressure on the market price. This enabled the government to choose cement as one of the first group of industrial goods to phase out the two-tier price in 1991.

Glass (44) includes producer goods as well as household glassware. The state ex-factory prices for plate glass were increased by 74 per cent in 1983. These prices affected about 75 per cent of total output from large and medium-sized enterprises. The prices for the remaining output from small enterprises were normally 30 per cent higher than the state prices. The domestic price of glass was further increased after the introduction of the two-tier price system in 1984; the figures from the Transaction Centres

Table 6.9 China's domestic price trends for petroleum and chemical products (32–

Product	1978	1979	1980	1981	1982	1983	1984
32. Petrol products	100.0	100.0	100.0	104.0	104.0	109.5	110.0
33. Coal products	100.0	100.0	123.3	123.3	123.3	123.3	164.4
34. Inorganic chemicals	100.0	100.8	100.4	98.9	99.4	121.4	133.6
35. Chem. fertilizers	100.0	100.0	100.0	100.0	113.4	113.4	126.8
36. Organic chemicals	100.0	93.8	90.6	86.7	82.8	80.0	86.6
37. Household chemicals	100.0	101.3	101.4	103.4	103.9	106.4	112.8
38. Other chemicals	100.0	99.8	102.4	100.6	101.5	102.5	113.0
39. Medicine	100.0	100.0	90.0	90.0	90.0	90.0	86.4
40. Chemical fibres	100.0	102.1	104.2	106.4	108.7	111.0	113.3
41. Rubber manufactures	100.0	100.8	101.6	102.4	103.2	104.1	104.9
42. Plastic articles	100.0	96.6	99.6	100.0	95.5	97.4	103.8

Sources: See Table 6.7.

indicated that the market prices of plate glass were normally 50–100 per cent higher than the state-list prices during 1984–87 (*Economic Information* 1984–7). Markets gained an increasing share of total sales when about 40 per cent of the total sales of plate glass were conducted by the enterprises themselves in the mid-1980s (State Council, Office for the Leading Group of National Industrial Census, 1989b:127).

The price of asbestos, a refractory material, was used to represent the domestic price of *Ceramic Products (45)*. Its state price was increased by 30 per cent in 1983. As information on market prices is not readily available, state-market price differences were assumed to be the same as those for other building materials. The domestic prices for *Other Building Materials (46)* were derived from the state ex-factory prices of asbestos–cement products and sanitary ceramic products. The state prices of the two groups of products were raised by 41 and 18 per cent in 1983 and 1982, respectively. Their domestic prices were even higher when the provincial prices and the market prices were taken into account.

State pricing dominated *Iron (47)* and *Steel (48)* for most years of this period. The state prices for pig iron and some basic steel products were adjusted twice in the 1980s. First, in 1980, the price of pig iron was raised by 33–47 per cent and the prices of basic steel products by 12–15 per cent. The second price rise occurred in 1984 when these prices were raised by another 26–30 per cent and 9–12 per cent, respectively. High-quality steel products received three major price adjustments. In 1980 and 1982, their prices were decreased and in 1984 they were increased. The state prices of ferrous alloys were increased by 8–9 per cent in 1979, 6 per cent in 1982 and 40–60 per cent in 1986. Permission to use markets combined with the introduction of the two tier-price system in 1984 led to a dramatic increase

42), 1978–95 (1978 = 100)

1985	1986	1987	1988	1989	1990	1991	1992	1993	1994	1995
110.1	110.6	110.3	127.0	146.4	168.8	194.8	224.9	259.9	300.5	347.8
179.6	209.4	215.0	237.8	266.9	283.4	320.5	372.1	519.9	635.3	707.1
142.3	161.6	169.2	180.5	192.6	205.5	219.3	234.0	249.6	266.4	283.9
127.8	127.8	127.8	182.5	208.5	238.2	272.0	310.8	355.0	405.5	506.9
82.5	81.5	81.3	100.4	128.1	135.1	134.0	147.7	173.6	206.8	262.5
126.7	133.7	148.0	169.3	200.1	195.3	179.4	183.1	199.2	219.8	258.3
114.1	116.3	119.5	149.0	191.9	204.2	204.4	227.4	269.7	324.3	415.5
86.4	86.4	86.4	93.9	104.9	98.0	88.3	87.8	90.9	96.6	102.5
115.7	118.1	120.6	140.3	176.8	180.5	171.5	175.6	201.5	241.5	330.6
105.7	107.4	109.1	123.7	155.9	168.0	146.1	158.4	178.1	208.3	262.2
113.2	120.8	131.7	161.0	166.5	151 8	135.3	136.0	143.2	151.1	177.3

in the market prices for steel products: some were double or even triple the state-list prices and remained high between 1984 and 1987, substantially raising the average domestic prices of these products. During 1989–92, the gap between the plan and market prices narrowed considerably for iron and steel products, and in the following three years, price control over iron and steel products was gradually lifted.

The price trend for *Non-ferrous Metals (49)* was similar. State prices covered about 90 per cent of total non-ferrous metal output. The prices of nine non-ferrous metals[18] were used to derive the domestic price trends for this category. Between 1978 and 1983, the state-list price dominated most non-ferrous metals. As the two-tier price system emerged after 1984, the state-list price covered only the planned output and the market price applied to the above-quota and non-plan or 'enterprise-self-marketing' output. In 1985, the latter accounted for 23 per cent of the total output of non-ferrous metals (State Council, Office for the Leading Group of National Industrial Census, 1989b). The market prices were normally 30–50 per cent higher than the state-list prices for most non-ferrous metals. The domestic price was thus estimated as an output value-weighted average of the state-list price and the market price for the sub-period 1984–7. For the post-1987 period, the output price deflator for the industry was used to represent the domestic price trend.

Metal Products (50) includes metal structures, wire, rope and various household metal products. The domestic prices for these products were heavily influenced by the changes in the basic metal prices, particularly steel prices. Steel prices were therefore used in the derivation of the price trend for metal manufactures.

Table 6.10   China's domestic price trends for building materials and metals

Product	1978	1979	1980	1981	1982	1983	1984
43. Cement	100.0	100.6	111.9	112.5	113.2	113.8	126.5
44. Glass	100.0	100.0	100.0	100.0	100.0	173.9	195.6
45. Ceramic products	100.0	100.0	100.0	100.0	100.0	130.0	135.2
46. Other bldg materials	100.0	101.1	106.6	107.3	143.7	148.9	152.0
47. Iron	100.0	103.0	132.8	132.8	135.3	135.3	183.4
48. Steel	100.0	107.6	107.1	111.9	113.6	118.1	148.3
49. Non-ferrous metals	100.0	100.7	101.3	100.1	101.8	101.8	109.2
50. Metal products	100.0	107.7	107.1	111.9	113.6	118.1	124.0

Sources: See Table 6.7.

The domestic price trends for all goods included in this group are reported in Table 6.10.

Mechanical, Electrical and Electronic products (51–61)

This group is composed of both producer and consumer goods. All producer goods followed a similar pattern of price changes over the reform period. In the past, their prices were regarded as being too high relative to primary or semi-manufactured products. From 1978 to 1983, no adjustments were made to their state prices; instead, the government introduced a 'floating' price for some over-supplied products in this group to allow producers to actually lower the prices for competition purposes. After 1984 an increasing proportion of enterprises was permitted to sell their own products to the market. A general rise in the prices of these goods was driven up further by the growing demand in the following years. Based on this information, the domestic prices for these products were assumed equal to the constant state-list prices for 1978–83 and to a weighted-average of state and market prices for 1984–7. The ratios of enterprise-self-marketing to total sales were used as the weights for market prices. After 1988, the output price deflator was used in deriving the domestic price trend for these group products.

Four popular consumer durables were selected in the estimation of the domestic price trend for *Household Mechanical and Electrical Goods (54)*: bicycles, sewing machines, washing machines and refrigerators. The state retail prices of bicycles and sewing machines were used here. For washing machines and refrigerators, only the average producer prices were available for 1983–5 from Chinese statistics. As the prices of these goods had been fairly stable, it was assumed that no price changes occurred for the rest of the decade. For the 1990s, on the other hand, the output deflator for the machinery industry was used.

Except for 1984 and 1985, domestic prices were not generally available for various types of transport equipment. To obtain an approximation for the

(43–50), 1978–95 (1978 = 100)

1985	1986	1987	1988	1989	1990	1991	1992	1993	1994	1995
146.1	216.4	210.7	232.4	256.3	282.7	311.8	344.0	379.4	418.5	461.5
206.4	220.3	234.2	266.3	302.8	344.2	391.4	445.0	506.0	575.3	650.4
139.4	147.7	156.0	187.6	239.9	250.4	270.0	321.5	424.0	470.9	549.8
153.9	160.1	162.4	195.3	249.8	260.7	281.2	334.8	441.5	490.4	572.6
187.8	217.6	215.6	242.2	286.8	307.0	334.1	381.8	601.3	583.5	560.3
204.0	199.1	204.9	230.1	272.6	291.7	317.5	362.8	571.4	554.5	532.4
113.5	130.1	131.3	151.5	183.3	202.2	230.9	263.6	415.8	444.0	468.5
145.1	159.6	175.5	198.0	236.6	249.5	256.9	282.7	343.6	369.5	415.9

domestic price trends for *Railway Equipment (55)* and *Ships (57)* , cost–profit ratios were used because the changes in these ratios were believed to be correlated with price changes. The cost–profit ratio in the railway equipment industry increased by 36 per cent between 1980 and 1985. The same ratio for the shipbuilding industry increased by 20 per cent (State Council, Office for the Leading Group of National Industrial Census, 1988). Based on this information, the annual growth rates were calculated and taken as a proxy for domestic price trends for these two industries in the 1980s.

The situation for *Motor Vehicles (56)* was different. Although there were no significant changes in the state prices for motor vehicles, market prices increased substantially following the introduction of the two-tier pricing system. The market prices for motor vehicles were therefore taken into account in deriving domestic price trends for this group. The domestic prices for *Other Transport Equipment (58)* were assumed to have followed a similar trend, but not to have risen as sharply as motor vehicle prices, between 1984 and 1987. The output deflators were used for the post-1987 period for all transport equipment industries.

Other Engineering Products (59) covers precision instruments and mechanical or electrical products not elsewhere classified. The domestic prices for this group did not increase until 1984. After 1988, the output price deflator was used to represent the domestic price trend.

The domestic prices for *Electronic Products (60)* were relatively high, as reflected in their high profit rates; some of these products were thus facing a downward pressure under the 'floating' prices in the early 1980s. After 1983, however, the electronics industry began to grow strongly. This trend was confirmed in the industry's cost–profit ratios. Between 1980 and 1985, the cost–profit ratios of the broadcasting and televising equipment industry and the electronic equipment industry increased by 58 and 6 per cent, respectively. As no statistics on the prices of these goods were available, these cost–profit ratios were used as proxies for the domestic price movements of this group for the 1980s. The output price deflator was used for the 1990s. The same

China's Trade Patterns

Table 6.11 China's domestic price trends for machinery products (51–61), 1978–95

Product	1978	1979	1980	1981	1982	1983	1984
51. Agri. machinery	100.0	100.0	100.0	100.0	100.0	101.0	102.5
52. Industrial equipment	100.0	100.0	99.0	99.0	99.0	100.0	104.1
53. Power equipment	100.0	100.0	100.0	100.0	100.0	100.0	100.0
54. Hshd mech/elect.gds	100.0	102.2	105.3	109.9	113.2	118.1	125.6
55. Railway equipment	100.0	100.0	100.0	106.4	113.1	120.3	128.0
56. Motor vehicles	100.0	100.0	100.0	100.0	100.0	100.0	103.1
57. Ships	100.0	100.0	100.0	103.6	107.4	111.3	115.3
58. Oth transp equip.	100.0	100.0	100.0	100.0	100.0	100.0	103.6
59. Other enging. prods.	100.0	100.0	100.0	100.0	100.0	100.0	118.0
60. Electronic products	100.0	100.0	100.0	101.2	102.4	103.6	104.9
61. Hshd Electronics	100.0	100.0	100.0	105.7	111.8	118.2	125.0

Sources: See Table 6.7.

method was also applied to *Household Electronics (61)* . The estimates for China's domestic price trends for machinery products are reported in Table 6.11.

BORDER PRICE TRENDS

The border price for tradables is defined as the world market price multiplied by the exchange rate. The estimation of border prices for industrial products was based on two sets of information. For those products whose international market prices were regularly published, the price movements were directly derived from their market price series. This applied to most standard agricultural products, energy products, major minerals and basic metals which are traded substantially in the world markets. For other products, the unit values of exports (f.o.b. price) or imports (c.i.f. price) were collected and used as an approximation for international market prices. The selection of unit values depended on whether the product concerned was mainly an exported or an imported good. The unit values of exports and imports were obtained from UN publications (International Economic Data Bank, ANU), the Ministry of Foreign Economic Relations and Trade (Editorial Board of ACFERT, 1984–96/7) and the Customs General Administration of China (1985–96). The information on international prices for some industrial products was obtained from the export price indices of China's major trade partners such as Japan, the Republic of Germany, the United States, Sweden and the Netherlands (State Statistical Bureau, Information Centre for International Statistics 1989).

International prices can fluctuate greatly within a short period of time. This may not always be caused by changes in permanent production conditions. To derive a reliable price trend, a three-year moving average was used to smooth

(1978 = 100)

1985	1986	1987	1988	1989	1990	1991	1992	1993	1994	1995
102.5	102.5	102.5	106.9	116.8	114.0	108.4	113.5	128.6	132.9	139.1
119.7	121.0	121.0	128.8	143.5	142.9	138.6	148.0	171.0	180.3	192.5
110.0	111.1	112.2	124.5	146.1	134.8	124.9	127.6	137.9	140.8	148.2
143.3	158.3	175.1	182.7	199.6	194.8	185.3	193.9	219.8	227.1	237.7
136.1	144.8	154.0	162.5	174.8	174.8	176.1	187.5	207.4	214.5	214.0
128.5	133.5	139.9	147.6	158.8	158.8	160.0	170.3	188.4	194.9	194.4
119.5	123.9	128.4	135.4	145.7	145.7	146.7	156.2	172.8	178.7	178.3
113.2	112.0	111.8	117.9	126.9	126.9	127.8	136.1	150.5	155.7	155.3
118.0	118.0	118.0	122.7	132.5	128.8	120.3	121.8	128.1	130.6	137.6
106.1	106.1	106.1	119.8	136.1	132.6	113.7	113.9	125.7	139.8	143.2
132.2	132.2	132.2	143.5	156.6	146.8	121.0	116.6	123.8	132.3	130.3

out annual fluctuations in the world market. Official exchange rates were used in calculation of border price equivalence of tradable goods.[19] The estimation results are presented in Table 6.12.

DIRECT PRICE COMPARISONS

Annual price comparisons were made for commodities for which information on domestic and border prices were both available. If price data were not available annually, the comparison was made instead for a specific year for which the relevant price data could be obtained and then the domestic and border price trends were used to derive the price ratios for the other relevant years. In fact, given domestic and international price trends, a single year's price comparison would be sufficient to infer the domestic–border price ratios for the whole period.

Price comparisons had to be carried out for the commodities whose domestic and international prices were both available. For those relatively homogeneous commodity categories, the price ratio was derived directly for a representative product j as ep_j^w/p_j^d where e denotes the exchange rate, p_j^w and p_j^d are the world price and the domestic price for good j, respectively. For multiple-commodity categories, the output value-weighted average of individual price ratios was calculated. The weight for the good i in category j was defined as the share of good i in the domestic output value of all the products included in the estimation for category j, that is,

$$w_{ij} = \frac{p_{ij}^d \, q_{ij}}{\sum_i p_{ij}^d \, q_{ij}} \tag{6.2}$$

Table 6.12 Border-price trends for China's tradable products, 1978–95
(1978 = 100)

Product	1978	1979	1980	1981	1982	1983	1984
1. Paddy rice	100.0	107.5	111.3	115.9	104.0	88.3	73.1
2. Wheat	100.0	106.5	117.2	116.7	112.7	107.2	101.8
3. Other grains	100.0	104.0	116.9	113.7	107.8	98.1	97.5
4. Oil-bearing crops	100.0	97.4	95.3	84.4	80.3	85.6	91.3
5. Cotton	100.0	108.5	114.0	111.9	107.6	106.2	100.5
6. Oth. industrial crops	100.0	99.4	93.8	86.8	77.9	74.9	71.6
7. Vegetables	100.0	98.5	97.9	96.6	98.5	102.5	103.0
8. Fruits	100.0	99.3	94.8	87.6	84.0	81.5	83.0
9. Forest products	100.0	101.4	107.0	109.8	111.0	109.0	93.3
10. Wool and hides	100.0	98.1	93.9	85.5	81.2	83.1	87.1
11. Meat, etc.	100.0	106.5	112.3	119.1	118.2	117.0	102.7
12. Fish	100.0	99.7	100.0	104.8	104.4	103.1	92.0
13. Other agri. products	100.0	100.0	100.0	101.6	101.3	97.7	86.0
14. Coal	100.0	98.8	106.1	119.6	120.7	106.6	96.8
15. Crude petroleum	100.0	141.1	179.6	183.6	169.5	156.8	144.8
16. Ferrous minerals	100.0	112.6	121.0	125.5	120.2	117 8	112 1
17. Non-ferrous minerals	100.0	112.1	117.1	108.5	99.3	95.3	94.0
18. Non-metal minerals	100.0	106.2	119.0	122.4	112 9	100.4	97.8
19. Timber	100.0	106.2	107.4	105.9	95.8	92.6	86 5
20. Sugar, tobacco, alcohol	100.0	112.1	123.6	130.2	127.3	125.2	127.5
21. Other processed food	100.0	102.5	106.6	106.8	100.2	95.3	91.5
22. Cotton textiles	100.0	99.5	98.8	94.8	86.9	83.7	77.2
23. Wool textiles	100.0	106.6	112.4	110.4	101.8	97.4	97.5
24. Hemp textiles	100.0	110.6	117.4	116.3	105.5	104.7	111.5
25. Silk textiles	100.0	106.8	108.7	105.6	95.3	90.9	80.4
26. Knitted goods	100.0	103.2	103.9	99.8	92.7	89.3	87.1
27. Other textiles	100.0	99.5	98.8	94.8	86.9	83.7	77.2
28. Clothing	100.0	99.4	106.7	109.5	113.2	115.6	102.5
29. Furniture	100.0	106.2	107.4	105.9	95.8	92.6	86.5
30. Paper	100.0	107.5	119.1	128.8	132.3	134.6	136.9
31. Cultural goods	100.0	97.2	94.1	91.7	79.8	75.0	65.0
32. Petrol. products	100.0	113.8	145.5	157.7	150.6	137.3	128.9
33. Coal products	100.0	108.0	111.3	112.8	105.6	100.1	107.0
34. Inorganic chemicals	100.0	120.1	142.7	157.6	148.0	132.5	116.2
35. Chem.fertilizers	100.0	117.4	116.9	113.0	96.8	98.9	102.6
36. Organic chemicals	100.0	104.9	107.6	104.5	93.9	85.7	82.8
37. Household chemicals	100.0	99.3	98.5	99.1	99.1	102.2	99.5
38. Other chemicals	100.0	110.4	119.1	117.8	107.6	102.5	98.5
39. Medicine	100.0	107.0	125.6	117.5	121.1	113.0	107.8
40. Chemical fibres	100.0	107.3	115.0	117.3	111.0	107.4	102.9
41. Rubber manufactures	100.0	106.4	112.9	114.7	110.7	106.5	102.9
42. Plastic articles	100.0	108.9	115.9	116.4	108.8	105.1	105.5
43. Cement	100.0	108.2	119.5	133.1	124.7	108.7	93.6
44. Glass	100.0	110.7	131.5	146.4	164.4	178.5	183.3
45. Ceramic products	100.0	104.0	108.5	105.5	101.5	98.2	98.9
46. Other bldg materials	100.0	106.0	116.6	126.6	137.9	144.6	137.8

1985	1986	1987	1988	1989	1990	1991	1992	1993	1994	1995
62.6	57.3	59.5	63.2	66.8	66.2	65.0	61.2	69.7	90.2	112.8
92.0	83.3	84.5	96.3	100.5	96.8	92.7	93.8	98.5	104.4	119.3
94.8	83.9	85.8	92.1	102.7	102.8	100.6	98.3	98.4	104.4	124.0
85.8	71.0	69.0	75.0	86.3	95.4	95.7	90.7	90.7	98.5	108.7
84.4	81.6	85.0	97.4	101.8	108.8	103.8	95.4	97.0	118.2	130.4
68.0	69.1	74.8	93.4	106.3	108.9	101.2	88.6	82.3	78.8	82.5
92.4	94.4	103.0	122.8	124.7	127.1	136.3	148.5	139.3	170.8	195.0
84.4	90.7	96.0	98.6	98.1	101.5	108.3	108.3	97.8	88.7	86.6
77.4	64.3	66.0	67.9	70.1	77.8	85.7	94.4	88.6	82.8	74.7
104.4	134.7	166.1	181.6	176.4	152.6	134.1	120.1	112.9	111.1	113.1
97.5	97.3	105.2	107.3	107.5	105.4	100.8	91.2	78.3	79.7	88.4
93.8	102.0	95.5	90.0	75.2	81.7	79.5	97.1	90.9	113.7	107.8
72.5	57.3	49.7	61.2	74.7	78.7	71.1	71.3	74.3	80.2	83.3
88.5	84.4	82.1	83.9	89.6	95.1	95.0	92.5	87.8	86.8	89.6
116.1	96.5	76.2	84.2	94.0	102.8	106.0	97.9	93.0	90.7	94.5
108.7	107.3	106.6	104.3	111.6	128.5	142.0	140.8	128.2	115.4	116.0
90.2	93.3	118.5	144.4	155.3	139.4	123.9	109.6	109.7	118.7	127.2
105.7	104.3	100.6	98.3	96.1	94.4	93.3	92.7	94.4	100.8	111.3
85.5	83.7	88.1	92.7	103.6	110.5	124 9	154.3	177.8	189.5	180 0
129.0	131.4	129.5	137.1	143.8	154.2	157.1	153.1	154.9	160.5	171.9
93.2	96.9	104.5	113.1	118.8	128.2	139.0	144.7	137.0	135.7	137.7
75.6	74.6	78.5	82.1	78.5	76.6	75.5	74.5	78.4	88.9	103.6
102.8	111.4	120.0	153.2	161.8	175.3	155.8	156.8	134.9	132.3	128.9
121.2	131.9	156.0	155.6	141.1	109.6	99.0	93.5	95.2	109.0	117.3
82.6	77.6	79.5	81.6	94.1	102.4	95.1	79.0	65.6	56.9	53.4
92.9	101.5	109.6	113.5	113.3	115.3	112.6	113.1	114.4	123.0	130.6
75.6	74.6	78.5	82.1	78.5	76.6	75.5	74.5	78.4	88.9	103.6
107.0	100.3	108.1	99.7	99.1	99.2	101.7	105.3	111.3	116.6	120.5
85.5	83.7	88.1	92.7	103.6	110.5	124.9	154.3	177.8	189.5	180.0
140.1	144.5	150.5	156.1	156.4	154.2	148.7	145.5	143.7	165.8	186.0
75.9	84.0	93.6	95.0	102.2	125.0	120.2	118.4	90.7	94.2	89.2
111.8	95.8	76.4	75.8	87.0	95.4	96.2	89.4	85.5	87.6	92.0
97.7	102.2	107.8	115.8	127.4	139.1	143.0	143.3	140.1	142.8	152.0
105.9	101.5	105.3	131.0	145.0	146.7	133.4	123.3	117.3	109.9	104.9
102.4	105.3	106.1	110.8	109.2	102.9	97.1	92.1	91.8	99.1	115.2
87.9	100.8	108.0	106.7	107.9	117.9	128.8	116.6	109.6	134.9	147.6
97.4	93.9	95.4	99.2	105.4	98.0	91.9	93.2	76.8	72.5	92.3
102.8	113.6	122.5	124.6	126.1	128.9	141.2	151.2	160.6	163.4	163.3
120.2	119.9	113.8	97.7	92.8	88.2	83.8	79.6	75.6	71.8	68.3
109.9	116.9	124.6	134.7	135.4	138.3	126.3	119.9	112.2	118.0	127.4
110.3	124.8	143.7	153.5	160.0	158.7	156.5	153.5	154.9	165.7	173.8
116.7	133.1	147.1	142.5	124.4	115.2	107.4	106.9	98.5	101.9	106.6
89.9	93.1	99.1	105.5	106.9	108.5	114.5	116.2	115.6	100.1	99.5
177.7	178.2	177.8	189.8	201.8	208.0	223.6	230.6	229.2	215.3	205.9
108.3	124.7	139.9	139.6	129.2	118.3	115.5	110.7	110.8	133.6	162.0
137.5	148.6	167.8	182.8	189.8	228.4	241.6	263.2	231.5	244.6	248.9

Table 6.12 (Continued)

Product	1978	1979	1980	1981	1982	1983	1984
47. Iron	100.0	111.4	119.3	115.3	103.6	96.2	94.8
48. Steel	100.0	100.0	100.2	103.9	110.0	118.3	127.2
49. Non-ferrous metals	100.0	112.1	117.1	108.5	99.3	95.3	94.0
50. Metal products	100.0	105.7	110.6	110.8	104.5	98.0	92.6
51. Agri. machinery	100.0	109.4	118.8	120.3	121.8	125.6	126.3
52. Industrial equipment	100.0	109.8	119.6	120.8	121.9	121.1	119.6
53. Power equipment	100.0	109.2	118.5	122.7	126.9	128.5	130.0
54. Hshd mech/elect.gds	100.0	101.3	100.5	98.0	92.7	96.3	100.9
55. Railway equipment	100.0	102.7	111.5	118.5	114.2	109.2	102.9
56. Motor vehicles	100.0	102.5	109.4	114.7	116.5	114.8	117.8
57. Ships	100.0	96.7	96.1	99.9	103.3	96.6	93.5
58. Oth transp. equipment	100.0	108.0	116.0	116.8	117.6	119.1	118.3
59. Other enging. prods.	100.0	108.7	117.4	116.3	115.2	115.9	114.4
60. Electronic products	100.0	107.7	115.4	112.5	109.6	106.7	105.8
61. Hshd Electronics	100.0	105.5	105.3	113.4	116.1	112.8	110.8

Sources: Handbook of Agricultural Technology and Economics Editorial Board (1983); Planning Office (MOA) (1989); Customs General Administration (1985–9, 1990–5); Editorial Board of ACFERT (1987–96/7); IMF (1981–96): International Economic Data Bank (ANU); Research Institute of Commodity Prices (SACP) (1985, 1988); Xiong Meihua (1991); State Administration of

where p_{ij}^d and q_{ij} denote the domestic price and quantity of good i in category j, respectively. The average price ratio for category j was derived by summing up the products of the individual price ratios and the output value weights w_{ij}

$$\frac{ep_j^w}{p_j^d} = \sum_i w_{ij} \frac{ep_{ij}^w}{p_{ij}^d} = \frac{\sum_i ep_{ij}^w q_{ij}}{\sum_i p_{ij}^d q_{ij}} \tag{6.3}$$

The price comparison was made for each category of tradable goods for every year from 1978 to 1995. The current year's output value weights were used whenever their data were available to take into account the rapid structural changes in many industries. To save space, however, we present here only the detailed price comparison results for a single year.

The Research Institute of the former State Administration of Commodity Price[20] has published a number of studies comparing China's domestic prices and foreign prices for more than 100 major agricultural and industrial products in the past ten years (SACP, Research Institute of Commodity Prices 1985 and 1988; Xiong Meihua 1991). These studies were also used to check the accuracy of the price comparison results for three particular years, 1985, 1988 and 1990.

Agricultural Products (1–13) . Table 6.13 reports the price comparison for 13 agricultural products.

Table 6.12 (Continued)

1985	1986	1987	1988	1989	1990	1991	1992	1993	1994	1995
98.3	101.9	106.7	109.4	113.3	127.1	117.7	118.2	106.1	114.5	120.6
134.3	139.0	139.6	151.8	161.9	172.7	162.6	147.8	132.1	140.7	156.1
90.2	93.3	118.5	144.4	155.3	139.4	123.9	109.6	109.7	118.7	127.2
97.7	108.5	116.2	126.6	134.0	142.9	140.4	145.9	127.0	132.7	131.9
127.8	136.8	136.8	130.0	123.5	117.3	111.5	105.9	100.6	95.6	90.8
120.8	137.7	137.7	137.7	130.8	124.3	118.1	112.2	106.6	101.2	96.2
132.3	152.3	152.3	144.7	137.5	130.6	124.1	117.9	112.0	106.4	101.0
111.3	118.9	129.5	127.5	127.5	127.5	127.5	127.5	127.5	127.5	127.5
119.1	109.3	115.3	118.6	116.2	113.9	111.6	109.0	103.6	96.8	88.9
130.8	142.7	149.5	144.6	137.3	130.5	123.9	117.7	116.0	106.3	97.0
87.2	90.2	91.9	85.6	81.8	78.2	74.8	71.5	68.4	65.5	62.7
121.4	145.0	145.0	137.8	130.9	124.4	118.1	112.2	106.6	101.3	96.2
122.1	133.3	133.3	128.0	124.2	118.0	114.4	109.8	104.3	88.1	76.1
100.0	122.5	122.5	116.4	110.6	105.0	99.8	94.8	90.0	85.5	81.3
109.3	125.1	130.1	123.6	117.4	111.5	105.9	100.6	95.6	90.8	86.3

Commodity Prices (1989); State Planning Commission (1987, 1994); United Nations, *Yearbook of International Trade Statistics* and *Commodity Trade Statistics*; UNCTAD, *Monthly Commodity Price Bulletin*; World Bank, *Commodity Trade and Price Trend.*

Natural Resource Products (14–19). Like agricultural commodities, prices were compared in each category because most products in this group were relatively homogeneous and heavily traded in the world markets. For the multiple-product categories, the output value-weighted average prices of the representative products were estimated (Table 6.14).

Light Industrial Products (20–31). This group of manufactured goods also contains highly diversified commodity categories. Price comparisons are therefore conducted for a specific year, mainly for the period between 1983 and 1986 depending on the data availability, and then inferred to other years. The results for 1984 are shown in Table 6.15.

Chemicals and Metal Products (32–50). This group contains industrial semi-processed materials, many of which are internationally tradable. Price comparisons for those goods can therefore be made for every year of the whole period. The results reported in Table 6.16 are for 1984.

Machinery Products (51–61). Unlike agricultural, natural resource, chemical and metal products, the products included in each category of machinery are highly diversified so that it is very difficult to conduct price comparisons on an annual basis. The estimates of price differentials were thus drawn from two sources: the shadow price estimates from the project evaluation guideline by the State Planning Commission (1987 and 1994) and import tariff rates. The use of tariff rates can be justified on the grounds that the products

Table 6.13   Price comparisons for China's agricultural products (1–13), 1984

Product	p^w	ep^w	p^d	ep^w/p^d	w
	US $	Yuan	Yuan		
1. Paddy rice (ton)	186.42	521.98	310.46	1.681	n.a.
2. Wheat (ton)	149.73	419.73	403.12	1.040	n.a.
3. Other grains (ton) (1986)					
– Corn	112.90	389.51	351.90	1.107	0.67
– Sorghum	77.00	265.65	413.20	0.643	0.06
– Millet	130.02	448.57	350.80	1.279	0.04
– Soybeans	210.38	725.81	798.10	0.909	0.23
Weighted average				1.039	1.00
4. Oil-bearing crops (ton) (1987)					
– Groundnuts	659.22	2 452.30	1 112.40	2.205	0.08
– Sesame seeds	512.27	1 905.64	1 695.30	1.124	0.02
– Sunflower seeds	237.31	882.79	859.50	1.027	0.08
– Rapeseed oil				1.716	0.43
– Cotton seeds	107.25	398.97	295.50	1.350	0.24
– Soybeans	252.10	937.81	825.30	1.136	0.15
Weighted average				1.514	1.00
5. Cotton (ton)	1 754.76	4 913.40	3 530.80	1.393	n.a.
6. Other industrial crops (ton) (1984)					
– Hemp	762.65	2 135.72	1 677.50	1.273	0.04
– Ramie	1 294.90	3 625.72	5 024.50	0.722	0.03
– Jute	472.50	1 323.00	476.00	2.779	0.07
– Sugarcane	16.73	46.84	60.00	0.781	0.24
– Sugar-beet	20.36	57.01	87.60	0.651	0.07
– Flue-cured tobacco	2 261.03	6 330.88	1 695.00	3.735	0.26
– Tea	2 618.51	7 331.83	3 744.00	1.958	0.16
– Silkworm cocoons	10 763.48	30 137.74	3 969.70	7.592	0.14
Weighted average				2.828	1.00
7. Vegetables (kg) (1986)					
– Potatoes	0 12	0.35	0.25	1.395	0.25
– Onions	0.12	0.35	0.25	1.405	0.25
– Turnips	0.16	0.47	0.18	2.611	0.25
– Cabbages	0.20	0.59	0.15	3.889	0.25
Weighted average				2.325	1.00
8. Fruits (ton)					
– Apples	326.30	913.64	586.10	1.559	0.59
– Oranges	441.73	1,236.84	807.40	1.533	0.41
Weighted average				1.575	1.00
9. Forest products (ton)					
– Natural rubber	894.49	2 504.57	6080.00	0.412	0.07
– Lacquer	20 903.17	58 528.88	12 797.50	4.573	0.02
– Tung oil	2 036.88	5 703.26	3 247.14	1.756	0.79
– Walnuts	938.96	2 629.09	1 388.36	1.894	0.12
Weighted average				1.743	1.00

Table 6.13   (Continued)

Product	p^w	ep^w	p^d	ep^w/p^d	w
	US $	Yuan	Yuan		
10. Wool and hides					
– Wool (ton)	4 306.22	12 057.42	4 228.89	2.851	0.63
– Cattle-hide (no.)	3.47	9.72	8.10	1.188	0.19
– Goat-hide (no.)	54.46	152.49	44.40	3.434	0.18
Weighted average				2.634	1.00
11. Meat, eggs and milk (ton)					
– Pork	1 603.07	4 488.60	1 821.00	2.516	0.82
– Beef	1 171.67	3 280.68	2 906.00	1.129	0.04
– Mutton	1 396.00	3 908.80	2 327.00	1.680	0.04
– Eggs	952.63	2 667.36	2 076.00	1.285	0.10
Weighted average				2.238	1.00
12. Fish (kg) (1986)					
– Pond fish	1.29	4.21	2.78	1.515	n.a.
13. Other agricultural products				2.861	n.a.

Notes:

a Exchange rate was 2.8 yuan per US dollar in 1984.

b Commodity specifications are provided in sources cited.

Sources:

1. p^d: Average procurement prices, State Statistical Bureau of China, (1988:209); p^w: Export unit value of rice, Editorial Board of ACFERT (1986). It is then multiplied by 0.73 to derive the unit value of paddy rice.
2. p^d: State Statistical Bureau (1988:209); p^w: United Nations (1989:370).
3. p^d: Average procurement prices, State Statistical Bureau of China (1988); Urban Social and Economic Survey Team (SSB) (1988); Planning Office (MOA) (1989); p^w: Export unit values, Editorial Board of ACFERT (1986).
4. p^d: Average procurement prices, State Statistical Bureau of China (1988); Urban Social and Economic Survey Team (SSB) (1988); p^w: Export unit values, Editorial Board of ACFERT (1988). p^w/p^d: Rapeseed oil, Research Institute of Commodity Prices (SACP) (1988:6)
5. Research Institute of Commodity Prices (SACP) (1985:375).
6. p^d: Average procurement prices, State Statistical Bureau of China (1988); Urban Social and Economic Survey Team (SSB) (1988) Research Institute of Commodity Prices (SACP) (1985); p^w: Export unit values, Editorial Board of ACFERT (1986); Research Institute of Commodity Prices (SACP) (1985).
7. p^d: Average retail prices, *Economic Information* (1986); p^w: Export unit values, Editorial Board of ACFERT (1987).
8. p^d: Average procurement prices, State Statistical Bureau of China (1988); Urban Social and Economic Survey Team (SSB) (1988); *Economic Information* (1986); p^w: Export unit values, Editorial Board of ACFERT (1986).
9. Natural rubber: Research Institute of Commodity Prices (SACP) (1985:381). Others: State Statistical Bureau of China (1988); Urban Social and Economic Survey Team (SSB) (1988); Editorial Board of ACFERT (1986).

10. p^d: Average procurement prices (State Statistical Bureau, 1988); State Statistical Bureau, Urban Social and Economic Survey Team, 1988. p^w: Export unit values, Editorial Board of ACFERT, 1986.
11. p^d: Average procurement prices, State Statistical Bureau of China (1988) Urban Social and Economic Survey Team (SSB) (1998); p^w: Export unit values, Editorial Board of ACFERT (1986): International Economic Data Bank (ANU).
12. p^d: Retail price, Urban Social and Economic Survey Team (SSB) (1988:123); p^w: Export unit values, Editorial Board of ACFERT (1986:973).
13. p^w/p^d: Output weighted average of eleven medicine herbs, State Statistical Bureau of China (1988); Editorial Board of ACFERT (1986, 1987): *Economic Information* (1985).

---

concerned were mainly importables and not subject to unified domestic pricing because the comparable domestic products could not be found. Most data cited in Table 6.17 refer to 1985.

AN ANALYSIS OF RELATIVE PRICES FOR TRADABLES

The price ratios for tradable products for the period 1978–95 were derived using the information from the above tables. The estimated results are presented in Table 6.18. As indicated in Table 6.18, China's relative price structure changed considerably between 1978 and 1995. During the same period, however, the international prices for most commodities had varied moderately. So it seems apparent that the changes in China's relative price structure were caused mainly by the dramatic changes in China's domestic prices induced almost exclusively by the economic reforms and open-door policy.

China's pre-reform commodity price structure was believed to be heavily distorted in two respects. First, the domestic prices of primary products–including agricultural, natural resource and semi-processed products such as basic metals and building materials–were much lower than their international prices. Second, the domestic prices of manufactured products–such as chemical products, machinery and electronics–were higher than their comparable international prices. This price structure was inherited from pre-1949 China and was later reinforced by the Soviet-style development strategies adopted. Such development strategies were biased towards industry and against agriculture and, within industry, biased towards manufacturing and against raw material extraction and processing activities.

This distorted price structure has been confirmed by the results in Table 6.18. To facilitate a comparison of China's pre-and post-reform relative price structures, the estimated price ratios for all 61 tradable categories for 1978, 1987 and 1995 are plotted in Figure 6.1. It can be seen that, in 1978, almost all agricultural and natural resource products and some semi-processed key industrial raw materials were located at the high end of the relative price spectrum, while most sophisticated manufactured products were located at the low end. Many agricultural products and industrial raw materials had a

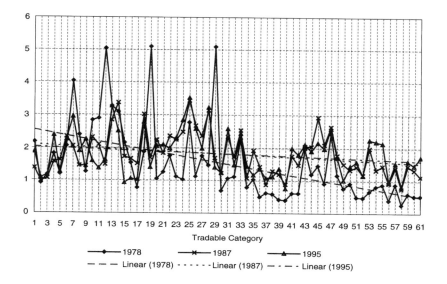

Figure 6.1   China's relative price structure for tradable goods, 1978, 1987 and 1995
Source: Table 6.18.

price ratio above unity in 1978. On the other hand, the prices of many chemical products (Sectors 34 and 36–42) and industrial manufactures (Sectors 49–61) were higher than their border prices. The level of price differentials appears to escalate with the degree of sophistication in processing or manufacturing activities. This escalated structure is typical in those developing countries that attempt to protect their domestic manufacturing industries at the expense of the primary sectors. China's old turnover tax-based taxation system was also partially responsible for such a distorted structure: the more a good was processed, the more it would be taxed and the higher its price would be. This pricing system played an important role in transferring resources from the primary sector to the manufacturing sector.

Figure 6.1 also shows the price structure for 1987, 10 years after the beginning of economic reforms. A visual inspection of Figure 6.1 reveals a sharp contrast between the two patterns. The prices of primary products had increased rapidly, relative to that of manufactured goods. A number of factors are responsible for these changes. The large-scale adjustments of state prices, commencing immediately after the announcement of economic reform in the late 1970s, substantially raised the prices of staple farm products and key industrial raw materials. The opening of the domestic markets and the introduction of a two-tier pricing system for most industrial products saw a rapid change in the domestic price structure in the mid-1980s. All these domestic changes were accompanied by the open-door policy which

Table 6.14   Price comparisons for China's industrial resources (14–19), 1984

Product	p^w	ep^w	p^d	ep^w/p^d	w
	US $	Yuan	Yuan		
14. Coal (ton)	50.00	140.00	38.92	3.60	n.a.
15. Crude petroleum (ton)	185.74	520.07	155.92	3.34	n.a.
16. Ferrous minerals (ton)					
– Iron ore, fine	29.73	83.24	62.50	1.33	n.a.
17. Non-ferrous minerals (ton)					
– Copper	1 644	4 603	5 575	0.83	0.408
– Lead	524	1 467	2 098	0.70	0.091
– Zinc	1 063	2 976	2 141	1.39	0.101
– Tin	13 794	38 623	20 116	1.92	0.058
– Nickel	6 056	16 957	22 227	0.76	0.084
– Aluminium	1 525	4 270	3 158	1.35	0.232
– Antimony	3 755	10 514	4 724	2.23	0.019
– Mercury	9 436	26 421	33 186	0.80	0.005
– Magnesium	3 371	9 439	4 535	2.08	0.002
Weighted average				1.12	1.000
18. Non metal minerals (ton)					
– Pyrites	41.64	116.59	55.00	2.12	0.429
– Phosphate minerals	31.92	89.38	30.00	2.98	0.412
– Asbestos	875.08	2 450.22	1 096.77	2.23	0.060
– Gypsum	16.72	46.82	14.68	3.19	0.024
– Talc	52.38	146.66	74.26	1.98	0.044
– China clay	63.54	117.91	82.21	1.43	0.031
Weighted average				2.21	1.000
19. Timber (cubic m)	82.16	230.05	117.2	1.963	n.a.

Notes:
a Exchange rate was 2.8 yuan per US dollar in 1984.
b Commodity specifications are provided in the sources.
Sources:
14. p^w and p^d: Research Institute of Commodity Prices (SACP) (1985:383).
15. p^d: weighted average of the planned price and the planned high price of crude petroleum from the Daqin Oil Field (Yang Songhao, 1988:79, 256), p^w: Unit value of China's crude petroleum export, Editorial Board of ACFERT (1984:1045, 1986:1057).
16. p^w and p^d: Research Institute of Commodity Prices (SACP) (1985:385).
17. p^d: Yang Songhao (1988:290–1), p^w: Research Institute of Commodity Prices (SACP) (1985:390–1)
18. p^d (sulphur iron pyrites and phosphate minerals): Yang Songhao (1988:309), p^d (asbestos, gypsum, talc and china clay): State Council: Office for Price Research Centre (1985), p^w (asbestos): import unit values, IEDB (ANU), p^w (others): export unit values, Editorial Board of ACFERT (1984, 1986).
19. p^d weighted average of the planned price (State Council: Office for the Leading Group of National Industrial Census, 1989b:292) and the market price (*Economic Information*, 1985; Urban Social and Economic Survey Team (SSB) 1988:71), p^w: import unit values, Editorial Board of ACFERT (1984:1091, 1986:1100).

Table 6.15   Price comparisons for China's light industrial products (20–31), 1984

Product	p^w	ep^w	p^d	ep^w/p^d	w
	US $	Yuan	Yuan		
20. Sugar tobacco and alcohol					
– Raw sugar (ton)	190.66	533.85	1 056.16	0.51	0.16
– Cigarette (box)	713.41	1 997.55	687.98	2.90	0.54
– Alcohol (ton)	1 396.89	3 911.29	1 854.20	1.92	0.30
Weighted average				2.03	1.00
21. Other processed food (ton) (1985)					
– Rice	216.36	636.11	367.48	1.73	0.49
– Wheat flour	181.47	533.51	437.30	1.22	0.16
– Peanut oil	818.55	2 406.54	2 517.30	0.96	0.03
– Drink	123.76	363.84	519.77	0.70	0.05
– Tea	2 149.29	6 318.91	5 739.25	1.40	0.14
– Cake	1 030.96	3 031.02	1 712.44	1.77	0.12
– Tinned food	1 413.87	4 156.78	2 892.68	1.44	0.01
Weighted average				1.53	1.00
22. Cotton textiles					
– Cotton yarn (kg)	4.60	12.88	6.58	1.96	0.75
– Cotton cloth (m2)	0.41	1.14	0.87	1.31	0.25
Weighted average				1.76	1.00
23. Wool textiles (1985)					
– Wool yarn (ton)	13.99	41.14	21.93	1.88	n.a.
24. Hemp textiles (1983)					
–Hemp cloth (m2)	1.21	3.39	2.01	1.69	n.a.
25. Silk textiles					
– Raw silk (kg)	53.59	150.05	42.40	3.54	n.a.
26. Knitted goods (1986)					
– Singlet, vest (no.)	0.72	2.52	1.45	1.74	n.a.
27. Other textiles (1983)				1.76	n.a.
28. Clothing					
– Sweaters, trousers (no.)	1.66	4.65	1.73	2.67	n.a.
29. Furniture				1.96	n.a.
30. Paper					
– News print (ton)	511.46	1 432.09	930.00	1.52	n.a.
31. Cultural goods (1985)				1.56	n.a.

Notes:

a The exchange rate was 2.8 yuan per US dollar in 1984.
b Commodity specifications are provided in the sources.
Sources:
20. p^d: Research Institute of Commodity Prices (SACP) (1985:377), State Council: Office for the Leading Group of National Industrial Census (1989b:293–4); p^w: export unit values, Editorial Board of ACFERT, (1986), IEDB (ANU); w. State Council: Office for the Leading Group of National Industrial Census (1989a).

21. p^d: State Council: Office for the Leading Group of National Industrial Census (1989b); State Council: Office for Price Research Centre (1985); p^w: Unit value of exports or imports, Customs General Administration of China (1986).
22. p^d and p^w: Research Institute of Commodity Prices (SACP) (1985:377–8); w: State Council: Office for the Leading Group of National Industrial Census (1988:96).
23. p^d (1985): State Council: Office for the Leading Group of National Industrial Census (1989b); p^w (1985): unit value of export, State Planning Commission (1987:473).
24. p^d (1983): State Council: Office for Price Research Centre (1985); p^w (1983): Export unit values, International Economic Data Bank (ANU).
25. p^d and P^w: Research Institute of Commodity Prices (SACP) (1985:378).
26. p^d: Urban Social and Economic Survey Team (SSB) (1988:174); p^w: unit value of exports, Editorial Board of ACFERT (1986:1004).
27. Assume the same as cotton textiles.
28. p^w: unit value of exports, Editorial Board of ACFERT (1986: 1004).
29. Assume the same as that of timber.
30. p^d and p^w: Research Institute of Commodity Prices (SACP) (1985:378).
31. p^w/p^d Assume approximate to the shadow price conversion factor for paper products (1.56) in State Planning Commission (1987:469).

---

encouraged trade and foreign investment. The gradual removal of trade barriers and the linking of the domestic market with the world market further accelerated the realignment of domestic and world prices. As a result, the distortions of the relative price structure were reduced markedly. As shown in Figure 6.1, from 1978 to 1987, the domestic prices of primary products increased considerably while that of manufactured products remained relatively stable or even declined slightly. These changes reduced the skewness of the domestic price structure which, as shown in Figure 6.1, had come to be more closely parallel to their border prices. In 1995, the above trends were further intensified, though at a comparatively lesser pace.

The convergence of China's domestic prices toward their international counterparts can also be seen from the variation of the standard deviation of the estimated price ratios over time. Table 6.19 provides the mean and standard deviation from the mean of the estimated price ratios. The results show a rapid decline in the deviation from the mean of the price ratios over the period 1978–95. The process of convergence slowed down thereafter, apparently due to serious inflation at the time, and then regained its momentum in the early 1990s. These results indicate a continuing trend of the convergence between China's domestic prices of tradables and their international counterparts. It is a clear sign that the economy is moving away from its pre-reform distorted structure toward a gradual integration with the rest of the world.

It can also be seen from Table 6.19 that China's domestic prices for most tradable goods, if converted at the nominal exchange rate, were below their border-price levels. This is the result of the repeated nominal exchange rate depreciation. Despite substantial increases in the domestic prices, their

Table 6.16   Price comparisons for China's chemical and metal product (32–50), 1984

Product	p^w US $	ep^w Yuan	p^d Yuan	ep^w/p^d	w
32. Petroleum products (ton)				2.03	
33. Coal products (ton)					
– Coke	95.04	266.11	123.00	2.16	
34. Inorganic chemicals (ton)					
– Sulphuric acid	38.00	106.40	190.10	0.63	0.337
– Nitric acid	128.54	359.91	447.29	0.63	0.029
– Hydrochloric acid	103.13	288.76	111.82	2.25	0.092
– Caustic soda	300.00	840.00	613.57	1.31	0.359
– Soda ash	135.00	378.00	374.15	1.26	0.182
Weighted average				1.16	1.000
35. Chemical fertilizers (ton)					
– Ammon sulphate	93.83	262.72	236.67	1.11	0.130
– Ammon nitrate	98.00	274.40	284.00	0.97	0.090
– Urea	223.57	626.00	410.00	1.53	0.724
– Superphosphate	146.00	408.80	375.00	1.09	0.173
Weighted average				1.43	1.000
36. Organic chemicals (ton)				0.79	
37. Household chemicals				0.91[a]	
38. Other chemicals (ton)				0.85	
39. Medicines				0.91	
40. Chemical fibres (ton)				0.66[a]	
41. Rubber manufactures				1.00	
42. Plastic articles					
– Plastic shoes (pair)	0.68	1.90	1.73	1.10[a]	
43. Cement (ton)					
– 525	69.89	195.69	80.00	2.46	
44. Glass (m2)					
– Plate glass (2mm)	1.74	4.87	2.53	1.92	
45. Ceramic products (ton)				1.82	
46. Other building materials (1985)				1.41	
47. Iron (ton)					
– Pig iron	238.27	667.16	312.00	2.14	0.660
– Ferro manganese	610.06	1708.17	1023.00	1.670	0.340
Weighted average				1.97	1.000
48. Steel (ton)				1.71	
49. Non-ferrous metals (ton)	2677.00	7496.00	6715.00	1.12	
50. Metal products (ton)					
– Steel wire rope	720.72	2018.02	2002.13	1.01	

Notes:

a. 1985 figure.

b. Exchange rate was 2.8 yuan per US dollar in 1984.

c. Commodity specifications are provided in the sources.

Sources:

32. p^w/p^d: output-value weighted average of shadow price conversion factors of 14 products in State Planning Commission (1987); adjusted by market price, State Council: Office for the Leading Group of National Industrial Census (1989b).

33. p^d: weighted average of planned price (Research Institute of Commodity Prices (SACP), 1985:385) and market price (State Council: Office for the Leading Group of National Industrial Census, 1989b); p^w: Research Institute of Commodity Prices (SACP) (1985:385).

34. p^d: weighted average of planned prices (Yang Songhao, 1988:311) and market prices (*Economic Information*, 1988); p^w: Sulphuric acid, caustic soda and soda ash, Research Institute of Commodity Prices (SACP) (1985:379). Nitric acid and hydrochloric acid, unit value of exports, IEDB (ANU); w: State Council: Office for the Leading Group of National Industrial Census (1989a).

35. p^d: Superphosphate, State Council, Office for Price Research Centre (1985); others, Yang Songhao (1988:309); p^w: Ammonium sulphate, export unit value (SITC 5611), International Economic Data Bank (ANU); others, Research Institute of Commodity Prices (SACP) (1985:379–80).

36. p^w/p^d: output value-weighted average of eight products in Research Institute of Commodity Prices (SACP) (1985:380–1); adjusted by market prices.

37. p^w/p^d: Assumed approximate to that of chemical products in Research Institute of Commodity Prices (SACP) (1985:378).

38. p^w/p^d: output value-weighted average of seven products in Research Institute of Commodity Prices (SACP) (1985:381–2), adjusted by market prices.

39. p^w/p^d: Derived from the import tariff rate, State Council: Office for Price Research Central (1985).

40. p^w/p^d: output value-weighted average of two products (polyamide and polyester long fibres) in Research Institute of Commodity Prices (SACP) (1985:378); adjusted by market prices.

41. p^w/p^d: The estimate for this category of products by the Research Institute of Commodity Prices (SACP) is 1.26 (1985) while that by the State Planning Commission is 0.5 (1987). Here, assume it equal to 1.

42. Plastic shoes: p^d (1983): State Council: Office for Price Research Centre (1985); p^w (1983): export unit value, Editorial Board of ACFERT (1984:1001).

43. p^d: weighted average of the planned price (Yang Songhao, 1988:325) and the market price (*Economic Information* 1988) of cement (525[a]); p^w: Research Institute of Commodity Prices (SACP) (1985:385).

44. p^d weighted average of planned prices (Yang Songhao, 1988:327) and market prices (*Economic Information*, 1988); p^w: Research Institute of Commodity Prices (SACP) (1985:385).

45. p^w/p^d: Assumed equivalent to other building materials.

46. p^w/p^d: output weighted average of shadow price conversion factor of four products in State Planning Commission (1987:457–58).

47. p^d: weighted average of planned prices (Yang Songhao, 1988:263–4) and market prices (*Economic Information* 1988); p^w: Research Institute of Commodity Prices (SACP) (1985:385), w: State Council: Office for the Leading Group of National Industrial Census (1988).

48. p^w/p^d: output value-weighted average of twenty steel products in Research Institute of Commodity Prices (SACP) (1985:386–90).

49. See 'Non-ferrous minerals', in Table 6.16.

50. p^d: State Council: Office for the Leading Group of National Industrial Census (1989b:300); p^w: Editorial Board of ACFERT (1986:1047).

Table 6.17   Price comparisons for China's machinery products (51–61), 1985

Product	w	ep^w/p^d
51. Agricultural machinery		
– Caterpillar tractors	0.06	0.59
– Wheel tractors	0.12	0.59
– Walking tractors	0.06	0.63
– Towed equipment	0.24	1.62
– Harvest equipment	0.16	1.62
– Transport equipment	0.20	1.35
– Dynamic equipment	0.11	1.14
– Water pumps	0.12	1.21
Weighted average	1.00	1.08
52. Industrial equipment		
– Machine tools	0.12	0.78
– Forge equipment	0.04	1.35
– Casting equipment	0.01	1.29
– Wool processing equipment	0.02	1.17
– Lifting equipment	0.14	1.02
– Industrial boilers	0.11	0.50
– Other general equipment	0.04	0.91
– Mining equipment	0.13	1.22
– Smelting equipment	0.06	1.06
– Petroleum drilling equipment	0.04	1.10
– Petro-chemical processing equipment	0.04	1.10
– Printing equipment	0.03	1.01
– Plastics machinery	0.14	1.03
– Electrically powered locomotives	0.02	1.00
– Textile equipment	0.02	1.03
– Papermaking equipment	0.02	1.03
– Other special equipment	0.04	0.91
Weighted average	1.00	0.98
Adjusted for market prices		0.85
53. Power station equipment	n.a.	1.41
54. Household mechanical/electrical goods	n.a.	1.13
55. Railway equipment	n.a.	1.37
56. Motor vehicles	n.a.	0.71
57. Ships	n.a.	1.15
58. Other transport equipment	n.a.	0.50
59. Other engineering products		
– Motors	0.22	0.86
– Transformers	0.07	1.25
– Other electric products	0.22	0.89
– Electric wires	0.33	1.16
– Automatic meters	0.06	0.83
– Electric meters	0.05	0.80
– Optical instruments	0.03	0.79
– Testing equipment	0.01	0.96
– Others	0.02	1.00
Weighted average	1.00	0.99

Table 6.17 (Continued)

Product	*w*	ep^w/p^d
60. Electronic products	n.a.	1.16
61. Household electronics	n.a.	1.43

Sources:

51. p^w/p^d: Output value-weighted average of shadow price conversion factors of eight products in State Planning Commission (1987:466–7); *w*: State Council: Office for the Leading Group of National Industrial Census (1989a).

52. p^w/p^d: Output value-weighted average of shadow price conversion factors of 17 products in State Planning Commission (1987:466–7), adjusted for market price, State Council: Office for the Leading Group of National Industrial Census (1989); *w*: State Council: Office for the Leading Group of National Industrial Census (1989a).

53. p^w/p^d: Shadow price conversion factors, State Planning Commission (1987:468), adjusted for market price, State Council: Office for the Leading Group of National Industrial Census (1989b).

54. p^w/p^d: Assume it approximates to shadow price conversion factors of light machinery and electrical equipment in State Planning Commission (1987:467).

55. p^w/p^d: Output value-weighted average of shadow price conversion factors of two products in State Planning Commission (1987:468). Weights from State Council: Office for the Leading Group of National Industrial Census (1988).

56. p^w/p^d: Shadow price conversion factors, State Planning Commission (1987:467).

57. p^w/p^d: Assumed higher than that of railway equipment.

58. The major products in this category are aircraft. Assume the NRP of this category is equivalent to the highest shadow-price conversion factor among industrial products (0.5) in State Planning Commission (1987).

59. p^w/p^d: Output weighted average of shadow-price conversion factors of nine products in State Planning Commission (1987:467); *w*: State Council: Office for the Leading Group of National Industrial Census (1989a).

60 p^w/p^d: Derived from the import tariff rate of electronic equipment, State Council: Office for Price Research Centre (1985).

61. p^w/p^d: Assume it approximates to the shadow-price conversion factor of automatic meter and optical instruments, State Planning Commissions (1987:468).

impact on China's price structure had largely been offset by the nominal exchange rate adjustments. During the period under investigation, China's nominal foreign exchange rate has been constantly devalued. In the beginning, the official exchange rate was 1.57 yuan per US dollar. By the end of the period, it was depreciated to 8.3 yuan per US dollar. The most dramatic devaluation occurred in 1981, when an internal settlement rate of 2.8 yuan per US dollar was introduced for merchandise trade, which effectively devalued the domestic currency by 64 per cent. The impact of this devaluation was a sharp drop in the mean price ratios for all China's tradable goods (Table 6.19). After the introduction of the two-tier price system, the domestic prices of industrial products increased rapidly. However, the continuing devaluation of the yuan prevented the domestic price of tradables from rising relative to their border price during the period 1984–95. Table 6.19 shows that the price ratios for that period were quite stable despite a rapid rise in the domestic price for many industrial products.

As documented earlier, during the reform period, China's domestic prices, on average, had increased much faster than their border counterparts. However, due to the continuous devaluation of the currency, China seems to have been able to keep the relative prices of tradable goods reasonably stable, especially in the late 1980s. Currency depreciation preserved the international competitiveness of many of China's traditional exports, even some farm products. However, the changes in domestic relative prices had made the opportunity costs of these traditional exports higher, which tended to diminish their international comparative advantage. As market reforms intensify, it can be expected that China will gradually move away from these traditional primary exports toward more manufactured exports.

CONCLUSION

This chapter has estimated the changes in China's relative price structure for tradable goods over the two decades of economic reforms. The estimates are based on direct comparisons between China's domestic prices and the border prices of tradable goods. The results have revealed that substantial changes have taken place in China's domestic markets, which have brought the domestic prices of tradable goods closer to international levels. In addition, the pre-reform bias of the relative price structure against primary products and in favour of manufactured products has been reduced substantially. These results indicate that the economic reforms and open-door policy have moved the Chinese economy toward a freer and more open economic system. The Chinese economy in 1995 was more integrated with the rest of the world than it was in 1978, implying a potential improvement of domestic resource-allocation efficiency. As a result of the linking of domestic and world prices, domestic firms were able to reallocate resources more easily to those industries in which China had a comparative advantage.

The chapter has shown that, for most tradable product groups, the domestic prices, converted at the nominal exchange rate, were lower than their border counterparts for the period concerned. Two facts related to the price comparison method may have contributed to this result. First, the price-comparison estimates of the price ratios covers only the domestically produced tradable goods, including exporting and import competing goods. It may exclude those imports which are not available domestically. It may

Table 6.18   Ratios of border to domestic prices for China's tradable goods,

Sector	1978	1979	1980	1981	1982	1983	1984
1. Paddy rice	2.18	1.84	1.84	3.58	3.05	2.31	1.68
2. Wheat	0.91	0.74	0.82	1.53	1.42	1.23	1.04
3. Other grains	1.18	0.98	1.06	1.86	1.54	1.27	1.16
4. Oil-bearing crops	1.83	1.17	1.03	1.60	1.54	1.72	1.82
5. Cotton	1.21	1.03	0.89	1.65	1.53	1.43	1.39
6. Other industrial crops	2.07	1.74	1.59	2.72	2.51	2.53	2.16
7. Vegetables	4.05	3.35	2.79	4.77	5.14	5.15	3.70
8. Fruits	2.41	2.29	1.76	2.92	2.59	2.30	1.60
9. Forest products	1.28	1.10	1.03	1.90	1.92	1.98	1.74
10. Wool and hides	2.85	2.47	2.16	4.06	3.12	2.93	2.31
11. Meal, etc.	2.90	2.10	1.92	3.61	3.48	2.59	2.24
12. Fish	5.05	3.13	2.57	4.44	4.17	3.63	2.19
13. Other agri. products	3.29	2.97	2.85	5.35	5.25	4.78	3.96
14. Coal	3.10	2.25	2.08	4.46	4.48	3.81	3.60
15. Crude oil	2.17	2.83	3.48	6.64	6.13	4.41	3.36
16. Ferrous minerals	1.56	1.63	1.13	2.19	2.10	2.06	1.33
17. Non-ferrous minerals	0.77	0.79	0.79	1.39	1.25	1.20	1.10
18. Non-metal minerals	1.90	1.74	1.89	3.80	3.42	2.52	2.46
19. Timber	5.11	3.89	3.78	5.18	3.47	2.36	1.96
20. Sugar, tobacco, spirit	1.07	1.10	1.17	2.13	1.92	1.78	2.03
21. Other processed food	1.28	1.16	1.12	2.04	1.87	1.73	1.62
22. Cotton textiles	1.78	1.63	1.57	2.81	2.57	1.91	1.76
23. Wool textiles	1.14	1.10	1.06	1.93	1.84	1.85	1.82
24. Hemp textiles	1.04	1.01	0.98	1.82	1.66	1.68	1.73
25. Silk textiles	2.79	2.83	2.71	4.91	4.43	4.11	3.54
26. Knitted goods	1.15	1.09	1.07	1.94	1.82	1.78	1.74
27. Other textiles	1.78	1.63	1.57	2.81	2.57	1.91	1.76
28. Clothing	1.50	1.38	1.44	2.79	2.92	3.02	2.67
29. Furniture	5.11	3.89	3.78	5.18	3.47	2.36	1.96
30. Paper	0.68	0.68	0.73	1.47	1.51	1.53	1.52
31. Cultural goods	1.08	0.99	0.94	1.73	1.52	1.49	1.30
32. Petro products	1.14	1.20	1.49	2.89	2.76	2.39	2.24
33. Coal products	2.30	2.29	1.86	3.51	3.29	3.12	2.50
34. Inorganic chemicals	0.80	0.88	1.01	2.12	1.98	1.45	1.16
35. Chem. fertilizers	1.06	1.15	1.11	2.00	1.51	1.54	1.43
36. Organic chemicals	0.49	0.51	0.52	0.99	0.93	0.88	0.79
37. Household chemicals	0.62	0.56	0.54	0.99	0.98	0.99	0.91
38. Synthetic chemicals	0.58	0.60	0.61	1.14	1.03	0.97	0.85
39. Medicine	0.42	0.41	0.52	0.91	0.94	0.88	0.87
40. Chemical fibres	0.39	0.38	0.39	0.72	0.67	0.64	0.60
41. Rubber products	0.61	0.60	0.61	1.14	1.09	1.04	1.00
42. Plastic articles	0.61	0.64	0.63	1.19	1.16	1.10	1.03
43. Cement	1.99	1.98	1.90	3.93	3.66	3.17	2.46
44. Glass	1.23	1.26	1.45	3.00	3.37	2.10	1.92
45. Ceramic products	1.49	1.43	1.44	2.62	2.52	1.88	1.82
46. Oth. bldg materials	0.93	0.90	0.91	1.83	1.49	1.50	1.40
47. Iron	2.46	2.49	1.97	3.55	3.13	2.91	2.12

1978–95 (%)

1985	1986	1987	1988	1989	1990	1991	1992	1993	1994	1995
1.46	1.41	1.39	1.24	1.01	1.37	1.57	1.57	1.50	1.88	1.89
0.97	0.92	0.98	0.97	0.84	1.11	1.26	1.20	1.25	1.30	1.08
1.04	0.99	1.06	1.07	0.95	1.23	1.44	1.28	1.11	1.32	1.18
1.78	1.64	1.59	1.46	1.43	2.03	2.32	2.40	2.08	2.30	2.39
1.27	1.44	1.63	1.54	1.33	1.40	1.45	1.45	1.39	1.58	1.28
1.98	2.22	2.35	2.21	2.31	2.88	2.86	2.63	2.40	2.82	2.27
2.07	2.33	2.06	1.97	1.98	2.67	2.84	2.77	2.36	3.31	2.96
1.25	1.42	1.47	1.16	1.29	1.74	1.93	2.16	2.03	2.29	1.92
1.50	1.40	1.46	1.17	1.16	1.94	2.32	2.47	2.18	2.73	2.27
2.03	1.82	2.33	1.89	1.69	2.07	2.07	1.87	1.64	1.83	1.62
1.80	2.30	2.11	1.53	1.37	1.80	2.07	1.79	1.30	1.13	1.39
1.51	1.81	1.51	1.11	0.84	1.22	1.30	1.59	1.32	2.03	1.66
2.86	3.40	2.85	2.95	2.56	3.37	3.21	3.04	2.95	3.96	3.28
2.95	3.26	3.39	3.13	3.01	3.83	3.76	3.27	2.32	2.81	2.52
2.42	2.17	1.75	1.81	1.89	2.45	2.36	1.96	1.14	1.11	0.93
1.36	1.57	1.68	1.41	1.25	1.64	1.75	1.56	0.93	1.16	1.06
1.07	1.13	1.54	1.62	1.46	1.51	1.31	1.05	0.70	1.05	1.05
2.52	2.92	3.03	2.62	2.09	2.62	2.72	2.52	1.88	2.79	2.80
1.81	1.82	1.72	1.23	1.20	1.40	1.56	1.79	1.80	1.89	1.43
2.01	2.29	2.26	1.31	1.17	1.58	1.81	1.75	1.66	2.28	2.08
1.53	1.73	1.86	1.75	1.60	1.93	2.28	2.27	2.00	2.52	2.11
1.81	2.10	2.38	2.10	1.63	1.88	1.93	1.87	1.82	2.16	2.00
1.88	2.25	2.26	2.53	2.27	3.02	3.19	2.97	2.46	2.87	2.31
1.81	1.96	2.50	2.21	2.01	1.94	2.11	2.12	2.20	3.18	2.86
3.36	3.49	3.46	3.21	3.23	4.45	5.07	4.57	3.95	4.42	3.54
1.93	2.39	2.69	2.33	1.87	2.23	2.47	2.49	2.42	3.10	2.59
1.81	2.10	2.38	2.10	1.63	1.88	1.93	1.87	1.82	2.16	2.00
2.90	3.09	3.16	2.72	2.26	2.65	2.75	2.97	2.74	3.80	3.24
1.81	1.82	1.72	1.23	1.20	1.40	1.56	1.79	1.80	1.89	1.43
1.32	1.32	1.26	1.06	0.87	1.07	1.12	1.10	1.04	1.69	1.27
1.56	2.01	2.36	2.14	2.10	3.03	3.07	3.06	2.22	3.15	2.60
2.03	2.03	1.75	1.51	1.52	1.84	1.79	1.49	1.29	1.71	1.50
2.19	2.31	2.56	2.48	2.46	3.22	3.25	2.91	2.13	2.66	2.46
1.04	1.03	1.10	1.28	1.35	1.62	1.54	1.38	1.29	1.69	1.47
1.49	1.79	1.95	1.43	1.24	1.30	1.20	1.03	0.94	1.33	1.20
0.92	1.26	1.45	1.16	0.93	1.23	1.51	1.28	1.07	1.65	1.38
0.83	0.89	0.88	0.80	0.73	0.89	1.01	1.03	0.82	1.05	1.10
0.92	1.17	1.33	1.08	0.86	1.05	1.28	1.27	1.19	1.51	1.14
1.02	1.20	1.23	0.97	0.83	1.08	1.26	1.25	1.20	1.60	1.39
0.66	0.80	0.90	0.84	0.68	0.86	0.92	0.88	0.75	0.99	0.76
1.12	1.46	1.78	1.68	1.41	1.64	2.07	1.94	1.82	2.49	2.01
1.10	1.38	1.51	1.20	1.02	1.32	1.54	1.58	1.44	2.11	1.83
2.14	1.76	2.08	2.00	1.86	2.18	2.32	2.21	2.08	2.45	2.14
1.85	2.04	2.07	1.94	1.84	2.12	2.23	2.09	1.91	2.36	1.94
2.03	2.59	2.96	2.46	1.80	2.01	2.02	1.69	1.34	2.17	2.18
1.45	1.77	2.13	1.93	1.58	2.32	2.53	2.40	1.67	2.38	2.01
2.26	2.35	2.67	2.44	2.17	2.89	2.73	2.49	1.48	2.46	2.62

Table 6.18 (Continued)

Sector	1978	1979	1980	1981	1982	1983	1984
48. Steel	1.20	1.03	1.00	1.86	1.93	2.00	1.71
49. Non-ferrous metals	0.77	0.79	0.79	1.39	1.25	1.20	1.10
50. Metal products	0.93	0.85	0.86	1.54	1.43	1.29	1.16
51. Agri.machinery	0.49	0.50	0.52	0.99	1.00	1.02	1.02
52. Industrial equipment	0.48	0.49	0.52	0.98	0.98	0.97	0.92
53. Power equipment	0.67	0.68	0.71	1.37	1.42	1.44	1.46
54. Hshd mech/elect. gds	0.83	0.76	0.71	1.24	1.14	1.13	1.12
55. Railway equipment	0.89	0.85	0.89	1.66	1.50	1.35	1.20
56. Motor vehicles	0.40	0.38	0.39	0.76	0.77	0.76	0.76
57. Ships	0.90	0.80	0.77	1.44	1.44	1.30	1.21
58. Oth.transp. equip.	0.27	0.27	0.28	0.52	0.52	0.53	0.51
59. Other enging. prods.	0.59	0.60	0.62	1.15	1.14	1.15	0.96
60. Electronic products	0.53	0.53	0.55	0.99	0.95	0.91	0.89
61. Hshd electronics	0.53	0.52	0.50	0.95	0.92	0.84	0.78

even exclude those imports that are imperfect substitutes to or differentiated from domestically produced goods, because of their non-comparability. As a consequence, the estimated results tend to depend more on domestically produced goods or exports than imported goods if the imports are composed mainly of the products which are unavailable domestically or non-comparable with domestic products.

The second problem with the estimates concerns the aggregation or classification of tradable goods. Tradable goods are grouped into 61 categories in this study. The price ratio is therefore estimated as the average of each tradable category. However, it is possible that, in a tradable category, the price ratio for some individual goods, especially importables, may be much higher than that for the group as a whole. As imports account for only a small proportion of the total value of the whole category, their impact on the price estimates for the whole group is unlikely to be significant. Again, the estimated price ratio tends to be dominated by the domestically produced goods or the exports.

Table 6.19 Mean and standard deviation of price ratios, 1978–95

	1978	1979	1980	1981	1982	1983	1984
Unweighted							
Mean	1.52	1.36	1.31	2.37	2.18	1.93	1.67
Standard deviation	1.16	0.90	0.83	1.40	1.26	1.04	0.79
Weighted							
Mean	1.51	1.34	1.32	2.42	2.25	1.96	1.72
Standard deviation	2.04	1.71	1.60	2.86	2.60	2.07	1.73

1985	1986	1987	1988	1989	1990	1991	1992	1993	1994	1995
1.38	1.72	1.81	1.75	1.60	2.02	1.94	1.60	0.95	1.56	1.75
1.07	1.13	1.54	1.62	1.46	1.51	1.31	1.05	0.70	1.05	1.04
1.10	1.30	1.37	1.32	1.19	1.52	1.62	1.58	1.18	1.72	1.47
1.08	1.36	1.46	1.33	1.17	1.45	1.61	1.51	1.33	1.82	1.60
0.85	1.12	1.21	1.14	0.98	1.19	1.30	1.19	1.03	1.38	1.19
1.41	1.89	2.02	1.73	1.42	1.85	2.11	2.04	1.87	2.61	2.28
1.13	1.28	1.36	1.29	1.19	1.55	1.82	1.80	1.66	2.40	2.22
1.37	1.39	1.48	1.47	1.39	1.76	1.95	1.89	1.73	2.38	2.17
0.71	0.88	0.94	0.86	0.77	0.93	0.98	0.90	0.84	1.12	0.99
1.15	1.34	1.42	1.26	1.13	1.37	1.45	1.35	1.22	1.69	1.57
0.50	0.71	0.77	0.69	0.62	0.74	0.78	0.72	0.65	0.89	0.82
0.99	1.38	1.49	1.37	1.25	1.55	1.79	1.76	1.66	2.06	1.63
0.88	1.26	1.36	1.14	0.97	1.20	1.48	1.45	1.31	1.67	1.50
0.77	1.03	1.16	1.01	0.89	1.15	1.47	1.51	1.41	1.87	1.75

As far as resource allocation is concerned, however, it is the relative price structure not the absolute magnitude of the price ratio that matters. Depreciation of nominal exchange rate can easily raise the border price of domestic goods; it is unlikely to change the relative price structure for tradable goods. The reallocation of domestic resources is, however, driven by changes in the relative price structure, or the opportunity costs of production, not the absolute level of prices. China's economic reforms and open-door policy have altered the relative prices of tradable goods in such a way as to reduce the pre-reform distortions. The resultant reduction of price distortions in the domestic commodity markets is expected to encourage a more efficient use of resources by tradable goods' producers and trading corporations. China's domestic firms, with their increasing decision-making autonomy, can now allocate their resources to minimize the opportunity costs and explore China's international comparative advantage. The gains from growing trade and more efficient allocation of resources, as a result of removing price

1985	1986	1987	1988	1989	1990	1991	1992	1993	1994	1995
1.55	1.74	1.83	1.64	1.47	1.85	1.97	1.88	1.61	2.09	1.84
0.62	0.65	0.64	0.60	0.57	0.75	0.77	0.71	0.62	0.77	0.65
1.56	1.76	1.82	1.62	1.46	1.84	1.99	1.89	1.62	2.11	1.87
1.50	1.68	1.67	1.47	1.31	1.63	1.73	1.68	1.50	2.01	1.84

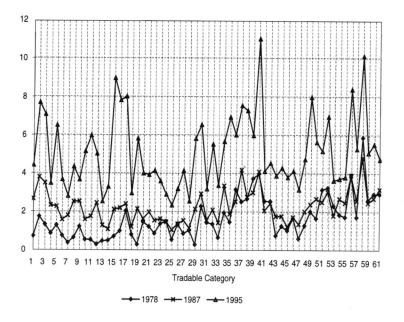

Figure 6A.1   Effective exchange rates for China's tradable goods, 1978, 1987 and 1995

distortions, have certainly contributed to the overall benefits that China has reaped during the reform period.

APPENDIX. EFFECTIVE EXCHANGE RATE

The information gathered above could be used to estimate the effective exchange rate (EER) for China's tradable goods. The EER for a tradable good can be defined as the ratio of its domestic price in the yuan to its world price in the foreign currency,

$$EER_j = \frac{P_j^d}{P_j^w} \qquad (6a.1)$$

For tradable goods, the EER shows the domestic value of one unit of foreign currency in exporting or importing tradable goods.

As shown in Table 6.19, the general level of the price ratios is heavily influenced by the changes in the nominal exchange rate. The repeated large scale depreciation of the Chinese currency during the period concerned may obscure the real relative price structure for tradable goods. The EER removes

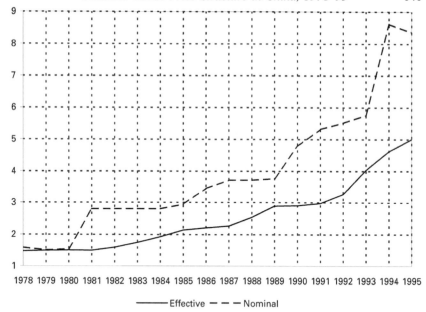

Figure 6A.2 China's nominal and effective exchange rates, 1978–95

the impact of the nominal exchange rate variations on the relative price structure. It may therefore provide a more accurate account for the changes in the ratio of domestic to international prices for China's tradable goods. Figure 6A.1 compares the EERs of all 61 tradable categories for 1978 and 1987, which can be taken as an alternative indicator of the changes of relative price distortions between the two periods.

In Figure 6A.1, the pre-reform distortions in the relative price pattern remains the same as in Figure 6.1, in which the prices of primary products are lower and that of intensively manufactured goods higher compared with their border price levels. Unlike Figure 6.1, however, the estimated EER for 1987 shows a more clear rise in the relative price of agricultural and natural resource goods and a more stable price for many industrial manufactures. In fact, the relative prices of some industrial manufactures were even lower in 1987 than in 1978. As a result, the domestic price structure had become more in line with the international pattern by the end of the period.

In recent years, there has been a growing interest in measuring the size of the Chinese economy in an internationally comparable way. It is well known that the nominal foreign exchange rate may not reveal the true international value of domestic output, especially for a developing country. A better alternative will be to calculate the international purchasing power of the Chinese currency through direct price comparison, similar to that used in this study. Normally, the direct price comparison should cover both tradable and non-tradable goods and services. International price comparisons for non-tradable goods are beyond the scope of this chapter; however, the estimation of the effective exchange rates for tradable goods in this study can be readily used to derive China's annual average EER, which could provide valuable information on the changes of the purchasing power of the Chinese currency over the reform period.

The average EER is defined as the output-weighted average of the EERs for all tradable goods. The estimated results for the period 1978–95 are plotted in Figure 6A.2. The nominal exchange rates are also included for comparison. Figure 6A.2 reveals a steady depreciation of the value of the Chinese currency. However, this real depreciation is not as rapid as the nominal exchange rate. In fact, the effective exchange rate was quite stable between 1978 and 1981 and rapid depreciation occurred only between 1981 and 1985 when the most rapid price changes took place. After 1985, the rise in the EER seems to have slowed down.

In 1987, China's EER was estimated to be 2.3 yuan per US dollar while the official exchange rate was 3.72 yuan per US dollar. This implies that the US dollar value of China's GDP, converted at the official exchange rates, actually under-estimates China's true output by at least 61 per cent. As the price differentials in non-tradable goods are believed to be much greater than in tradable goods, the real value of Chinese national output should be even higher. By 1995, the EER increased to 5 yuan per US dollar. It implies that the official exchange rate of 8.3 may under-estimate the value of the RMB by about 66 per cent. Although this estimate is based on tradable goods alone, it is still indicative about the true level of the real exchange rate.

Compared with the earlier studies, this estimate appears to be quite close to those based on a similar method. Taylor (1986), for instance, calculated the purchase power parity of the Chinese currency on the basis of tradable goods alone. He used the ratio of the sum of China's imports and exports at the domestic prices in yuan to the sum of the same at the world prices in US dollar. He reached an estimate of 2.23 yuan per US dollar for 1986, which is very close to that reported in this chapter.

7 Shadow Prices of Primary Factors of Production, 1978–95

In Chapter 6, we estimated the ratios of domestic to border prices for China's tradable goods. Distortions also exist in the markets for non-traded goods and primary factors. To calculate the domestic resource productivity for China's tradable goods, the shadow prices for non-tradable goods and the primary factors of production have to be estimated.

PRIMARY-FACTOR SHADOW PRICING

The conventional approach to shadow pricing for primary factors of production is mainly concerned with the social costs involved in reallocating an additional unit of the factor concerned to a new project. The major component of the social opportunity costs of employing one more worker or unit of capital is the output forgone at the margin in some sector of the economy from which the factor is withdrawn. In practice, consideration is also given to some other components of the social costs, such as the possible reduction of savings as a result of a rise in consumption by the worker, the increase in urban infrastructure needed if the worker migrates into the city, and the disutility of increased effort required by the worker in the new job (Lal 1974; Squire and van der Tak 1975).

The shadow-pricing method used in this study is not exactly the same as that used in the practical project evaluations. The DRP measure deals with a hypothetical situation of free trade in which goods prices are determined by the global market and factor prices are determined by their social opportunity costs valued at border prices. The primary concern is thus with the main component of social opportunity costs, the marginal social product forgone. As the marginal products of primary factors can only be estimated under the existing production conditions which are unlikely to be removed easily, the shadow price thus estimated is often referred to as the second-best shadow price.[1]

The distortions in domestic factor markets can arise from two sources: domestic factor market imperfections and domestic goods market distortions. The former may be reflected in the deviation of domestic factor returns from their marginal products while the latter may be reflected in the deviations of domestic goods prices from their border prices. Further deviations can be caused by government intervention, factor market monopoly or monoposony on the one hand and trade barriers and price controls in the goods market on the other. A proper shadow factor pricing should be able to correct both distortions.

In principle, the shadow price of a primary factor of production could be defined as its marginal product valued at the border price. In a multiple commodity economy with non-tradable goods, however, the shadow price of a factor may be defined as the weighted average of its marginal tradable products, valued at their border prices, and its marginal non-tradable products, valued at their shadow prices. To convert the existing factor returns into their shadow returns in the DRP estimation, we also need the shadow-price conversion factor. The shadow-price conversion factor for a given primary factor of production is the ratio of its shadow price to its prevailing domestic price. Given domestic factor prices at unity, the shadow-price conversion factor for primary factor s, P_s^S, can be expressed as

$$P_s^S = \sum_j \alpha_{sj} P_j^T m_{sj}^T + \sum_k \beta_{sk} P_k^N m_{sk}^N \tag{7.1}$$

where α_{sj} and β_{sk} are, respectively, the shares of factor s used in producing tradable good j and non-tradable good k in the total returns to factor s^2; m_{sj}^T and m_{sk}^N are, respectively, the ratio of the marginal tradable product j and the ratio of the marginal non-tradable product k of factor s to the prevailing returns to factor s; P_j^T is the ratio of domestic to border prices for tradable good j and P_k^N is the shadow price conversion factor for non-tradable good k. It can be seen in (7.1) that if there are no distortions, P_s^S will equal unity. Otherwise, it could be greater or smaller than unity which indicates possible distortions in the goods or factors markets.

Both labour and capital are normally considered for shadow pricing. This practice is based on an implicit assumption of homogeneous labour. However, in a labour-abundant developing country such as China, labour is not homogeneous. There are at least two different types of labour in China. The majority of the labour force consists of unskilled workers, mainly living in rural areas. Skilled workers constitute a small proportion of the total labour force. Until recently, there has been little labour mobility in China, which precluded the existence of a properly functioning labour market. Under such circumstances, the observed wage rates or labour income were unlikely to be related in any significant way to the social opportunity costs of labour. During the prolonged central-planning period, wage rates for the two different types of labour could be distorted in opposite directions. For instance, unskilled labour could be over-valued while skilled labour could be under-valued. Thus, it would be very misleading to apply a single shadow wage rate for the entire labour force. There is a strong case for applying different shadow prices for the two types of labour.

In the following, the shadow price conversion factors will be estimated for three primary factors: skilled labour, unskilled labour and capital. To estimate these shadow-price conversion factors, three sets of information are needed: the factor shares (α_{sj} and β_{sk}), the tradable and non-tradable good price ratios (P_j^T and P_k^N) and the marginal product ratios (m_{sj}^T and m_{sk}^N) . The tradable price ratios could be taken from estimates of China's relative price structure in Chapter 6. The other two will be estimated in this chapter.

INPUT–OUTPUT COEFFICIENTS: SKILLED AND UNSKILLED LABOUR

The factor shares can be derived readily from China's input–output tables.[3] To apply the separate shadow prices for different types of labour, however, requires a division of China's total labour force and the total labour income in each sector into two parts. In the Chinese input–output tables, there is no distinction between the income earned by skilled and unskilled labour. In the absence of any data on labour skills in the Chinese statistics, we have to find an alternative way to derive a proxy for unskilled and skilled labour and their separate incomes. In this section, we will adopt some simple assumptions to separate sectoral wages into unskilled and skilled wages.

The ratio of the unskilled wage to the sectoral wage bill, u_j, is derived using the formula

$$u_j = \frac{W_j^u}{W_j^t} = \frac{s_j^u}{s_j^u + \alpha(1 - s_j^u)} \tag{7.2}$$

where W_j^u and W_j^t denote the wage of unskilled labour and the total wage bill in industry j; s_j^u denotes the share of unskilled labour in the total labour force in industry j; and α is the ratio of the average wage rate of skilled labour to that of unskilled labour in industry j. Equation (7.2) is derived from

$$u_j = \frac{W_j^u}{W_j^t} = \frac{w_j^u L_j^u}{w_j^u L_j^u + w_j^s L_j^s}$$

where w_j^u and w_j^s denote, respectively, the average wage rates of unskilled and skilled labour; and L_j^u and L_j^s are the respective numbers of sectoral unskilled and skilled workers. Since $W_j^s = \alpha\, w_j^u$ and $L_j^u = L_j^t - L_j^s$, where L_j^t denotes the total number of sectoral workers, the above equation can be expressed as

$$\frac{w_j^u L_j^u}{w_j^u L_j^u + \alpha w_j^u(L_j^t - L_j^u)} = \frac{L_j^u}{L_j^u + \alpha(L_j^t - L_j^u)} \tag{7.3}$$

Dividing the numerator and the denominator by L_j^t and letting $s_j^u = L_j^u/L_j^t$ yields (7.2). Now we need to estimate only two parameters, s_j^u and α, to derive u_j.

As no information on the skills composition of the labour force is available, we take the educational structure of the labour force as a proxy for labour skills. 'Unskilled labour' is defined as those workers who have attended only the lower-middle school, primary school or received no schooling–that is, those who have no more than nine years of schooling. Workers with a higher level of education are considered as 'skilled'. Information on the educational structure of the labour force is drawn from *Data on the 1985 Industrial Census of the PRC* (State Council, Office for the Leading Group of National Industrial Census 1988), *1982 Population Census of China* (State Council, Population Census Office, and State Statistical Bureau, Statistical Department of Population 1985) and *Summary Survey of the Third National Industrial Census of the PRC* (*1995*) (State Statistical Bureau, Office for the Third National Industrial Census 1996).

As information on education is available only for 1982, 1985 and 1995, a further assumption has to be made to obtain the estimates for other years of the period. It is assumed that the sectoral division of skilled and unskilled labour was fairly stable, but that the proportion of unskilled workers in the total labour force steadily declined at the rates derived from the average annual changes between 1982 and 1985 and between 1985 and 1995. According to the 1982 population census and the 1985 industrial census, the average share of unskilled labour was 78 per cent in mid-1982 and 77 per cent at the end of 1985. The average annual rate of decline was thus 0.73 per cent. The results for 1987 are presented in column (1) of Table 7.1. A similar approach was also used to obtain the labour shares for the period 1988–95.

Table 7.1   Share of unskilled labour in sectoral labour force and wage bill, 1987

Sector	Labour share (s^u) (*1*)	Wage share (u) (*2*)
1. Paddy rice	0.941	0.899
2. Wheat	0.941	0.899
3. Other grains	0.941	0.899
4. Oil-bearing crops	0.941	0.899
5. Cotton	0.941	0.899
6. Other industrial crops	0.941	0.899
7. Vegetables	0.941	0.899
8. Fruits	0.875	0.794
9. Forest products	0.875	0.794
10. Wool and hides	0.937	0.892
11. Meat, eggs, etc.	0.937	0.892
12. Fish	0.938	0.894
13. Other agricultural products	0.875	0.794
14. Coal	0.808	0.700
15. Crude petroleum	0.629	0.484

Table 7.1   (Continued)

Sector	Labour share (s^U) (1)	Wage share (u) (2)
16. Ferrous ores	0.810	0.703
17. Non-ferrous ores	0.743	0.615
18. Non-metallic minerals	0.867	0.783
19. Timber	0.774	0.655
20. Sugar, tobacco and alcohol	0.787	0.671
21. Other processed food	0.800	0.689
22. Cotton textiles	0.725	0.593
23. Wool textiles	0.689	0.550
24. Hemp textiles	0.747	0.620
25. Silk products	0.802	0.691
26. Knitted goods	0.756	0.632
27. Other textiles	0.882	0.805
28. Clothing	0.805	0.695
29. Furniture	0.810	0.702
30. Paper	0.785	0.669
31. Cultural goods	0.778	0.660
32. Petroleum products	0.600	0.453
33. Coal products	0.771	0.650
34. Inorganic chemicals	0.748	0.621
35. Chemical fertilizer	0.763	0.641
36. Organic chemicals	0.693	0.555
37. Household chemicals	0.740	0.611
38. Other chemicals	0.702	0.566
39. Medicines	0.679	0.539
40. Chemical fibres	0.612	0.466
41. Rubber manufactures	0.743	0.616
42. Plastic articles	0.794	0.681
43. Cement	0.814	0.708
44. Glass	0.774	0.654
45. Ceramic products	0.830	0.730
46. Other building materials	0.865	0.780
47. Iron	0.770	0.649
48. Steel	0.718	0.584
49. Non-ferrous metals	0.676	0.536
50. Metal manufactures	0.798	0.686
51. Agricultural machines	0.745	0.618
52. Industrial equipment	0.708	0.573
53. Power station equipment	0.690	0.552
54. Household mechanical/electrical goods	0.725	0.594
55. Railway equipment	0.611	0.465
56. Motor vehicles	0.705	0.569
57. Ships	0.697	0.560
58. Other transport equipment	0.540	0.393
59. Other engineering products	0.714	0.580

Table 7.1 (Continued)

Sector	Labour share (s^{u}) (1)	Wage share (u) (2)
60. Electronic products	0.614	0.467
61. Household electronic appliances	0.606	0.460
62. Repairs	0.412	0.578
63. Electricity and water	0.667	0.526
64. Construction	0.775	0.656
65. Transport	0.754	0.629
66. Commerce	0.732	0.601
67. Public utilities	0.775	0.655
68. Finance	0.508	0.363
69. Other services	0.457	0.317

Sources: Tables 7A.1 and 7A.2.

Wage differentials are derived from the sample surveys of employees in the state-owned industrial enterprises and the sample surveys of the income and expenditure of urban households conducted annually by the State Bureau of Statistics. The results show that, in 1985, for instance, skilled labour accounted for 30 per cent of the total industrial labour force and, on average, earned about 83 per cent more than unskilled labour.

The shares of unskilled wages in the sectoral wage bill, u_j, can now be estimated using (7.2) for every year of the period 1978–95. The estimated results for 1987 are presented in column (2) of Table 7.1. Skilled labour was unevenly distributed across industries. The majority of unskilled labour was in agricultural sectors while most skilled labour was employed in more sophisticated manufacturing industries.

With the above information we can break up the aggregated labour income reported in the input–output tables into skilled and unskilled components. The shadow prices can now be estimated for the three primary factors of production: unskilled labour, skilled labour and capital.

FACTORS' MARGINAL-PRODUCT ESTIMATION

As the first step in the shadow price estimation, we need to find the marginal products for unskilled labour, skilled labour and capital for the reform period.

Estimation Approach

The marginal products of factors differ across industries. However, the available data prevent us from estimating the individual marginal products for all the factors concerned over the entire period 1978–95. As an alternative, a single marginal product ratio will be estimated for each factor for a particular year. This could be justified on the grounds of a long-run assumption that the marginal product of a factor tends to be equalized across industries. This assumption, though simple, is consistent with that used in our DRP estimation.

Marginal product will be estimated for unskilled labour, skilled labour and capital, respectively.[4] If the shadow prices of skilled and unskilled labour are to be derived from their marginal products forgone elsewhere in the economy, it is necessary to ascertain the sector or sectors from which the skilled and unskilled labour are most likely to come. The above estimates indicate that over 80 per cent of unskilled labour lived in the countryside, constituting about 95 per cent of the total rural labour force. It seems reasonable to assume that any additional requirements for unskilled labour in the industrial sector would have come from the agricultural sector. The agricultural labour force could thus be taken as a proxy for unskilled labour as a whole. The marginal product forgone in rural areas, as a result of moving labour into urban industrial sectors, can be an important indication of the shadow price of unskilled labour for the economy as a whole. In addition, during the process of resource reallocation, some industries that have no international comparative advantage will contract and release some labour to other sectors. Marginal products forgone in these sectors should also be taken into consideration in the shadow pricing for unskilled labour. The marginal product of unskilled labour should be estimated from the production functions of both agricultural and non-agricultural sectors. Similarly, it could be reasonably assumed that skilled labour comes mainly from non-agricultural sectors and thus only non-agricultural production functions are needed in the estimation of marginal product of skilled labour.

Like skilled labour, any additional unit of capital comes most likely from non-agricultural sectors as well. Skilled labour and physical capital could thus be estimated together. This is because skilled labour has some features more akin to capital than to unskilled labour: both are regarded as scarce resources in China and are believed to have been under-valued over the period concerned, and both skilled labour and physical capital are normally employed intensively in the same part of the economy. Their marginal products can therefore be derived from the same set of data.

Functional Form Specification

To estimate the marginal products of capital, skilled and unskilled labour, the production functions for the agricultural and the major non-agricultural sectors are now specified and estimated. The Cobb–Douglas production function is selected as the basic functional form used in the estimates; the variables included in each of the functions may vary depending on the data availability.

The specification of production functions begins with the agricultural sector. An agricultural production function normally contains the variables of common agricultural inputs such as labour, land, capital and chemical fertilizers. An agricultural production function with variables for sown areas, farm household-owned capital, and the quantities of chemical fertilizer used as well as labour was tried, but the estimated results were not acceptable statistically. This could have been due to the incompleteness and inconsistency of the data used. For instance, the aggregate value of agricultural output includes four major agricultural activities: farming, forestry, animal husbandry and fishing. Not all of the explanatory variables are relevant to these four activities–for instance, the sown area and the quantity of chemical fertilizer used are relevant to farming activities but not to fishing or animal husbandry. The data on capital are even more dubious: they include only private capital, some of which may be used by farm households in non-agricultural activities.[5]

The lack of information makes it difficult to achieve data consistency. Since the primary concern of this exercise is to derive the marginal product of labour, we need to include only two basic explanatory variables in the production function: labour and other non-labour inputs. In the Chinese statistics, the value of gross agricultural output is the sum of two components: net output value and material costs. The former is equivalent to value-added, the latter includes the costs of all items spent in the process of production, including intermediate inputs and fixed-capital depreciation. In agriculture, the material costs cover, among other things, seeds, fertilizers, machinery, electricity and the use of other agricultural facilities. It seems that the material costs provide a relatively good indication of the contribution of all non-labour inputs to agricultural output. They may also be taken as a proxy for capital. In China, farm households are both labour and capital owners. The intermediate inputs are, therefore, chosen as the non-labour variable in the production function.

The basic functional form used for the non-agricultural sectors is also of a Cobb–Douglas type. There are four non-agricultural sectors. The industrial production function includes four explanatory variables: skilled labour, unskilled labour, fixed capital and variable capital. The production functions for the other three non-agricultural sectors contain three explanatory variables: skilled labour, unskilled labour and capital, which is the sum of fixed and variable capital stock.

Data Issues

The data used in the empirical estimates are all cross-section data. For agriculture, they include the net value of agricultural output, the number of agricultural workers and the value of material costs for China's 29 provinces for each year between 1979 and 1995.[6] Agricultural labour is measured in terms of able-bodied persons. The data on agricultural net output, labour and material costs are obtained from the *Statistical Yearbooks of China* (State

Statistical Bureau 1984–96a).[7] Prior to 1984, the classification included some non-agricultural activities, such as small rural industries in the value of agricultural output. For the data to be comparable, adjustments have been made to deduct the non-agricultural components from the net output value, labour and non-labour inputs.

For the industrial sector, we use the cross-sectional data on the 40 industries that cover all mining and manufacturing industries. The definition of skilled and unskilled labour is the same as that discussed above. As educational statistics for the sectoral labour force are available only for 1980, 1985 and 1995, the decomposition of the labour force can be conducted only for these three years. This restricts the estimation of the marginal industrial products of capital and labour to these years. The factor's marginal products for other years have to be extrapolated from these three sets of the estimates.

The data on skilled and unskilled labour in the industrial sector are estimated from China's 1982 population census (State Council, Population Census Office, and State Statistical Bureau, Statistical Department of Population, 1985) and the 1985 and 1995 national industrial censuses (State Council, Office for the Leading Group of National Industrial Census 1988 and State Statistical Bureau, Office for the Third Industrial Census, 1997). The data on the net industrial output and capital stock are also drawn from the two industrial censuses. Net industrial output is the value of gross output net of material inputs. The capital data include the values of fixed capital assets and the values of variable or working capital. The data cover all the independent accounting units of the industrial enterprises at or above the township level.

One of the problems associated with the Chinese industrial output data is that the price structure was heavily distorted so that the observed profit might not necessarily reflect the true returns to the capital. In many industries, profits and losses resulted, to a great extent, from the existing centrally determined price structure. To correct this bias, the reported net output values were readjusted using the average profit–capital ratio. It was intended to reduce the possible impacts the distorted prices might have on the net outputs of various industries. The implicit assumption is that, in the long run, price distortions will diminish and all industries will enjoy approximately the same profit ratio.

Three other non-agricultural sectors are also included in the estimation of factor's marginal products. They are construction, transport and commerce. The data on net output, capital and labour for the construction sector were taken from the *Statistical Yearbook of China*, covering only the state-owned construction enterprises. The data were aggregated into 29 provinces and 15 central government's departments or large national construction companies.

The data on the transport and commercial sectors were mainly drawn from various provincial *Statistical Yearbooks*. Most provinces began publishing

Table 7.2 OLS estimation results for the agricultural production function,

	1979	1980	1981	1982	1983	1984	1985	1986
Labor $(L)^b$	0.14	0.12	0.13	0.15	0.15	0.14	0.24	0.22
	$(2.72)^a$	(2.35)	(2.34)	(2.82)	(2.82)	(2.83)	(4.31)	(4.14)
Material $(M)^b$	0.91	0.93	0.93	0.91	0.92	0.92	0.78	0.77
	(15.82)	(15.44)	(15.21)	(14.79)	(15.66)	(16.07)	(11.59)	(11.53)
Dummy^c	0.32	0.27	0.33	0.29	0.36	0.26	0.56	0.36
	(2.82)	(2.17)	(2.5)	(2.27)	(2.64)	(2.08)	(3.33)	(1.98)
Intercept	0.14	0.18	0.21	0.13	0.09	0.17	-0.06	0.07
	(1.58)	(0.92)	(1.01)	(0.63)	(0.46)	(0.96)	(0.30)	(0.37)
Mean of Y^{Ab}	4 132	4 427	5 202	5 900	6 052	7 679	8 592	9 380
Mean of L^b	989	1 006	1 029	1 066	1 076	1 093	1 047	1 051
Adjusted R^2	0.98	0.98	0.98	0.98	0.98	0.98	0.98	0.97
Log-likelihood	-68.78	-74.02	-78.07	-80.71	-82.68	-89.21	-100.07	-104.23
DW-statistic	1.91	1.48	1.83	1.73	1.64	1.52	1.61	1.87
RESET (2)	0.51	0.02	0.01	0.07	0.04	0.26	0.01	0.32

Notes: *a* Figures in parentheses are *t* ratios.
b The unit of Y^A and *M* are in million RMB yuan; the units of *L* are in 10 000 workers.
c Dummy variables for 1988–95 were statistically insignificant and were dropped from the equations.

annual statistics in the mid- or late 1980s. The quality and consistency of provincial statistical yearbooks vary substantially, and this creates serious difficulties for data-gathering and data-processing. The data on capital and labour owned and employed by the transport sector cover the state-owned railway system, and the road and water transport enterprises and are aggregated at the provincial level. As these statistics are not available for all provinces, the data coverage varies from sector to sector. The sample data used in the estimation cover 12 provinces' railway transport, 18 provinces' road transport and 7 provinces' water transport. The net outputs were calculated as the sum of the total wage bills, tax payments, interest payments, depreciation funds and profits. The data are presented as an Appendix in Table 7A.1 (p.164).

The commercial sector includes domestic wholesalers and retailers. The data on net output, labour and capital for the commercial sector were taken from the state-owned and cooperative commercial companies in 29 provinces. Net output was estimated as the sum of wage, tax, interest payments and profit earnings. Skilled and unskilled labour is defined in the same way as above. The levels of educational attainment of the labour force

1987	1988	1989	1990	1991	1992	1993	1994	1995
0.24	0.25	0.33	0.33	0.32	0.33	0.31	0.33	0.33
(4.29)	(4.01)	(6.93)	(6.02)	(5.82)	(6.38)	(5.82)	(4.82)	(4.58)
0.76	0.68	0.62	0.63	0.63	0.63	0.63	0.59	0.64
(11.19)	(9.68)	(11.33)	(9.91)	(9.73)	(10.3)	(10.47)	(8.06)	(8.12)
0.44								
(2.32)								
-0.03	0.24	-0.03	0.01	0.02	0.00	0.16	0.27	0.05
(0.13)	(1.08)	(0.16)	(0.04)	(0.13)	(0.00)	(0.80)	(1.01)	(0.17)
10 875	12 988	14 253	16 846	17 657	19 284	22 779	30 899	39 854
1 094	1 078	1 111	1 145	1 173	1 168	1 144	1 112	1 100
0.97	0.96	0.97	0.97	0.96	0.97	0.96	0.94	0.94
-109.33	-126.69	-123.26	-132.27	-134.78	-136.79	-144.21	-161.00	-168.66
1.76	1.98	1.87	2.01	2.04	2.11	2.08	2.20	2.00
0.19	0.78	0.39	0.00	0.21	0.07	0.85	0.41	0.01

employed in the construction, transport and commercial sectors were derived from *Data on China's One Per Cent Population Sample Survey 1987* (Provincial Statistical Bureaus and Population Sample Survey Offices 1989). The data for the commercial sector are given in Table 7A.2 (p.166). Because the provincial statistics are inconsistent and incomplete, the data for the construction, transport and commerce sectors are available only for 1985. Nevertheless, with one year's complete data on all five major sectors of the economy, we can estimate the contribution of each sector to the overall marginal products of primary factors. Assuming that these contributions are fairly stable over time, we can use them in estimating a factor's marginal products for other years.

Regression Results

The equation to be estimated for the agricultural production function is in logarithmic form

$$\log Y_i^A = a_0 + a_1 \log L_i + a_2 \log M_i + e_i \tag{7.4}$$

where Y_i^A denotes agricultural net output value for province i, L_i is the labour force and M_i is material cost, a_0, a_1 and a_2 are parameters to be estimated, and e_i is an error term. Net output also depends on some omitted region-specific variables, such as weather, soil quality, irrigation system, the composition of various agricultural activities and so on. In this regard, Tibet may be an extreme case. A regional dummy variable for Tibet is therefore included to obtain consistent estimates.[8]

The Ordinary Least Squares (OLS) estimation of (7.4) for each year from 1979 to 1995 is reported in Table 7.2. The elasticity of agricultural net output with respect to labour increased from 0.14 in 1979 to 0.24 in 1985 and 1987 and then to 0.31–0.33 between 1989 and 1995. As we will show later, the marginal product of labour during this period demonstrated a similar trend.

The estimation equation for the industrial production function is also in logarithmic form, that is,

$$\log Y_i^I = b_0 + b_1 \log L_i^S + b_2 \log K_i^F + b_3 \log K_i^V + b_4 \log L_i^U + e_i \qquad (7.5)$$

where Y_i^I denotes the net output value of sub-sector i, L_i^S and L_i^U are skilled and unskilled labour, respectively, K_i^F and K_i^V are fixed and variable capital, respectively, the b_s are the coefficients and e_i is an error term. The OLS

Table 7.3   OLS estimation results for the industrial production function, 1980, 1985 and 1995

	1980	1985	1995
Skilled labour (L_i^s)	0.20	0.17	0.21
	(3.74)	(3.17)	(1.30)
Fixed capital (K_i^E)	0.48	0.48	0.31
	(27.94)	(26.53)	(3.54)
Variable capital (K_i^V)	0.22	0.25	0.43
	(5.91)	(7.93)	(4.07)
Unskilled labour (L_i^U)	0.10	0.08	0.13
	(3.34)	(2.62)	(1.18)
Intercept	2.57	2.33	-0.38
	(6.63)	(5.81)	(1.14)
Mean of Y_i^I (10 000 yuan)	399 566	684 158	5 193 494
Mean of L_i^S (1000 person)	250 276	347 693	942 574
Mean of L_i^U (1000 person)	1 006 807	1 303 432	1 419 943
Mean of K_i^F (10 000 yuan)	710 843	1 181 191	10 832 168
Mean of K_i^V (10 000 yuan)	448 373	817 709	9 972 686
No. of observations	40	40	34
Adjusted R^2	0.98	0.98	0.95
Log-likelihood	-433.92	-456.27	-199.19
DW-statistic	1.72	2.07	1.99
RESET(2)	4.88	0.09	5.67

estimation results of (7.5) for 1980, 1985 and 1995 are reported in Table 7.3. The production functions for other non-agricultural sectors are also of Cobb–Douglas and expressed in the logarithmic form as

$$\log Y_i = b_0 + b_1 \log L_i^S + b_2 \log K_i + b_3 \log L_i^U + e_i \tag{7.6}$$

The OLS estimation results of (7.6) for the construction, transport and commercial sectors are reported in Table 7.4.

The marginal products of primary factors for the economy as a whole are defined as the weighted averages of marginal products for individual sectors. According to the assumptions made above, the marginal product of unskilled labour for the economy as a whole is defined as the weighted average of the marginal products of agricultural labour and the marginal product of unskilled labour from the four non-agricultural sectors. The marginal products of skilled labour and capital are the weighted averages of marginal products of the factors from the four non-agriculture sectors. The weights for labour are the shares of the sectoral labour forces in China's total labour force while the weights for capital are the shares of sectoral capital stock in total non-agricultural capital stock. The weighted average can be calculated only for 1985 because of the lack of data on some non-agricultural sectors for other years. To obtain the estimates for other years, we assume that the difference between the weighted average marginal product and the individual

Table 7.4   OLS estimation results for the production functions of other non-agricultural sectors, 1985

	Construction	Transport	Commerce
Capital (K_i)	0.38	0.78	0.56
	(6.17)	(22.78)	(6.14)
Skilled labour (L_i^S)	0.38	0.13	0.22
	(4.53)	(2.06)	(2.69)
Unskilled labour (L_i^U)	0.22	0.11	0.16
	(2.42)	(1.78)	(2.91)
Intercept	-0.65	-1.19	-0.61
	(-2.95)	(-6.37)	(-1.66)
Mean of Y	31 471	24 614	119 539
Mean of K_i	85 443	103 509	1 063 625
Mean of L_i^S	41,403	11 911	86 959
Mean of L_i^U	89 731	30 984	268,415
No. of observations	44	37	29
Adjusted R^2	0.98	0.99	0.98
Log-likelihood	-484.76	-313.49	-311.63
DW-statistic	2.26	1.90	2.32
RESET(2)	0.70	2.44	0.56

Table 7.5   Sectoral and the aggregate marginal products of unskilled labour, skilled labour and capital, 1985

	MPL^U	LW	MPL^S	LW	MPK	YW
Agriculture	195	0.69	n.a.	n.a.	n.a.	n.a.
Industry	436	0.18	3,335	0.60	0.25	0.75
Construction	765	0.05	2,923	0.15	0.14	0.13
Transport	840	0.03	2,620	0.09	0.19	0.04
Commerce	729	0.05	3,041	0.16	0.06	0.08
Weighted average	311	1.00	3,162	1.00	0.22	1.00

Notes: MPL^U, MPL^S and MPK: the marginal products of unskilled, skilled labour and capital in RMB yuan, respectively; LW: labour weights (share of sectoral labour in total labour force); YW: output weights (share of sectoral gross output in total non-agricultural gross output).
Sources: MPL^U: calculated from Tables 7.3–7.5; MPL^S and MPK: calculated from Tables 7.4–7.5; LW and YW: State Statistical Bureau (1989).

sectoral marginal products remained constant during the whole period. The sectoral and the weighted average marginal products of primary factors in 1985 are shown in Table 7.5.

Marginal Product Conversion Factors for Primary Factors

Using the above information, the marginal products of the factors concerned can be estimated. Together with the prevailing returns to the factors, we can also determine the ratio of marginal products to prevailing factor returns which are needed to convert the actual factor returns to their marginal products.

To derive the marginal-product ratios for unskilled labour, the average wage rate for unskilled labour is required. The average wage rate should be a weighted average of the wage rates in various sectors. It is so defined as to be compatible with the estimated marginal products. Since the majority of unskilled labour comes from agriculture, we use the average income per able-bodied person engaged in agricultural production as the wage rate for unskilled labour. The data are drawn from the Rural Household Survey conducted by the State Statistical Bureau and published annually in the *Statistical Yearbook of China* since 1981. The results of the estimated marginal product, the average wage rate and the marginal product conversion factors for unskilled labour over the period 1978–95 are reported in Table 7.6.

As mentioned above, an additional unit of skilled labour or capital is likely to be drawn from one of four non-agricultural sectors: industry, construction, transport or commerce. The social opportunity cost of using an additional unit of skilled labour or capital should be equal to the weighted average of

Table 7.6   Ratio of marginal product to average income for unskilled labour, 1978–95

Year	A-MPL	AWR^U	MPC^U
1978	n.a.	418.05	0.165
1979	58.18	351.62	0.165
1980	52.39	383.10	0.137
1981	63.36	414.58	0.153
1982	82.98	467.08	0.178
1983	81.59	469.46	0.174
1984	97.28	520.24	0.187
1985	194.89	687.15	0.284
1986	200.16	747.17	0.268
1987	242.40	803.73	0.302
1988	303.67	899.03	0.338
1989	429.03	994.33	0.431
1990	482.86	1 128.18	0.428
1991	485.07	1 179.25	0.411
1992	547.34	1 293.72	0.423
1993	622.77	1 605.90	0.388
1994	925.91	1 918.08	0.483
1995	1,205.40	2 454.26	0.491

Notes: A-MPL: Marginal product of agricultural labour in current RMB yuan;
   AWR^U: Average wage rate of unskilled labour, five sector-weighted average;
   MPC^U: Shadow-wage conversion factor for unskilled labour.
Sources: A-MPL: Calculated from Table 7.3. AWR^U: State Statistical Bureau,
   Statistical Yearbook of China (1981–97); State Statistical Bureau, Statistical
   Department of Rural Areas, *Rural Statistical Yearbook of China* (1986–96).

the marginal products of skilled labour or capital from these non-agricultural sectors. Since the data on construction, transport and commerce are available only for 1985, we can only derive the weighted average of marginal products for skilled labour and capital for that single year. For the industrial sector, the estimates of marginal products can be made for three separate years–1980, 1985 and 1995. An average annual growth rate can then be calculated and used to derive the estimates for other years over the period. It is also assumed that the ratio of industrial marginal products to the weighted average of all four non-agricultural sectors' marginal products remains constant over the whole period. So the weighted average marginal products for skilled labour and capital can be derived for every year. This procedure may be justified by the fact that the industrial sector is by far the dominant one among all non-agricultural sectors, accounting for 75 per cent of the gross output and 60 per cent of the labour force. In view of the large shares of the industrial sector, it is unlikely that the estimated results will be greatly biased.

As illustrated in Table 7.5, the marginal product of skilled labour, defined as a weighted average of the four non-agricultural sectors' marginal products, was RMB 3162 yuan in 1985. It is also known from the above estimates that the marginal product of skilled labour in the industrial sector rose at an average annual rate of 0.77 per cent, from RMB 3211 yuan in 1980 to RMB 3335 yuan in 1985. The corresponding annual estimates can therefore be obtained by assuming that the marginal product of skilled labour increased at the similar rate for the entire period 1978–85. The similar approach can be used to derive the marginal product for the period 1986–95. The estimated marginal prices will then be compared with the average wage rates to arrive at the marginal product conversion factor for skilled labour, which are reported in Table 7.7.

Table 7.7   Ratio of marginal product to average income for skilled labour, 1978–95

Year	$I\text{-}MPL^S$	MPL^S	AWR^S	MPC^S
1978	3 162	2 998	1 069	2.80
1979	3 186	3 021	1 306	2.31
1980	3 211	3 044	1 196	2.55
1981	3 235	3 067	1 465	2.09
1982	3 260	3 091	1 492	2.07
1983	3 285	3 114	1 514	2.06
1984	3 310	3 138	1 883	1.67
1985	3 335	3 162	1 792	1.76
1986	3 361	3 187	2 023	1.58
1987	3 387	3 211	2 248	1.43
1988	3 905	3 702	2 718	1.36
1989	4 503	4 269	3 064	1.39
1990	5 191	4 922	3 382	1.46
1991	5 986	5 674	3 722	1.52
1992	6 901	6 543	4 248	1.54
1993	7 957	7 543	5 327	1.42
1994	9 174	8 697	6 838	1.27
1995	10 578	10 028	8 309	1.21

Notes: $I\text{-}MPL^S$: marginal product of industrial skilled labour in *RMB* yuan; MPL^S: marginal product of skilled labour, four non-agricultural sector-weighted average; AWR^S: average annual wage rate for skilled labour, four non-agricultural sector-weighted average; MPC^S: ratio of marginal product to average wage rate for skilled labour.
Sources: $I\text{-}MPL^S$: the figures for 1980, 1985 and 1995 are calculated from Table 7.4; MPL^S: the figure for 1985 is derived from Table 7.6; AWR^S: estimated from State Statistical Bureau, *Statistical Yearbook of China* (various issues 1981–96); State Statistical Bureau, Statistical Department of Society (1989); Office for the Leading Group of National Industrial Census (State Council) (1988, vol.3); Office for the Third National Industrial Census (SSB) (1996).

The shadow-price conversion factor for capital is derived similarly to that for skilled labour. The marginal product of capital, defined as a weighted average of the marginal products of capital used in four non-agricultural sectors, was RMB 0.22 yuan in 1985 (Table 7.5). It implies that one yuan of additional capital investment should increase total output by 0.22 yuan at the 1985 price. The marginal product of capital in the industrial sector was RMB 0.24 yuan in 1980 and 0.25 yuan in 1985, implying an average annual growth rate of 0.90 per cent between 1980 and 1985. The marginal product of industrial capital in 1995 was RMB 0.17 yuan, which implies an annual growth rate of -3 per cent. The two growth rates are used to obtain the estimates of MPK for other years in the period concerned (Table 7.8).

The marginal product of capital is then compared with the prevailing (market) return to capital to obtain the ratio of marginal product to actual

Table 7.8   Ratio of marginal product to average return for capital, 1978–95

Year	I-MPK (1)	MPK (2)	ARK (3)	MPC^K (4)
1978	0.236	0.206	0.205	1.01
1979	0.238	0.207	0.201	1.03
1980	0.240	0.209	0.197	1.06
1981	0.242	0.211	0.193	1.09
1982	0.245	0.213	0.189	1.13
1983	0.247	0.215	0.185	1.16
1984	0.249	0.217	0.181	1.20
1985	0.251	0.219	0.178	1.23
1986	0.242	0.211	0.174	1.21
1987	0.233	0.203	0.171	1.19
1988	0.224	0.196	0.163	1.20
1989	0.216	0.189	0.156	1.21
1990	0.208	0.182	0.149	1.22
1991	0.201	0.175	0.143	1.23
1992	0.193	0.169	0.136	1.24
1993	0.186	0.163	0.130	1.25
1994	0.180	0.157	0.125	1.26
1995	0.173	0.151	0.119	1.27

Notes: *I-MPK*: Marginal product of capital in the industrial sector; *MPK*: Marginal product of capital, four non-agricultural sector-weighted average; *ARK*: Average return to capital; *MPC^K*: Marginal price conversion factor for capital.
Sources: *I-MPK*: Calculated from Table 7.4; *MPK*: Calculated from Table 7.6 and 7.7; *ARK*: Estimated from office for the Leading Group of National Industrial Census (State Council) (1988, vol.3); Office for the Third National Industrial Census (SSB) (1996); Statistical Department of Industry and Communications (SSB), (1988–95) and State Statistical Bureau, (1981–97).

return to capital. The market return to capital used here is the ratio of profits and taxes to total capital stock, which includes the value of fixed capital assets (net of depreciation) and the value of variable capital.

To derive the price of capital from its marginal product, a social discount rate is required. This is the rate at which future consumption ought to be discounted to make it equivalent in value to present consumption. To take into account savings and investment, each year's consumption is revalued in terms of savings or investment. The single combined stream is then discounted at an appropriate rate– for example, the accounting rate of interest for investment. The accounting rate of interest can be regarded as a budgetary device which balances the supply of, and the demand for, public investible resources (UNIDO 1978). Theoretically, it can be obtained by ranking all investment projects by their net present values (NPVs) and using the internal rate of return (IRR) of the marginal project as the accounting rate of interest. Since this approach involves some practical difficulties, it has been suggested that the government be asked for a national decision on the accounting rate of interest. The State Planning Commission (SPC) of China issued a project appraisal guideline in 1987, in which the accounting rate of interest was set at 10 per cent, close to what Little and Mirrlees recommend for developing countries (Little and Mirrlees 1974: 296–7). In 1993, the SPC renewed its project appraisal guideline and raised the social discount rate to 12 per cent. However, the capital market in China is still in its infancy and interest rates remain under government control. During the period investigated, the market interest rates for bank loans had been largely fixed at low levels which did not deviate very much from the social discount rate set by the SPC. To simplify the calculation, we therefore use only marginal-product estimates, instead of the price (present value) of capital, to derive the ratio of marginal to average return to capital. The estimated results are shown in column (4) of Table 7.8.

As shown in the above tables, the wages of unskilled labour were upwardly biased while those of skilled labour were downwardly biased over the entire period under investigation. The distortions in the labour market were serious at first: the actual income for an unskilled labourer was six times the average marginal product, while the actual income for a skilled worker was only one-third of the average marginal product. These distortions have been gradually reduced. For skilled labour, the actual return was 20 per cent higher than the marginal product by 1995; for unskilled labour, however, the actual income was still more than double the marginal product in 1995 despite a dramatic decline from the early 1980s. This is probably due to the existence of surplus labour in both rural and urban areas. The marginal product of unskilled labour is expected to remain below its average income for many years to come, simply because of this large surplus-labour population.

The situation in the capital market differed markedly. At the beginning of the reforms, the actual return to capital was found to be quite close to its marginal product. A possible explanation for this may lie in the fact that the marginal product of capital was very low in the pre-reform era while the return to capital was relatively high. The high return to capital, to a large extent, included monopoly profits, resulting mainly from price distortions. The marginal product of capital increased in the 1980s and declined in the 1990s, while the actual return to capital declined steadily. The decline in the marginal product of capital in the 1990s might indicate some over-investment in certain sectors of the economy. The rapid decline in the actual returns to capital was the result of the removal of state monopoly in the economy and the intensified competition among domestic producers.[9] These two trends have led to a steady divergence between the marginal product of capital and actual return to capital. As shown in Table 7.8, by 1995, the marginal product of capital was estimated to be 27 per cent higher than its actual return. The divergent performance between China's labour and capital markets also reflects the fact that economic reforms have moved faster in the labour than in the capital market. There is an urgent need to reform China's capital market, including the banking and financial system and the fixed capital investment system.

SHADOW PRICES FOR NON-TRADABLE GOODS AND PRIMARY FACTORS

The estimated marginal products of capital and labour are all measured in domestic prices that were also distorted during this period. To correct these distortions, the estimated marginal products should be converted into their border-price equivalents. The estimated marginal tradable products can be readily converted to border prices using the ratios of border to domestic goods prices that were estimated in Chapter 6. To convert the marginal non-tradable products, however, the shadow prices of non-tradable goods have to be estimated. In an input–output framework, the price of a non-tradable good can be decomposed into three components:

$$P_j^N = \sum_i a_{ij}^{TN} P_i^T + \sum_k a_{kj}^{NN} P_k^N + \sum_S a_{sj}^{FN} P_s^F \qquad (7.7)$$

where a_{ij}^{TN} and a_{kj}^{NN} are the respective shares of tradable good i and non-tradable good k used in the production of non-tradable good j; a_{sj}^{FN} is the share of factor s in the production of non-tradable good j and P_s^F is the price of factor s. Given the marginal products of factors and the border prices of tradable goods, the shadow prices of non-tradable goods can be derived.

We know from (7.1) that shadow factor prices can be decomposed into the value of marginal tradables and the value of marginal non-tradable products. This implies that the shadow prices of a non-tradable goods can be expressed in terms of the border prices of tradable goods and the factor's marginal products, that is,

$$P_j^N = \sum_i (a_{ij}^{TN} + a_{ij}'^{TN}) P_i^T + \sum_k (a_{kj}^{NN} + a_{kj}'^{NN}) P_k^N \qquad (7.8)$$

Table 7.9   Shadow-price conversion factors for non-tradable goods, 1978–95

	1978	1979	1980	1981	1982	1983	1984	1985
62. Repair	1.59	1.39	1.39	2.48	2.32	2.06	1.78	1.56
63. Electricity	1.98	1.81	1.77	3.47	3.30	2.86	2.59	2.16
64. Construction	1.67	1.45	1.45	2.61	2.38	2.10	1.78	1.60
65. Transport	1.81	1.62	1.64	3.02	2.83	2.48	2.18	1.88
66. Commerce	1.95	1.72	1.69	3.06	2.84	2.47	2.09	1.80
67. Public utilities	1.80	1.59	1.60	2.90	2.74	2.41	2.10	1.83
68. Finance	1.82	1.72	1.69	3.22	3.03	2.68	2.44	2.06
69. Other services	2.64	2.10	2.15	3.55	3.25	2.81	2.24	1.97

Sources: Calculated using (7.8).

where $a_{ij}^{\prime TN}$ and $a_{kj}^{\prime NN}$ are the shares of tradable good i and non-tradable good k used in measuring factor contributions to the production of non-tradable good j, respectively. They can be further expressed as

$$a_{ij}^{\prime TN} = \sum_s m_{si}^T a_{sj}^{FN}$$

and

$$a_{kj}^{\prime NN} = \sum_s m_{sk}^N a_{sj}^{FN}$$

where m_{si}^T and m_{sk}^N are the respective marginal tradable product i and the marginal non-tradable product k of factor s as defined earlier. This suggests that, given the border prices of tradable goods and the marginal products of factors, the shadow prices of non-tradables could be calculated. Shadow prices are estimated for eight categories of non-tradable goods and services:

Table 7.10   Shadow-price conversion factors for primary-factor incomes,

	1978	1979	1980	1981	1982	1983	1984	1985
Depreciation	1.86	1.87	1.85	3.71	3.51	3.11	2.92	2.39
Unskilled wage	0.36	0.32	0.25	0.53	0.56	0.48	0.45	0.54
Skilled wage	6.22	4.61	4.86	7.46	6.72	5.77	4.10	3.47
Tax	1.52	1.38	1.37	2.51	2.31	2.02	1.86	1.70
Profit	1.85	1.84	1.77	3.54	3.37	3.03	2.81	2.29
Other	1.78	1.66	1.68	3.01	2.78	2.35	2.01	1.75

Sources: Author's own calculation using (7.1).

Table 7.9 (Continued)

1986	1987	1988	1989	1990	1991	1992	1993	1994	1995
1.77	1.82	1.80	1.72	2.44	2.47	2.23	1.82	2.31	2.03
2.33	2.34	1.95	1.60	1.86	1.93	1.76	1.47	1.91	1.67
1.76	1.88	1.73	1.56	1.98	2.07	1.92	1.58	2.08	1.85
2.07	2.08	1.84	1.62	2.04	2.15	1.98	1.67	2.12	1.82
1.98	2.04	1.78	1.59	2.00	2.23	2.09	1.79	2.32	2.06
2.03	2.11	1.91	1.71	2.19	2.25	2.07	1.76	2.25	1.97
2.29	2.29	2.06	1.76	2.30	2.36	2.18	1.85	2.36	2.05
2.20	2.29	1.99	1.77	2.29	2.40	2.21	1.81	2.25	1.92

repairs, electricity, construction, transport, commerce, public utilities, finance and other services.[10] The results are reported in Table 7.9.

Given the border prices of tradable goods and the shadow prices of non-tradable goods, the shadow prices of factors can be determined. The estimated marginal products of capital, unskilled and skilled labour can now be applied to the four of the six value-added items in China's input–output table: depreciation, profits, unskilled labour income and skilled labour income. The values of taxes and other costs[11] are assumed to be undistorted because they represent returns to the society. The shadow-price conversion factors for all the value-added items are presented in Table 7.10.

As mentioned above, shadow pricing was intended to correct two distortions in the factor markets: the deviation of factor returns from their marginal products and the deviation of domestic good prices from their (free trade) border prices. It can be seen in Table 7.10 that the second correction could be demonstrated most clearly in the shadow-price conversion factor for 'Tax' or 'Other' because these two items had no marginal price distortions. The first correction is reflected in the difference between the shadow-price conversion

1978–95

1986	1987	1988	1989	1990	1991	1992	1993	1994	1995
2.67	2.70	2.46	2.11	2.67	2.65	2.39	2.07	2.67	2.39
0.57	0.65	0.64	0.70	0.89	0.86	0.81	0.66	1.02	0.93
3.94	4.08	3.39	2.88	3.70	3.74	3.32	2.59	2.86	2.32
1.88	1.93	1.64	1.51	1.83	1.96	1.84	1.61	2.13	1.89
2.57	2.51	2.32	1.90	2.58	2.59	2.36	2.08	2.73	2.46
1.87	1.96	1.74	1.56	1.97	2.09	1.98	1.68	2.14	1.89

factors for the items other than 'Tax' and 'Other' and the shadow-price conversion factors for 'Tax' and 'Other'. The trends of changes in the shadow-price conversion factors are not the same as the marginal-product conversion factors because of the changes in the relative price structure. For capital, it increased until 1987 and then declined. For unskilled labour, it almost continuously increased over time while, for skilled labour, it declined over time. This indicates a decline in the distortions in China's labour markets. The distortions in the capital market have changed very little in recent years: fundamental reforms are needed in this area.

CONCLUSION

Certain trends have emerged from these estimations. The average wage rates for unskilled and skilled labour were markedly different from their estimated shadow rates: the average wage rates for unskilled labour were higher while those of skilled labour were lower than their shadow rates. During the two decades of economic reforms, average wage rates can thus be seen to have moved closer to their shadow wage rates. This indicates a reduction of distortions in the labour market.

A similar trend has not been seen in the capital market. On the contrary, the deviation between the estimated shadow prices and the market return for capital was still relatively high towards the end of this period and showed no sign of convergence. This is probably because the capital market remained largely under the control of the government.

The shadow-price conversion factor estimates for non-tradable goods and services suggest that the output from these non-traded sectors was under-priced which, in turn, indicates under-development in these sectors. The divergences between the estimated shadow and market prices for most goods and services in this group have not declined in the 1990s.

APPENDIX

Table 7A.1   China's provincial net output, capital, skilled and unskilled labour, transport sector, 1985

Province	Net output	Capital	Skilled labour	Unskilled labour
Railway transport				
Beijing	51 387	207 310	18 562	29 438
Shanxi	73 359	274 197	25 816	54 309
Inner Mongolia	35 690	176 188	18 308	34 616
Liaoning	150 590	688 971	54 238	105 285

Table 7A.1 (Continued)

Province	Net output	Capital	Skilled labour	Unskilled labour
Jilin	50 643	216 164	24 077	40 821
Heilongjiang	87 727	351 932	47 380	80 226
Zhejiang	18 353	76 545	3 545	14 178
Henan	3 465	20 214	1 391	3 304
Hunan	55 589	281 104	25 288	54 712
Guangdong	24 191	86 623	10 064	19 535
Guizhou	25 870	155 206	8 140	27 797
Yunnan	35 154	201 058	10 457	32 860
Road transport				
Hebei	17 648	60 094	14 836	43 992
Shanxi	6 049	24 254	3 992	12 176
Heilongjiang	3 693	13 758	4 306	9 981
Anhui	7 976	34 732	6 589	25 869
Jiangxi	4 373	16 014	4 227	11 370
Shandong	12 842	52 493	9 372	27 037
Henan	12 841	48 335	11 998	30 144
Hubei	15 644	55 024	14 049	38 866
Hunan	7 539	28 143	6 957	22 019
Guangdong	10 126	33 287	6 996	21 628
Guangxi	5 578	20 533	5 317	15 916
Sichuan	34 360	114 238	21 105	105 802
Guizhou	4 662	17 725	2 863	17 501
Yunnan	20 109	76 126	8 367	53 659
Gansu	4 599	18 073	5 795	9 973
Qinghai	2 415	9 894	991	4 411
Ningxia	1 186	4 371	1 031	3 045
Xinjiang	25 009	92 030	13 539	49 344
Water transport				
Anhui	1 141	4 737	656	2 576
Jiangxi	1 124	3 647	918	2 469
Shandong	4 646	16 958	2 646	7 635
Hunan	2 632	11 450	1 329	4 208
Guangdong	81 124	304 830	35 966	100 063
Guangxi	11 015	32 105	9 472	29 283
Yunnan	373	1 465	120	653

Notes: Net output and capital are in 10 000 RMB yuan and labour force in workers.

Sources: State Statistical Bureau, (1986); Almanac of China's Transport Editorial Board, (1987); Provincial Statistical Bureaus and Population Sample Survey Offices, (1989); Economic Information Centre for the Northeast Economic Zone, (1988); Beijing Statistical Bureau (1987); Hebei Statistical Bureau, (1988); Shanxi Statistical Bureau, (1987); Inner Mongolia Statistical Bureau, (1989); Liaoning

Table 7A.1 (Continued)

Statistical Bureau, (1987); Economic Information Centre for the Northeast Economic Zone, (1988); Zhejiang Provincial Committee (CCP), Policy Research Office, and Provincial Government, Research Centre for Technological, Social and Economic Development, (1987); Almanac of Anhui Economy Editorial Board, (1987); Jiangxi Statistical Bureau, (1989); Shangdong Statistical Bureau, (1990); Henan Statistical Bureau, (1990); Hubei Statistical Bureau, (1988); Human Statistical Bureau, (1989); Guangdong Statistical Bureau, (1989); Guangxi Statistical Bureau, (1988); Sichuan Statistical Bureau, (1989); Guizhou Regional Annals Compilatory Committee, (1987); Yunnan Statistical Bureau, (1991); Gansu Statistical Bureau, (1989); Qinghai Statistical Bureau, (1987); Ningxia Statistical Bureau, (1988); Xinjiang Statistical Bureau, (1990).

Table 7A.2   China's provincial net output, capital, skilled and unskilled labour, commercial sector, 1985

Province	Net output[b]	Capital[b]	Skilled labour[c]	Unskilled labour[c]
Beijing	68 559	261 582	106 601	179 962
Tianjing	92 359	1 075 381	55 396	141 955
Hebei[a]	2 000	17 416	971	3 475
Shanxi	124 696	1 308 932	76 592	233 623
Inner Mongolia	120 947	1 098 516	1 02 770	219 596
Liaoning	178 715	1 551 458	129 017	555 790
Jilin	118 941	1 095 529	145 432	252 033
Heilongjiang	144 108	1 526 418	152 397	369 867
Shanghai	139 668	1 003 513	101 263	202 740
Jiangsu	218 393	2 519 122	151 128	491 969
Zhejiang	103 120	1 212 569	61 108	288 478
Anhui	65 180	299 889	53 123	205 888
Fujian	66 513	588 570	47 686	206 235
Jiangxi	93 181	1 197 022	65 394	240 188
Shandong	314 950	3 104 105	185 656	532 273
Henan	257 031	2 433 716	204 879	519 586
Hubei	288 060	2 609 380	177 248	506 051
Hunan	120 492	1 073 800	102 773	341 172
Guangdong	284 505	2 405 176	216 694	682 453
Guangxi	72 798	668 358	59 069	215 416
Sichuan	224 117	2 050 996	112 474	634 368
Guizhou	29 472	210 407	24 516	134 987
Yunnan	98 944	915 936	36 587	196 751
Tibet	5 317	47 006	1 981	10 654
Shaanxi	67 325	744 716	62 717	122 181
Gansu	48 687	921 507	41 399	106 453
Qinghai	15 594	146 335	8 222	25 254
Ningxia	10 105	90 521	6 424	25 037
Xinjiang	92 839	864 490	32 281	139 611

Table 7A.2 (Continued)

Notes: a. The data on Hebei province refer only to major state retail commercial companies.
b. Net output and capital are in 10 000 RMB yuan.
c. Labour force is in persons.

Sources: Tianjing Statistical Bureau, (1987); Shanghai Statistical Bureau, (1987); Jiangsu Statistical Bureau, (1989); Fujian Statistical Bureau, (1988); Tibet Statistical Bureau, (1990); Shaanxi Statistical Bureau, (1987). See Table 7A.1 for the sources of other provincial statistics.

8 China's International Comparative Advantage, 1978–95: DRP Results

The estimates in previous chapters of China's relative price structure for tradable goods and shadow conversion factors for primary factors make it possible to adopt the domestic resource productivity (DRP) method to measure China's international comparative advantage at a commodity or sectoral level. This chapter presents the estimated results and discusses the impact of China's recent economic reforms on the country's comparative advantage over the period 1978–95.

METHOD AND DATA ISSUES

The basic principle of the DRP and its relevance for measuring comparative advantage were elaborated in Chapter 5. Here, we briefly restate the formula to be used in the estimation of China's comparative advantage and the related data issues.

DRP Formula for the Estimation

As noted in Chapter 5, the DRP method adopted in this study divides all commodities into tradables and non-tradables and decomposes non-tradable intermediate inputs into tradable inputs and primary factor requirements.[1] This method is based on an input–output table. We can express the DRP formula in the matrix form. Suppose that an economy produces t tradable goods and n non-tradable goods with f primary factors. The intermediate input matrix $\mathbf{A}$ may be partitioned as follows

$$A = \begin{pmatrix} \mathbf{A}_{TT} & \mathbf{A}_{TN} \\ \mathbf{A}_{NT} & \mathbf{A}_{NN} \end{pmatrix}$$

where $\mathbf{A_{TT}}$ is a $t \times t$ sub-matrix of the unit requirements for tradable intermediate inputs in the production of tradables and $\mathbf{A_{TN}}$ is an $t \times n$ sub-matrix of the unit requirements for tradables in the production of non-tradables. $\mathbf{A_{NN}}$ and $\mathbf{A_{NT}}$ are $n \times n$ and $t \times n$ sub-matrices of the unit requirements for non-tradables in production of non-tradables and tradables, respectively.

The sub-matrix of unit factor requirement coefficients (value-added) F may be, accordingly, partitioned as $\mathbf{F}_T$, the $f \times t$ sub-matrix of the factor inputs in production of tradables, and $\mathbf{F}_N$, the $f \times n$ sub-matrix of the factor inputs in the production of non-tradables, that is,

$$\mathbf{F} = (\mathbf{F}_T \ \mathbf{F}_N)$$

The general formula of the DRP method in matrix form is

$$\mathbf{DRP} = [\mathbf{I}_{TT} - \mathbf{A}_{TT}^T - \mathbf{A}_{NT}^T(\mathbf{I}_{NN} - \mathbf{A}_{NN}^T)^{-1}\mathbf{A}_{TN}^T]\mathbf{P}_T\{[\mathbf{A}_{NT}^T(\mathbf{I}_{NN} - \mathbf{A}_{NN}^T)^{-1}$$
$$\mathbf{F}_N^T\mathbf{P}_F + \mathbf{F}_T^T\mathbf{P}_F]^D\}^{-1} \tag{8.1}$$

where $\mathbf{I}_{TT}$ and $\mathbf{I}_{NN}$ are $t \times t$ and $n \times n$ identity matrices, respectively; $\mathbf{P}_T$ and $\mathbf{P}_F$ are the column vectors of the border and domestic price ratios of tradable goods and the shadow-price conversion factors for the primary factors, respectively. The superscripts of T, D and -1 indicate a transposed matrix, a diagonal matrix and an inverse matrix, respectively.[2]

The calculation of the DRP for Chinese tradable commodities requires three sets of data: the input–output coefficients (**A** and **F**), the border and domestic price ratios of tradable goods ($\mathbf{P}_T$) and the shadow-price conversion factors for primary factors of production ($\mathbf{P}_F$).

Input–output Coefficients

Since the early 1980s, a number of input–output tables have been constructed for China. One of the early tables (1981) was published by the World Bank (World Bank 1985b). The State Planning Commission compiled the first published national input–output table of 1981, which divided the economy into 24 sectors. The second input–output table made up of 117 sectors, compiled for 1987, was published in 1991 by the State Statistical Bureau. It was the most disaggregated input–output table ever published for China. The table was constructed on the basis of a comprehensive survey involving about 500 000 enterprises and institutions as well as 80 000 households nationwide. This table marked a significant improvement in the compilation of Chinese input–output data. Since then, the State Statistical Bureau has published China's input–output tables regularly. The second detailed table of 1992 was published in 1995 which was also based on a fresh nationwide survey and had similar disaggregation as the 1987 table. Between 1987 and 1995, two more tables were also published by the State Statistical Bureau, one for 1990 and the other for 1995. Unlike the 1987 and 1992 tables, however, these two tables were the extensions of the 1987 and 1992 tables and had only 33 sectors. The regular publication of these detailed input–output tables provides valuable information about China's changing economic structure, and facilitates empirical studies on changes in China's trade and possible industrial structural changes.

It should also be pointed out, however, that these published tables have some undesirable features in terms of the present study. The classification criterion used in China's input–output tables is based on China's industry classification system which focuses on productive activities rather than individual commodities. There is also an apparent imbalance in the structure of these tables in the sense that they concentrate more on industry (83 sectors) and less on agriculture (six sectors). In view of these problems, the tables have been modified to suit this study. The six agricultural sectors are broken down into 13 commodity groups. An input–output table compiled by the former Price Research Centre of the State Council was used in the decomposition of the agricultural sectors.[3] Of the remaining 104 sectors, 81 tradables are aggregated into 48 groups.[4] As the emphasis of this study is on tradable goods, the 23 non-tradable sectors are aggregated and reduced to eight groups. This results in a 69-sector input output table.[5]

While the DRP measures of China's comparative advantage in this study focus on the reform years between 1978 and 1995, input–output tables are not available on an annual basis for the entire period. An alternative option would be to make a strong assumption that the intermediate input coefficients were static over the period studied. This assumption could only be made on the grounds that underlying technologies are unlikely to change markedly over a relatively short period of time. This implies that the major changes in DRP measures during this period resulted solely from the changes in the relative prices of goods and factors. In practice, however, the goods-price changes led to factor-price changes and eventually caused possible adjustments in the input demands and underlying technologies adopted. As no annual tables are available, the input–output coefficients for the missing years have to be estimated from the published tables and other available information on the Chinese economy.

The (RAS) approach is used in this study to derive the input–output coefficients for other years.[6] This approach is usually referred to as a non-survey or partial-survey method because all data needed are drawn from published sources. More specifically, the RAS technique estimates the coefficients using three pieces of information for the year of interest: gross output of each sector; intermediate input sales of each sector; and intermediate input purchases of each sector. Using this information, the input–output coefficients for the target year can be derived from a series of iterations of bi-proportional adjustments of the direct coefficient table for the base year. Using this approach, we have compiled 18 consecutive input–output tables for the period 1978–95, in which the 1987 and 1992 tables are compiled and modified directly from the published tables and the 1981, 1985, 1990 and 1995 tables are based on the disaggregation of the published but more aggregated tables. The other tables are also compiled on the basis of these published tables and the additional data on the economic structure gathered from various Chinese statistical sources.

Table 8.1   DRP measure of China's comparative advantage for tradable goods,

Product	1978	1979	1980	1981	1982	1983	1984	1985
1. Paddy rice	2.15	2.06	2.16	2.30	2.05	1.74	1.42	1.30
2. Wheat	1.11	1.01	1.20	1.23	1.22	1.15	1.08	1.02
3. Other grains	1.19	1.12	1.27	1.19	1.01	0.91	0.95	0.86
4. Oil-bearing crops	2.00	1.42	1.27	1.04	1.08	1.43	1.80	1.87
5. Cotton	1.11	1.05	0.92	0.96	0.99	1.08	1.27	1.24
6. Other industrial crops	3.32	3.09	2.93	2.96	2.64	3.28	2.98	3.02
7. Vegetables	3.31	3.03	2.67	2.47	2.89	3.43	2.90	1.84
8. Fruits	1.52	1.62	1.27	1.14	1.14	1.17	0.93	0.90
9. Forest products	0.78	0.77	0.74	0.77	0.84	1.02	1.09	1.07
10. Wool and hides	2.31	2.54	2.73	2.62	2.27	2.16	2.30	2.04
11. Meat, etc.	3.91	3.21	2.91	3.02	3.02	2.41	2.37	1.97
12. Fish	4.94	3.23	2.69	2.48	2.52	2.55	1.69	1.25
13. Other agri. products	2.57	2.39	2.31	2.25	2.38	2.49	2.39	2.06
14. Coal	2.01	1.62	1.50	1.82	1.98	1.94	2.16	2.04
15. Crude petroleum	1.28	2.25	2.46	2.36	2.30	1.86	1.74	1.37
16. Ferrous minerals	0.92	1.07	0.69	0.72	0.73	0.83	0.54	0.67
17. Non-ferrous minerals	0.25	0.33	0.34	0.32	0.28	0.34	0.39	0.41
18. Non-metal minerals	0.89	0.87	0.90	0.87	0.96	0.97	1.14	1.48
19. Timber	3.16	2.65	2.61	1.90	1.31	0.96	0.89	0.97
20. Sugar, tobacco, alcohol	0.49	0.59	0.65	0.62	0.60	0.62	0.97	1.14
21. Other processed food	-1.36	-0.71	-0.56	-0.50	-0.48	-0.05	0.41	0.82
22. Cotton textiles	1.22	1.24	1.24	1.18	1.16	0.91	0.95	1.19
23. Wool textiles	0.08	0.15	0.07	0.11	0.22	0.48	0.63	0.95
24. Hemp textiles	-0.45	-0.22	-0.17	-0.16	-0.11	-0.15	0.26	0.48
25. Silk textiles	1.87	2.14	2.04	2.02	1.99	2.16	2.09	2.19
26. Knitted goods	0.45	0.48	0.48	0.47	0.50	0.71	0.84	1.25
27. Other textiles	-0.36	0.47	0.72	0.76	0.98	0.12	0.41	0.91
28. Clothing	-0.02	-0.03	0.11	0.31	0.67	1.18	1.16	1.76
29. Furniture	3.96	3.29	3.26	2.28	1.44	0.94	0.85	0.92
30. Paper	-0.50	-0.30	-0.17	-0.05	0.08	0.23	0.43	0.45
31. Cultural goods	0.23	0.20	0.17	0.19	0.14	0.25	0.22	0.72
32. Petrol products	0.23	-0.24	-0.11	0.00	0.03	0.32	0.56	0.91
33. Coal products	0.71	1.76	1.04	0.81	0.64	1.08	0.56	0.79
34. Inorganic chemicals	0.27	0.39	0.52	0.61	0.59	0.40	0.26	0.24
35. Chem. fertilizers	0.44	0.60	0.55	0.46	0.18	0.37	0.41	0.66
36. Organic chemicals	-0.08	0.00	-0.01	-0.01	0.00	0.05	0.05	0.23
37. Household chemicals	-0.29	-0.21	-0.21	-0.20	-0.16	-0.06	-0.04	-0.07
38. Other chemicals	-0.21	-0.16	-0.14	-0.13	-0.17	-0.12	-0.09	0.10
39. Medicine	-1.11	-0.78	-0.54	-0.51	-0.41	-0.37	-0.22	0.04
40. Chemical fibres	-0.10	-0.07	-0.06	-0.07	-0.07	-0.05	-0.03	0.01
41. Rubber manufactures	-0.14	-0.09	-0.05	-0.04	-0.06	0.01	0.07	0.28
42. Plastic articles	0.19	0.26	0.26	0.26	0.31	0.37	0.43	0.56
43. Cement	1.27	1.48	1.44	1.64	1.61	1.57	1.28	1.30
44. Glass	0.70	0.84	1.03	1.23	1.62	0.99	1.06	1.21
45. Ceramic products	0.87	0.98	1.00	0.97	1.00	0.76	0.88	1.25
46. Other bldg materials	0.35	0.43	0.45	0.50	0.33	0.47	0.5 1	0.73

1978–95

1986	1987	1988	1989	1990	1991	1992	1993	1994	1995
1.22	1.17	0.99	0.83	0.93	1.12	1.27	1.49	1.34	1.55
0.79	0.66	0.69	0.61	0.70	0.86	0.91	1.20	0.83	0.76
0.74	0.77	0.83	0.76	0.81	0.99	0.97	1.00	0.82	0.82
1.54	1.37	1.40	1.43	1.62	1.83	2.03	2.11	1.66	1.98
1.33	1.40	1.54	1.35	1.09	1.10	1.18	1.38	1.07	0.94
1.54	2.39	2.23	2.49	2.44	2.40	2.39	2.64	2.22	1.96
1.98	1.72	1.80	1.91	2.00	2.15	2.29	2.34	2.41	2.42
0.94	0.95	0.80	1.02	1.11	1.27	1.63	1.87	1.55	1.45
0.91	0.87	0.82	0.89	1.19	1.43	1.68	1.81	1.71	1.61
1.58	1.66	1.48	1.43	1.33	1.44	1.41	1.50	1.13	1.10
2.42	1.95	1.34	1.25	1.32	1.51	1.31	0.99	0.31	0.81
1.44	1.38	0.83	0.61	0.74	0.77	1.12	1.09	1.30	1.16
2.44	2.15	2.47	2.30	2.37	2.14	2.18	2.64	2.77	2.62
2.04	2.03	2.16	2.65	2.42	2.28	2.11	1.67	1.59	1.64
0.82	0.92	1.03	1.27	1.34	1.07	0.89	0.51	0.29	0.26
0.71	0.76	0.68	0.68	0.70	0.71	0.65	0.28	0.23	0.28
0.35	0.37	0.82	0.86	0.59	0.39	0.26	0.09	0.18	0.28
1.58	1.64	1.75	1.61	1.61	1.62	1.63	1.35	1.64	1.98
0.86	0.73	0.56	0.64	0.47	0.55	0.80	1.00	0.73	0.57
1.35	1.24	0.62	0.58	0.67	0.78	0.80	0.94	1.06	1.13
0.88	1.02	1.53	1.65	1.35	1.62	1.82	1.83	1.78	1.43
1.27	1.39	1.43	1.21	1.09	0.99	1.02	1.28	1.16	1.35
1.23	1.09	1.76	1.85	2.09	2.08	2.07	1.97	1.83	1.61
1.11	0.96	1.30	1.18	0.40	0.60	0.85	1.45	2.19	2.49
2.19	2.34	2.37	2.80	3.14	3.50	3.41	3.54	3.09	2.83
1.53	1.75	1.60	1.40	1.24	1.38	1.62	2.10	2.28	2.19
1.67	1.57	1.65	0.99	0.82	0.65	0.66	1.01	0.93	1.41
1.66	2.02	2.10	1.94	1.70	1.64	2.20	2.40	2.85	2.65
0.72	0.52	0.39	0.53	0.37	0.46	0.81	1.12	0.66	0.43
0.35	0.25	0.11	-0.05	-0.15	-0.04	0.05	0.11	0.40	0.22
1.06	1.37	1.41	1.74	2.17	2.03	2.28	1.70	2.09	2.02
1.11	0.79	0.62	0.69	0.59	0.47	0.36	0.78	0.95	0.93
0.69	0.93	1.45	2.01	2.40	2.10	1.63	1.46	1.44	1.78
0.11	0.11	0.29	0.50	0.33	0.34	0.39	0.59	0.54	0.46
0.85	0.87	0.60	0.52	0.18	0.08	0.04	0.15	0.21	0.23
0.44	0.57	0.44	0.31	0.33	0.51	0.39	0.37	0.60	0.53
-0.16	-0.21	-0.14	-0.08	-0.09	-0.07	0.00	-0.05	-0.11	0.13
0.25	0.37	0.24	0.09	-0.03	0.16	0.29	0.44	0.35	0.14
0.17	0.17	0.01	-0.12	-0.16	0.12	0.26	0.37	0.40	0.39
0.04	0.06	0.11	0.04	0.04	0.05	0.08	0.03	0.00	-0.11
0.56	0.76	1.04	0.95	0.62	0.96	0.88	1.05	1.30	1.10
0.66	0.66	0.54	0.56	0.58	0.67	0.82	0.93	1.27	1.41
0.77	1.02	1.19	1.33	1.13	1.14	1.18	1.46	1.20	1.17
1.23	1.18	1.33	1.43	1.23	1.19	1.18	1.36	1.22	1.05
1.55	1.75	1.64	1.22	0.95	0.87	0.68	0.62	0.98	1.25
0.89	1.14	1.23	1.07	1.38	1.40	1.41	1.00	1.17	1.09

Table 8.1 (Continued)

Product	1978	1979	1980	1981	1982	1983	1984	1985
47. Iron	1.50	1.84	1.35	1.34	1.20	1.30	0.90	1.33
48. Steel	0.37	0.29	0.36	0.33	0.45	0.64	0.65	0.51
49. Non-ferrous metals	0.19	0.26	0.28	0.24	0.20	0.27	0.32	0.34
50. Metal products	0.35	0.33	0.37	0.33	0.30	0.26	0.28	0.37
51. Agri.machinery	0.04	0.08	0.10	0.09	0.11	0.16	0.24	0.42
52. Industrial equipment	0.03	0.06	0.09	0.09	0.11	0.13	0.18	0.19
53. Power equipment	0.22	0.27	0.30	0.33	0.39	0.48	0.64	0.79
54. Hshd. mech/elect.gds	0.39	0.37	0.33	0.28	0.26	0.32	0.40	0.51
55. Railway equipment	0.31	0.36	0.41	0.42	0.37	0.34	0.34	0.69
56. Motor vehicles	0.00	0.00	0.00	0.01	0.03	0.05	0.09	0.09
57. Ships	0.39	0.38	0.33	0.35	0.40	0.36	0.43	0.50
58. Oth transp. equip.	-0.10	-0.11	-0.11	-0.13	-0.14	-0.16	-0.17	-0.18
59. Other enging. prods.	0.13	0.17	0.20	0.19	0.22	0.30	0.24	0.35
60. Electronic products	0.18	0.20	0.20	0.18	0.18	0.22	0.26	0.30
61. Hshd. Electronics	0.18	0.19	0.15	0.18	0.19	0.17	0.15	0.16

Source: Author's own calculation.

Tradable Goods Price Ratios

The ratios of the border to domestic prices for the 61 tradable goods are taken from Chapter 6. These price ratios are used in the DRP estimation to convert the domestic prices for tradable goods into their border prices so the value-added could be measured at their respective border prices.

Shadow-price Conversion Factors for Primary Factors

The shadow-price conversion factors are taken from Chapter 7 and applied to all the six value-added items in China's input–output tables: (1) depreciation, (2) unskilled wages, (3) skilled wages, (4) profits, (5) taxes and (6) others. The concept of profit in a planned economy is more complicated than in a market economy. Its level may be determined by capital market distortions such as depressed interest rates and depreciation rates or distorted prices. Depreciation and profits are both treated as the payments for capital services, and hence shadow-priced. Similarly, skilled and unskilled labour income should also be assigned to their relevant shadow-wage conversion factors. Although tax revenue and other transfer payments are the revenues to the society, they still need shadow pricing to take account of the general deviation of the domestic prices from the free trade border prices.

Table 8.1 (Continued)

1986	1987	1988	1989	1990	1991	1992	1993	1994	1995
1.21	1.35	1.65	1.63	1.75	1.38	1.32	0.81	1.27	1.69
0.68	0.70	0.78	0.83	0.82	0.67	0.50	0.20	0.41	0.74
0.29	0.3 1	0.78	0.80	0.49	0.34	0.26	0.11	0.20	0.29
0.42	0.41	0.44	0.43	0.46	0.50	0.69	0.66	0.73	0.51
0.51	0.54	0.46	0.46	0.41	0.45	0.48	0.55	0.58	0.59
0.30	0.32	0.32	0.27	0.19	0.22	0.21	0.25	0.24	0.19
0.82	0.88	0.96	0.81	0.88	1.04	1.14	1.38	1.53	1.51
0.49	0.52	0.53	0.58	0.62	0.77	0.89	1.11	1.37	1.52
0.49	0.44	0.63	0.73	0.72	0.83	0.94	1.20	1.32	1.39
0.11	0.13	0.07	0.06	0.00	-0.01	-0.01	0.06	0.01	0.00
0.48	0.49	0.40	0.43	0.35	0.32	0.32	0.46	0.53	0.64
-0.12	-0.14	-0.21	-0.21	-0.26	-0.26	-0.27	-0.26	-0.29	-0.25
0.61	0.66	0.60	0.62	0.59	0.77	0.90	1.20	1.06	0.82
0.48	0.51	0.40	0.35	0.33	0.50	0.56	0.63	0.60	0.64
0.17	0.24	0.26	0.29	0.33	0.53	0.65	0.77	0.84	0.97

DRP ESTIMATES OF CHINA'S INTERNATIONAL COMPARATIVE ADVANTAGE

The DRP is estimated for all Chinese tradable goods over the period 1978–95 and the results are reported in Table 8.1. The benchmark of unity may be used to divide all tradable goods into two groups. A DRP estimate in excess of unity suggests an area of potential comparative advantage, otherwise, disadvantage. In the following, we will first discuss some general trends that characterize China's changing comparative advantage over the reform period and then examine in detail the individual tradable goods in the five broad categories.

General Trends

To see the changes in China's comparative advantage structures over the reform period, we select the DRP estimates for 1978, 1987 and 1995 and present them in Figures 8.1–8.3. The 61 tradable goods are clustered in five broad categories according to their factor intensities.

Figure 8.1 shows China's comparative advantage structure as it was in 1978, selected to represent the pre-reform Chinese economy. It can be seen in Figure 8.1 that China's comparative advantage was almost exclusively confined to agricultural and natural resource-intensive goods. A handful of physical capital and unskilled labour-intensive products displayed some degree of comparative advantage, such as Cotton Textiles (22), Silk Textiles (25) and Furniture (29), Cement (43) and Iron (49). These goods all relied heavily on some agricultural products and other natural resources as their main intermediate inputs. In 1978, no comparative advantage was found in

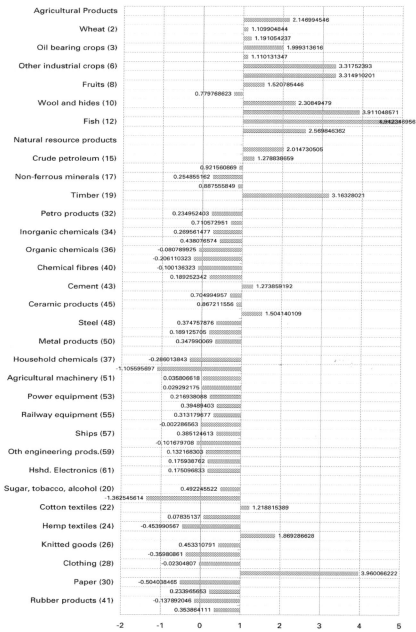

Figure 8.1 DRP Estimates for China's comparative advantage: 1978
Source: Table 8.1.

most tradable industries, even in many unskilled labour-intensive manufacturing. This result seems to run counter to the prediction of the Heckscher–Ohlin trade theory – that is, with a vast population of unskilled labour, China should have a strong comparative advantage in unskilled labour-intensive manufacturing industries. This is certainly not the case in 1978 as the DRP results indicated. This puzzle could be explained by the severe distortions observed in China's domestic goods and factors markets at that time.

Under the centrally planned system prior to 1978, China's domestic goods-price structure was skewed against primary products and in favour of manufactured products. Compared with their international counterparts, the domestic prices of primary goods were low while that of manufactured goods were high. The skewness of the goods prices escalated as one moved upstream along the production lines toward more sophisticated manufactured final products. In the primary-factor markets, as indicated in the shadow-price estimation in Chapter 7, the wages for unskilled labour are found to be higher and the wages for skilled labour and rental returns for capital lower than their marginal products. The distortions in goods and factors markets encouraged an excessive use of scarce factors and an insufficient use of redundant resources such as unskilled labour. As a result, China's advantage in unskilled labour-intensive manufacturing was largely offset by relatively high labour costs in the state-run manufacturing sector. Moreover, during the plan period, many industries had relied heavily on cheap domestic raw materials and intermediate inputs. Over time, they developed an input requirement much higher than international standards. This over-use of under-valued inputs tends to reduce the international value-added generated in these industries. As indicated in Table 8.1, 13 industries are so inefficient that their value-added would be negative if their output and inputs were valued at international free trade prices. It is not surprising that these inefficient industries are not confined merely to those industries using China's scarce resources. The distortions in the goods and factors markets prevented China from using its most abundant resources efficiently. Even the most labour-intensive industries may not be able to survive in a free and more open market environment.[7]

To show the changes in China's comparative advantage during the reform period, we also present the DRP estimates for 1987 and 1995 (Figures 8.2 and 8.3, respectively). The results for 1987 represent the outcome of the first while the results for 1995 represent the outcome of the second decade of economic reforms. The stark contrast between the 1978 pattern and the 1987 or 1995 patterns is evident. Four general trends of changes are noteworthy.

First, there is a sharp decline in the variation of the DRP estimates for 1987 and 1995, compared with that for 1978. It can be seen in Figure 8.1 that the estimates of DRP for 1978 vary widely, ranging from a minimum of -1.36 for Other Processed Food (21) to a maximum of 4.94 for Fish (12). The variance of the DRP estimates for 1987 reduces considerably, ranging from -0.21 for

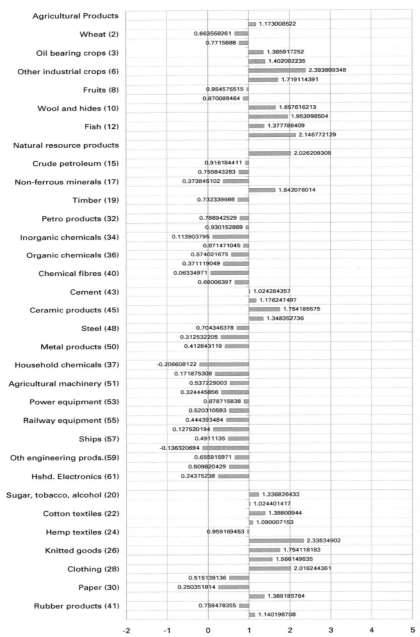

Figure 8.2 DRP Estimates for China's comparative advantage: 1987
Source: Table 8.1.

Household Chemicals (37) to 2.34 for Silk Textiles (25). Similarly, the DRP estimates for 1995 vary modestly between -0.25 for Other Transport Equipment (58) and 2.83 for Silk Textiles (25). A comparison between the DRP estimates for 1978 and 1987 or 1995 reveals a trend of convergence for all tradable goods. This can be seen more clearly from the standard deviation of DRP estimates reported in Table 8.2. The standard deviation of DRP estimates was 1.26 in 1978. It reduced to 0.61 in 1986 and then bounced back slightly in the early 1990s. By 1995, it remained at 0.75, much lower than that in 1978.

This convergence can be interpreted as the result of a fall in domestic distortions through tradable price realignments between China and the rest of the world. As mentioned in Chapter 5, the deviation of DRP from unity can be seen as a measurement of domestic price distortions. The larger the differences between the domestic and international relative price structures, the greater the divergence of the DRP estimates from unity. So, the high level of variation in the DRP estimates for 1978 actually reveals a high level of distortions in the domestic goods and factors markets at that time. The high variation in DRP estimates for 1978 could also be read as evidence of considerable domestic resource misallocation. It suggests that greatest allocative efficiency could be achieved by encouraging resources to shift from activities with relatively low to activities with relatively high DRPs. If these plan-induced distortions were reduced and free markets were allowed to play a larger role, considerable potential gains could be reaped from policy reforms.

Since 1978, China has come a long way toward abolishing its centrally planned domestic price system and lifting controls over domestic prices to allow a realignment of the relative price structure with the rest of the world. The effects of the price reforms and trade liberalization are captured in the DRP estimates. Tables 8.1 and 8.2 show that the DRP estimates for tradable goods on average are much closer in 1987 and 1995 than in 1978.

Further examination reveals that the most rapid changes occurred between 1984 and 1988, when the two-tier price system was introduced. The results also show an increase in the variation in the DRP estimates between 1989 and 1991, which coincides with the aftermath of high inflation and subsequent austerity period. During these years, there was a temporary halt to the price-alignment process and, in certain sectors, even reversals to the old price structures. This may have been caused by a slowdown in the price-reform process and the repeated devaluation of China's currency. Currency devaluation was intended to boost export competitiveness during the three years of austerity policies. In the context of China's partially reformed economy, devaluation had a detrimental impact on domestic prices. On the one hand, it did not affect the relative price of those tradable goods whose prices had been liberalized because they could adjust flexibly to the changed market conditions. On the other, the devaluation further widened the gap between domestic prices and border prices for those products whose domestic

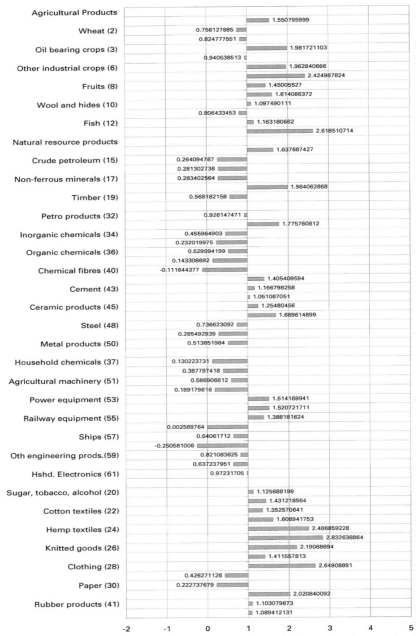

Figure 8.3 DRP Estimates for China's comparative advantage: 1995
Source: Table 8.1

prices were still fixed by the state. Because most of these were key agricultural products, the devaluation also distorted again the relative prices between primary products and manufactured goods, which, in the early years, had been adjusted. This is reflected in a temporary rise in the dispersion of DRP estimates over this period. Nonetheless, compared with the early 1980s, the variation in the DRP estimates in 1995 was still much lower.

Second, there is a slow but steady increase in the DRP measures of China's comparative advantage in the period, implying a steady rise in China's international competitiveness. As Table 8.3 indicates, in 1978, only 20 of 61 Chinese tradable commodity groups had a DRP estimate above unity. The number increased steadily and reached 32 by 1995. In 1978, the comparative advantage group accounted for only 43.4 per cent of the total value of gross output of Chinese tradables. By 1995, however, it amounted to almost 52 per cent of total tradable output values.

Third, the most important change in the DRP estimates over this period, revealed in Figures 8.1–8.3, are those of structural changes. The post-reform patterns of comparative advantage considerably differ from the pre-reform one. The general structural changes can be detected by comparing the Spearman's rank correlation coefficients of DRP estimates for the base year, 1978, with those for subsequent years. The rank correlation matrix of the DRP estimates for the period 1978–95 are presented in Table 8.4. A low level of correlation coefficient implies weak or no similarity between the DRP estimates for the base and that for the current year. Substantial structural changes have taken place in the comparative advantage patterns over time. As indicated in Table 8.4, the structure of China's comparative advantage in 1995 was significantly different from that in 1978: the two structures show very little rank correlation.

The pace of change in the structure of China's comparative advantage was not uniform during this period. Structural change, measured as annual changes in the rank correlation coefficient, was relatively slow prior to 1983. Before 1983, major reforms were introduced only in the agricultural sector while the non-agricultural sectors remained subject to the readjustment policy implemented in 1979. This policy was designed to overcome the structural imbalances in the economy that arose during Cultural Revolution. After 1983, major steps were taken to speed up the process of economic reforms in non-agricultural sectors as well as in the agricultural sector. These reforms included, among other things, the abolition of the state purchasing system for agricultural products, further reduction in the reliance on central plans and the opening up of the secondary markets for most producer goods. The introduction of market mechanisms helped speed up the realignment of irrational domestic prices with international prices and thus stimulated more efficient utilization of domestic resources. This resulted in substantial changes in China's comparative advantage structure in the second half of this period.

The changes in the rank correlation coefficient of DRP estimates accelerated after 1983 and reached a peak in 1988. Between 1989 and 1992,

Table 8.2 Descriptive statistics of DRP estimates, 1978–95

	1978	1979	1980	1981	1982	1983	1984	1985
Mean	0.847	0.861	0.834	0.810	0.796	0.815	0.818	0.898
Standard deviation	1.256	1.058	0.980	0.914	0.876	0.857	0.761	0.657
Sample variance	1.578	1.119	0.961	0.835	0.767	0.734	0.579	0.431
Minimum	-1.363	-0.784	-0.560	-0.512	-0.477	-0.371	-0.220	-0.182
Maximum	4.942	3.293	3.262	3.019	3.020	3.429	2.979	3.023

Source: Author's own calculations.

however, the structure of China's comparative advantage remained largely unchanged and, to some extent, even returned to the previous patterns. The situation began to change in 1993 with a modest alteration recorded in the comparative advantage structure. In 1994, another large structural change occurred. It seems quite clear that substantial structural changes in China's comparative advantage coincided with China's domestic economic growth cycles and the reform process; the periods 1985–7 and 1993–4 were both when China had its most rapid growth and its most sweeping reforms. There seems to be a clear link between economic growth and reform on the one hand and economic reform and changes in comparative advantage on the other.

Fourth, the most significant structural change is the shift of comparative advantage away from primary products, agricultural and natural resource goods towards manufactures, especially labour-intensive goods. In 1978, China's comparative advantage was confined mainly to primary commodities–namely, agricultural products, minerals and timber. As Table 8.5 shows, of the 20 commodity groups in which China had a comparative advantage, 12 were from the agricultural sector. Together with three natural resource goods, primary products as a group accounted for 67 per cent of the output value of comparative advantage goods. In 1987, although nine agricultural products and two natural resource-intensive goods remained in the group of 25

Table 8.3   Number of tradable commodities with comparative advantage and their percentage share in total tradable output, 1978–95

	1978	1979	1980	1981	1982	1983	1984	1985
No. of goods	20	22	21	20	21	19	18	23
Output share (%)	43.4	44.6	43.4	43.3	44.1	35.2	34.7	44.0

Source: Author's own calculations.

1986	1987	1988	1989	1990	1991	1992	1993	1994	1995
0.924	0.950	0.969	0.968	0.932	0.973	1.025	1.083	1.083	1.094
0.614	0.622	0.651	0.695	0.750	0.734	0.740	0.767	0.759	0.747
0.377	0.387	0.424	0.483	0.563	0.538	0.548	0.589	0.576	0.558
-0.156	-0.207	-0.212	-0.214	-0.256	-0.261	-0.269	-0.255	-0.286	-0.251
2.437	2.394	2.470	2.803	3.137	3.496	3.414	3.539	3.089	2.833

commodities with comparative advantage, their share in the output value of this group dropped to 37 per cent. Over the same period, manufactured goods, particularly unskilled labour-intensive ones, replaced primary products: by 1995, nine agricultural goods and two natural resource goods remained in the advantage group, their combined share declining to less than 26 per cent. By 1995, comparative advantage had been gained in 12 out of 14 unskilled labour-intensive manufactures. The labour-intensive goods alone accounted for more than 53.4 per cent of the output value of the advantage group in 1988 and their share further increased to 54.8 per cent in 1995. Comparative advantage was also found in six physical capital-intensive and three human capital-intensive manufactured goods over this period.

Table 8.5 also shows that physical and human capital-intensive manufactured goods dominated the group in which China had comparative disadvantage over the entire period studied. The combined share in total output value of this group expanded from 59.2 to 72.2 per cent; at the same time, the share of unskilled labour-intensive manufactures in this group shrank sharply.

In Table 8.6, the DRP estimates are aggregated in the five broad groups of tradable commodities, which provides a general picture for the changing pattern of China's comparative advantage over time. It is clear that the DRP estimates for agricultural and natural resource goods constantly declined over time while the DRP estimates for other manufactured goods increased. In 1978, agricultural and resource products were on top of the list, followed by physical capital-intensive and unskilled labour-intensive products. Human

1986	1987	1988	1989	1990	1991	1992	1993	1994	1995
24	25	26	25	24	25	26	32	32	32
41.9	49.4	45.2	44.0	43.9	42.4	45.5	55.0	56.9	51.9

Table 8.4   Spearman's rank correlation matrix of DRP estimates, 1978–95

1978	1							
1979	0.960	1						
1980	0.954	0.991	1					
1981	0.945	0.977	0.991	1				
1982	0.912	0.942	0.962	0.983	1			
1983	0.908	0.888	0.898	0.926	0.943	1		
1984	0.838	0.812	0.836	0.875	0.907	0.951	1	
1985	0.778	0.764	0.788	0.829	0.856	0.894	0.954	1
1986	0.604	0.610	0.629	0.671	0.705	0.727	0.823	0.916
1987	0.578	0.595	0.607	0.649	0.678	0.717	0.793	0.897
1988	0.464	0.506	0.518	0.559	0.597	0.649	0.715	0.824
1989	0.491	0.512	0.521	0.555	0.589	0.670	0.708	0.805
1990	0.567	0.583	0.587	0.624	0.656	0.740	0.758	0.837
1991	0.553	0.555	0.558	0.592	0.626	0.719	0.741	0.815
1992	0.546	0.542	0.545	0.576	0.612	0.702	0.719	0.793
1993	0.458	0.453	0.464	0.488	0.532	0.602	0.649	0.730
1994	0.311	0.294	0.296	0.325	0.377	0.471	0.524	0.632
1995	0.348	0.350	0.351	0.380	0.433	0.506	0.557	0.675
	1978	1979	1980	1981	1982	1983	1984	1985

Source: Author's own calculations.

capital-intensive products were China's most disadvantaged goods, whose combined international value-added was negative. In 1995, the average DRP estimate for China's tradables increased, driven by a sharp rise in unskilled labour-intensive products and an impressive rise in both physical and human capital-intensive products on the ladder of DRP estimates. On the other hand, DRP estimates for two primary product groups fell considerably, though agricultural products still maintained their top ranking.

In identifying structural changes in a country's comparative advantage over time, it is the *relative ranking position*, rather than the absolute level, of the DRP estimates that is most important. This is because, as the domestic prices are realigned toward the world price in the domestic reform process, the dispersion in the DRP estimates declines and the DRP estimates for individual tradable goods tend to converge to unity. Using the changes in the level of DRP estimates to capture the changing comparative advantage could be misleading. To accurately describe the changes in comparative advantage, we need to consider the relative ranking of individual tradable products.

Changes in the commodity composition of China's comparative advantage are further illustrated in Table 8.7 which reveals the shifts in the DRP ranking between 1978 and 1995. The commodities are arranged in descending order of their DRP ranking and divided equally into three groups. The top 20 commodity groups (Top 20) have the highest DRP estimates, implying highest level of comparative advantage.

Table 8.4 (Continued)

1986	1987	1988	1989	1990	1991	1992	1993	1994	1995
1									
0.972	1								
0.878	0.925	1							
0.812	0.865	0.962	1						
0.808	0.862	0.921	0.955	1					
0.795	0.849	0.886	0.921	0.969	1				
0.776	0.815	0.839	0.876	0.928	0.974	1			
0.746	0.758	0.767	0.796	0.802	0.876	0.933	1		
0.690	0.718	0.748	0.756	0.760	0.831	0.884	0.931	1	
0.747	0.773	0.807	0.797	0.797	0.839	0.864	0.882	0.961	1

Table 8.7 indicates that the relative positions of natural resource and capital-intensive goods were fairly stable during the whole period. The major shifts occurred between the agricultural and labour-intensive goods. The number of agricultural commodities in the Top 20 group dropped from 12 to seven while six labour-intensive goods moved from the Bottom 21 and the Middle 20 groups to the Top 20 group to replace those agricultural products that had dropped out. The five agricultural products that had lost comparative advantage are Wheat (2), Other Grains (3), Cotton (5), Meat (11) and Fish (12), in which, except Fish (12), all four goods had a DRP estimate below unity. The six labour-intensive goods which had gained comparative advantage are Other Processed Food (21), Wool Textiles (23), Hemp Textiles (24), Knitted Goods (26), Clothing (28) and Cultural Goods (31).

The agricultural sector held or even increased its comparative advantage in the early 1980s. After the mid-1980s, comparative advantage in agriculture began to drop very rapidly, especially in wheat and other grains, mainly due to increasing costs of production as a result of the increase in the industrial prices after the two-tier price system was introduced. The decline of comparative advantage in China's agriculture bottomed out at the end of the 1980s. In the early 1990s, there was a temporary rise in comparative advantage in some agricultural products. Since 1992–3, however, the decline in comparative advantage in agriculture has resumed, most evidently in grains; this pattern of changes has largely coincided with China's agricultural production cycles.

Table 8.5   Composition of commodity groups with and without comparative

	1978	1979	1980	1981	1982	1983	1984	1985
Tradable group with DRP > 1								
Agricultural	57.5	59.9	59.3	62.5	63.9	74.3	73.2	53.8
	(12)[a]	(12)	(11)	(11)	(11)	(12)	(11)	(11)
Natural resource	9.8	9.4	9.2	8.9	8.4	8.9	10.3	8.2
	(3)	(4)	(3)	(3)	(3)	(2)	(3)	(3)
Physical capital	3.0	4.1	6.1	5.3	6.7	6.2	5.8	7.4
	(2)	(3)	(4)	(3)	(4)	(3)	(2)	(4)
Human capital	0.0	0.0	0.0	0.0	0.0	0.0	0.0	0.0
	(0)	(0)	(0)	(0)	(0)	(0)	(0)	(0)
Unskilled labour	29.7	26.5	25.4	23.4	21.1	10.6	10.7	30.6
	(3)	(3)	(3)	(3)	(3)	(2)	(2)	(5)
Tradable group with DRP < 1								
Agricultural	1.6	1.8	4.4	4.7	5.0	7.3	8.1	7.8
	(1)	(1)	(2)	(2)	(2)	(1)	(2)	(2)
Natural resource	1.8	1.5	1.7	1.7	1.7	2.2	1.5	1.8
	(3)	(2)	(3)	(3)	(3)	(4)	(3)	(3)
Physical capital	33.7	32.8	30.6	30.7	29.5	26.8	27.0	30.7
	(13)	(12)	(11)	(12)	(11)	(12)	(13)	(11)
Human capital	25.5	26.2	26.2	26.4	27.1	24.1	24.6	30.6
	(13)	(13)	(13)	(13)	(13)	(13)	(13)	(13)
Unskilled labour	37.5	37.7	37.0	36.5	36.7	39.6	38.8	29.1
	(11)	(11)	(11)	(11)	(11)	(12)	(12)	(9)

Note: *a* Figures in parentheses are numbers of commodities.
Source: Author's own calculations.

The fall of agricultural products in China's comparative advantage structure gave way to the rise of manufactured products, especially labour-intensive ones. Starting in the early 1980s, labour-intensive manufactured goods gained comparative advantage very quickly. Thanks to the structural adjustment

Table 8.6   DRP estimates of China's comparative advantage for five groups of

	1978	1979	1980	1981	1982	1983	1984	1985
Agricultural	2.23	1.99	1.85	1.81	1.81	1.90	1.76	1.54
Natural resources	1.46	1.51	1.48	1.38	1.30	1.17	1.15	1.16
Physical capital	0.45	0.54	0.52	0.54	0.53	0.54	0.50	0.66
Human capital	0.06	0.09	0.11	0.11	0.12	0.15	0.20	0.30
Unskilled labour	0.55	0.60	0.62	0.56	0.52	0.55	0.69	0.96

Source: Author's own calculations.

advantage, 1978–95 (%)

1986	1987	1988	1989	1990	1991	1992	1993	1994	1995
45.0	37.1	30.3	32.3	34.0	38.3	35.4	25.9	21.5	21.3
(9)	(9)	(7)	(8)	(9)	(10)	(11)	(11)	(10)	(9)
4.9	4.1	7.5	7.9	8.0	8.9	5.7	4.8	4.2	4.7
(2)	(2)	(3)	(3)	(3)	(3)	(2)	(2)	(2)	(2)
8.9	7.2	8.7	9.4	9.0	9.1	8.3	5.6	10.5	13.0
(4)	(4)	(5)	(5)	(4)	(4)	(4)	(3)	(5)	(6)
0.0	0.0	0.0	0.0	0.0	2.8	2.8	17.8	16.2	6.2
(0)	(0)	(0)	(0)	(0)	(1)	(1)	(4)	(4)	(3)
41.2	51.6	53.4	50.4	49.0	40.9	47.8	45.9	47.6	54.8
(9)	(10)	(11)	(9)	(8)	(7)	(8)	(12)	(11)	(12)
14.5	15.3	23.3	21.4	18.4	10.6	7.8	12.9	17.0	16.3
(4)	(4)	(6)	(5)	(4)	(3)	(2)	(2)	(3)	(4)
4.3	5.0	2.0	2.0	2.1	1.6	4.0	4.9	5.3	5.0
(4)	(4)	(3)	(3)	(3)	(3)	(4)	(4)	(4)	(4)
29.2	34.6	31.0	30.5	32.4	33.3	36.5	46.0	41.8	36.2
(11)	(11)	(10)	(10)	(11)	(11)	(11)	(12)	(10)	(9)
30.7	36.8	32.7	31.7	32.4	33.2	37.6	25.5	27.2	36.0
(13)	(13)	(13)	(13)	(13)	(12)	(12)	(9)	(9)	(10)
21.3	8.3	11.1	14.4	14.7	21.2	14.2	10.7	8.6	6.5
(5)	(4)	(3)	(5)	(6)	(7)	(6)	(2)	(3)	(2)

policies introduced in the late 1970s and early 1980s, the light industrial sectors achieved a rapid expansion. Many textile products increased their comparative advantage dramatically during this early period; the introduction of the two-tier pricing system in the mid-1980s further stimulated the development of manufacturing industries, and many labour-intensive manufactured goods moved up quickly on the comparative advantage ladder. By the end of 1980s, however, the momentum of labour-intensive

tradable goods, 1978–95

1986	1987	1988	1989	1990	1991	1992	1993	1994	1995
1.44	1.40	1.32	1.30	1.37	1.47	1.59	1.72	1.51	1.50
1.05	1.06	1.15	1.26	1.19	1.09	1.03	0.80	0.74	0.79
0.70	0.75	0.80	0.80	0.71	0.68	0.67	0.67	0.78	0.83
0.34	0.36	0.33	0.32	0.29	0.39	0.46	0.59	0.62	0.66
1.15	1.21	1.26	1.22	1.17	1.25	1.37	1.45	1.55	1.47

Table 8.7   Commodity composition of DRP rankings, 1978–95

	1978	*1979*	*1980*	*1981*	*1982*	*1983*	*1984*	*1985*
Top 20								
Agricultural	12	10	11	11	11	12	11	9
Natural resources	3	4	3	3	3	2	3	3
Physical capital	2	3	3	3	3	4	2	4
Human capital	0	0	0	0	0	0	0	0
Unskilled labour	3	3	3	3	3	2	4	4
Middle 20								
Agricultural	1	3	2	2	2	1	2	4
Natural resources	3	2	3	3	3	4	2	2
Physical capital	8	7	7	6	6	6	7	4
Human capital	4	4	4	4	4	3	2	3
Unskilled labour	4	4	4	5	5	6	7	7
Bottom 21								
Agricultural	0	0	0	0	0	0	0	0
Natural resources	0	0	0	0	0	0	1	1
Physical capital	5	5	5	6	6	5	6	7
Human capital	9	9	9	9	9	10	11	10
Unskilled labour	7	7	7	6	6	6	3	3

Source: Author's own calculations.

manufactures had eased, and in the early 1990s, the comparative advantage in some labour-intensive products even declined to some extent. During this period, more sophisticated manufactured products began to emerge as new comparative advantage goods. In 1994 and 1995, capital-intensive manufactured goods with a DRP estimate greater than unity included such product groups as Railway Equipment (53), Household Mechanical/ Electrical Goods (54), Power Station Equipment (55), and Other Engineering Products (59).

The trends revealed in Table 8.7 imply that, if the current trends continue, the unskilled labour-intensive and some capital-intensive manufactures will overtake primary products to become China's next most important advantage product group. Although some of the more labour-intensive agricultural products and natural resource products with abundant domestic supplies may still maintain their relative positions, most primary products will fall into the disadvantage group. This situation will surely be intensified by soaring domestic demand for farm products and raw industrial materials as China's high economic growth persists.

These four trends represent the most important features of China's changing comparative advantage over the reform period, revealed in the DRP estimate results. To highlight these changes at the commodity level, we list in Table 8.8 the DRP estimates for all tradable goods in descending

1986	1987	1988	1989	1990	1991	1992	1993	1994	1995
7	8	7	7	7	8	9	9	7	7
2	2	2	3	3	2	2	1	2	2
4	3	3	4	3	4	2	2	1	2
0	0	0	0	0	0	0	1	3	2
7	7	8	6	7	6	7	7	7	7
5	5	6	5	6	5	4	4	5	6
3	3	3	3	2	2	2	2	1	0
5	6	5	4	4	4	5	4	7	6
2	1	2	3	4	4	4	4	2	3
5	5	4	5	4	5	5	6	5	5
1	0	0	1	0	0	0	0	1	0
1	1	1	0	1	2	2	3	3	4
6	6	7	7	8	8	8	9	7	7
11	12	11	10	9	9	9	8	8	8
2	2	2	3	3	2	2	1	2	2

ranking order for the period 1978–95. This table is designed to highlight the structural changes in China's comparative advantage during its two decades of economic reforms, and is useful for tracing the changing positions in comparative advantage for individual products over the entire reform period. The table shows that unskilled labour-intensive manufacturing industries benefited the most from the reform policies in terms of comparative advantage. This can be seen in the changes in the ranking orders of tradable goods or sectors in Table 8.8. Between the DRP estimates for 1978 and 1995, there are 28 ascending sectors, 32 descending sectors and one unchanged sector. Included in the ascending group are three agricultural sectors, one natural resource sector, 11 unskilled labour-intensive manufacturing industries, five physical capital-intensive industries and eight human capital-intensive industries. In other words, most agricultural and natural resource-producing sectors are among the descending group and, have more or less, lost their comparative advantage. On the other hand, almost all unskilled labour-intensive industries[8] have gained comparative advantage to a large extent. The eight sectors with the highest DRP ranking order rises are all unskilled labour-intensive ones–that is, the textiles, clothing and food processing industries. This trend may help explain why there has been a big surge in labour-intensive manufactured exports from China over the period after 1978.

It should be noted that not all changes in ranking order are of equal importance. The ranking of some industries could be passively driven by

Table 8.8   Descending ranking orders of DRP estimates for all tradables, 1978-95

Rank	1978	1979	1980	1981	1982	1983	1984	1985	1986
1	12	29	29	11	11	7	6	6	13
2	29	12	6	6	7	6	7	25	11
3	11	11	11	10	6	12	13	13	25
4	6	6	10	12	12	13	11	10	14
5	7	7	12	7	13	11	10	14	7
6	19	19	7	15	15	25	14	11	27
7	13	10	19	1	10	10	25	4	28
8	10	13	15	29	1	14	4	7	10
9	1	15	13	13	25	15	15	28	18
10	14	25	1	25	14	1	12	18	45
11	4	1	25	19	44	43	1	15	6
12	25	47	14	14	43	4	43	47	4
13	8	33	43	43	29	47	5	1	26
14	47	8	47	47	19	28	28	43	12
15	15	14	8	2	2	8	18	45	20
16	43	43	4	44	47	2	9	12	5
17	22	4	3	3	22	5	2	26	22
18	3	22	22	22	8	33	44	5	44
19	5	3	2	8	4	9	20	44	23
20	2	16	33	4	3	44	22	22	1
21	16	5	44	45	45	18	3	20	47
22	18	2	45	5	5	19	8	9	24
23	45	45	5	18	27	29	47	2	32
24	9	18	18	33	18	3	19	19	31
25	33	44	9	9	9	22	45	23	8
26	44	9	27	27	16	16	29	29	9
27	20	35	16	16	28	45	26	32	46
28	26	20	20	20	33	26	48	27	21
29	35	26	35	34	20	48	53	8	19
30	54	27	34	46	34	20	23	3	35
31	57	46	26	26	26	23	33	21	53
32	48	34	46	35	48	53	32	53	15
33	46	57	55	55	57	46	16	33	2
34	50	54	50	57	53	34	46	46	43
35	55	55	48	48	55	35	30	31	3
36	34	50	17	50	46	42	42	55	29
37	17	17	54	53	42	57	57	16	16
38	32	48	57	17	50	17	21	35	33
39	31	53	53	28	17	55	27	42	48
40	53	42	49	54	54	32	35	54	42
41	42	49	42	42	59	54	54	48	59
42	49	31	60	49	23	59	17	57	41
43	60	60	59	31	49	49	55	24	51
44	61	61	31	59	61	50	49	30	54
45	59	59	61	61	35	31	50	51	55
46	23	23	28	60	60	30	34	17	57

1987	1988	1989	1990	1991	1992	1993	1994	1995
6	13	25	25	25	25	25	25	25
25	25	14	6	6	6	13	28	28
13	6	6	14	14	7	6	13	13
14	14	13	33	7	31	28	7	24
28	28	33	13	13	28	7	26	7
11	7	28	31	33	13	4	6	26
45	23	7	23	23	14	26	24	31
26	18	23	7	31	23	23	31	18
7	27	31	47	4	4	8	23	4
10	47	21	28	28	21	21	21	6
18	45	47	4	21	9	9	9	33
27	26	18	18	18	18	31	4	47
5	5	4	46	11	33	14	18	14
22	21	44	21	10	8	10	14	9
12	10	10	15	9	26	1	8	23
31	33	26	10	46	46	33	53	1
4	22	5	11	26	10	43	33	54
47	31	43	26	47	47	24	54	53
20	4	15	44	8	11	5	1	8
44	11	11	9	44	1	53	55	21
1	24	45	43	43	5	44	41	27
46	44	22	8	1	44	18	12	42
23	46	24	5	5	43	22	42	55
21	43	46	22	15	53	59	47	22
43	41	8	45	53	12	2	44	45
24	15	27	1	3	22	55	43	43
8	1	41	53	22	3	29	46	12
33	53	9	27	41	55	54	22	20
15	12	17	48	45	2	12	10	41
53	3	48	3	2	59	41	5	10
35	9	1	12	55	15	27	20	46
9	17	53	55	20	54	46	59	44
32	8	49	16	54	41	19	45	61
3	48	3	2	12	24	3	32	5
41	49	55	20	59	42	11	27	32
16	2	32	54	16	29	20	61	3
19	16	16	41	42	20	42	2	59
48	55	19	59	48	19	47	3	11
2	20	59	32	27	50	32	50	2
42	32	12	17	24	45	61	19	48
59	35	2	42	19	27	50	29	57
36	59	54	49	61	16	60	60	60
51	19	20	19	36	61	45	36	51
54	42	42	50	50	60	34	51	19
29	54	29	51	60	48	51	34	36
60	51	35	24	32	51	15	57	50

Table 8.8 (Continued)

Rank	1978	1979	1980	1981	1982	1983	1984	1985	1986
47	51	51	51	23	31	60	24	50	60
48	52	52	52	51	52	61	60	59	36
49	56	56	23	52	51	51	51	49	50
50	28	36	56	56	30	52	59	60	17
51	36	28	36	32	32	27	31	41	30
52	40	40	41	36	56	36	52	34	52
53	58	41	40	41	36	56	61	36	49
54	41	58	58	30	41	41	56	52	38
55	38	38	32	40	40	40	41	61	39
56	37	37	38	38	24	21	36	38	61
57	27	24	30	58	58	37	40	56	34
58	24	32	24	24	37	38	37	39	56
59	30	30	37	37	38	24	38	40	40
60	39	21	39	21	39	58	58	37	58
61	21	39	21	39	21	39	39	58	37

Source: Author's own calculations.

changes in others. For instance, a rise of the DRP ranking for Other Textiles (27) from 57th position in 1978 to 21st in 1995 could force all 36 sectors in between down one level. Thus, the structural changes in DRP rankings may be seen to be dominated by the large movers – that is, the rapidly descending and ascending sectors. Again, Table 8.8 shows that the rapidly ascending sectors are the unskilled labour-intensive manufacturing industries. At the bottom are the rapidly descending ones, many of which are agricultural and natural resource sectors.

The driving forces behind the structural changes in the DRP estimates for China's tradable goods-producing sectors stem from the ascendance of unskilled labour-intensive industries and the decline of natural resource and agricultural goods. The economic reforms have removed market distortions and granted sufficient autonomy to enterprises and trading corporations that have made the industries that use China's abundant resources more efficient and internationally competitive.

Individual Commodity Groups

How have the relative positions of individual tradable goods changed on the ladder of comparative advantage over the reform period? As before, we cluster all the 61 tradable goods into five groups according to their factor intensities and discuss individual commodities in each group in turn. We present only the ranking orders of the DRP estimates here, because it is relative position that reveals intertemporal changes of DRP estimates.[9]

Table 8.8 (Continued)

1987	1988	1989	1990	1991	1992	1993	1994	1995
57	36	34	29	29	34	57	48	34
55	50	51	57	51	36	38	39	29
50	60	57	36	17	32	39	30	39
17	57	50	34	49	57	36	38	49
38	29	60	61	34	38	16	11	17
52	52	36	60	57	39	52	15	16
49	34	61	52	52	49	48	52	15
30	61	52	35	38	17	35	16	35
61	38	38	40	39	52	49	35	30
39	30	56	56	35	40	30	49	52
56	40	40	38	40	30	16	17	38
34	56	30	37	56	35	56	56	37
40	39	37	30	30	37	40	40	56
58	37	39	39	37	56	37	37	40
37	58	58	58	58	58	58	58	58

Agricultural Products

The descending ranking of DRP estimates for 13 agricultural commodity groups are presented in Table 8.9. It can be seen that, except for Oil-bearing Crops (4), Vegetables (7), Forest Products (9) and Other Agricultural Products (13), all agricultural commodity groups show a declining DRP ranking order, indicating a rising comparative cost of production in these products. For instance, in 1978, one yuan worth of domestic primary factors put into paddy rice production could generate 2.15 yuan worth of US dollars added value while in 1995 the same input could only produce 1.55 yuan worth of US dollars. As a result, the DRP ranking order for rice production dropped from ninth position to 16th. In 1978, 12 agricultural commodities had a DRP estimate above unity, whereas in 1995, nine of them still did so. China has lost its comparative advantage in Wheat (2), Other Grains (3) and Meat (11) over the past two decades. More importantly, ranking positions have fallen sharply for many agricultural products for which China had a comparative advantage.

However, China has not lost comparative advantage in all agricultural products and has actually maintained its comparative advantage in agricultural products such as vegetables, fruit and forest products. China's advantage in unlimited supplies of rural unskilled labour may continue to contribute to the low comparative cost of producing in these more labour-intensive agricultural products.

In any case, losses are not irreversible. Given that China's domestic production costs remain constant, for instance, a rise in world grain prices

Table 8.9   DRP ranking order for agricultural products, 1978–95

Product	1978	1979	1980	1981	1982	1983	1984	1985
1. Paddy rice	9	11	10	7	8	10	11	13
2. Wheat	20	22	19	15	15	16	17	23
3. Other grains	18	19	17	17	20	24	21	30
4. Oil-bearing crops	11	17	16	20	19	12	8	7
5. Cotton	19	21	23	22	22	17	13	18
6. Other industrial crops	4	4	2	2	3	2	1	1
7. Vegetables	5	5	6	5	2	1	2	8
8. Fruits	13	14	15	19	18	15	22	29
9. Forest products	24	26	25	25	25	19	16	22
10. Wool and hides	8	7	4	3	7	7	5	4
11. Meat,etc.	3	3	3	1	1	5	4	6
12. Fish	1	2	5	4	4	3	10	16
13. Other agri. products	7	8	9	9	5	4	3	3

Source: Author's own calculations.

may lower the comparative cost of grain production in China again and therefore increase its comparative advantage. As indicated in the DRP estimates, wheat and other grains, for example, actually increased their comparative advantage ranking positions in some years. An increase in the world price relative to domestic price was certainly a contributing factor. With its huge population, China is unlikely to give up its grain production and rely solely on imports even if it may have lost comparative advantage in producing grains. When China increases its imports of grains, the world price of grains may increase, too, and domestic grain production may once again become internationally competitive.

Table 8.10   DRP ranking order for natural resource products, 1978–95

Product	1978	1979	1980	1981	1982	1983	1984	1985
14. Coal	10	15	12	12	10	8	6	5
15. Crude petroleum	15	9	8	6	6	9	9	11
16. Ferrous minerals	21	20	27	27	26	26	33	37
17. Non-ferrous minerals	37	37	36	38	39	38	42	46
18. Non-metal minerals	22	24	24	23	24	21	15	10
19. Timber	6	6	7	11	14	22	24	24

Source: Author's own calculations.

1986	1987	1988	1989	1990	1991	1992	1993	1994	1995
20	21	27	31	26	22	20	15	19	16
33	39	36	41	34	30	29	25	37	39
35	34	30	34	30	26	27	34	38	36
12	17	19	13	11	9	9	6	12	9
16	13	13	17	23	23	21	19	30	34
11	1	3	3	2	2	2	3	6	10
5	9	6	7	8	4	3	5	4	5
25	27	33	25	22	19	14	9	15	19
26	32	31	28	20	15	11	11	11	14
8	10	15	15	16	14	17	14	29	30
2	6	20	20	17	13	19	35	51	38
14	15	29	40	31	34	25	29	22	27
1	3	1	4	5	5	6	2	3	3

Natural Resource Goods

Table 8.10 presents the DRP ranking orders for natural resource goods. In 1978, China had comparative advantages in Coal (14), Crude Petroleum (15) and Timber (19) while, in 1995, it had comparative advantages only in Coal (14) and Non-metal Minerals (18). Except for Non-metal Minerals (18), all natural resource products had lost their DRP ranking positions during 1978–95, implying a fall in their comparative advantage. The highest fall is recorded in Timber (19) and Crude Petroleum (15). The DRP ranking for Coal (14) was relatively stable. The DRP ranking for Crude Petroleum (15) drops sharply with some unusual fluctuations, apparently due to the up-and-downs in the world petroleum market. The biggest decline in comparative advantage in this category occurred in Timber (19): a drop from sixth position to 44th over the period. A possible explanation may be found in the dramatic changes in the

1986	1987	1988	1989	1990	1991	1992	1993	1994	1995
4	4	4	2	3	3	7	13	14	13
32	29	26	19	15	24	31	46	52	53
37	36	37	37	33	36	42	51	54	52
50	50	32	29	40	49	54	57	57	51
9	11	8	12	12	12	12	22	13	8
29	37	43	38	43	41	38	33	40	44

domestic and world prices of timber. In 1978, timber was one of the cheapest industrial raw materials in China, compared with the world market. In 1995, the domestic timber price had moved up closer to the world price.

Physical Capital-intensive Goods

As China does not have abundant capital, it could be expected that China is unlikely to have a comparative advantage in capital-intensive goods. However, this is true only in a general sense. As indicated in this study, if individual products are considered, the comparative cost structure of capital-intensive goods is more complicated than expected (Table 8.11).

The DRP estimates for most products in this group were below unity during the entire period studied. These included Petroleum Products (32), various chemicals products (34, 35, 36, 38, 40 and 42) and most metals and their products (48, 49, 50). However, some products in this group, such as Coal Products (33), Plastic Articles (42), Cement (43), Glass (44), Ceramic Products (45) and Iron (47), had maintained or gained comparative advantage over the period concerned. This phenomenon reflects the complexity of China's comparative advantage structure. One obvious explanation lies in the fact that China has relatively rich endowments of the natural resources used as key inputs in those industries–such as coal, iron ore and many non-metal minerals. Another possible explanation may be found in the established industrial structure. China had invested extensively in capital-intensive heavy industries for a long time prior to the reform

Table 8.11   DRP ranking order for physical capital-intensive product, 1978–95

Product	1978	1979	1980	1981	1982	1983	1984	1985
32. Petrol products	38	58	55	51	51	40	32	27
33. Coal products	25	13	20	24	28	18	31	33
34. Inorganic chemicals	36	32	30	29	30	34	46	52
35. Chem. Fertilizers	29	27	29	32	45	35	40	38
36. Organic chemicals	51	50	51	52	53	52	56	53
38. Other chemicals	55	55	56	56	59	58	59	56
40. Chemical fibres	52	52	53	55	55	55	57	59
42. Plastic articles	41	40	41	41	37	36	36	39
43. Cement	16	16	13	13	12	11	12	14
44. Glass	26	25	21	16	11	20	18	19
45. Ceramic products	23	23	22	21	21	27	25	15
47. Iron	14	12	14	14	16	13	23	12
48. Steel	32	38	35	35	32	29	28	41
49. Non-ferrous metals	42	41	40	42	43	43	44	49
50. Metal products	34	36	34	36	38	44	45	47

Source: Author's own calculations.

period. Although these investments seemed premature in the sense that they were well in advance of China's level of development and were sponsored at high social opportunity costs, these industries, once established, could provide certain gains for the production of some capital-intensive products. This was particularly the case for those products that require only standard technologies and can be produced on a massive scale–such as iron, steel, cement and glass. China's vast internal market also permits these industries to take advantage of economies of scale. In this respect, the impact of the existing industrial structure, or past investments, on China's current comparative advantage should not be overlooked. It could actually help to determine in which industries China has a potential for import competing or substituting.[10]

Overall, the DRP rankings for most products in this group were quite stable over the period studied compared with that for agricultural and natural resource goods.

Human Capital-intensive Goods

Unlike physical capital-intensive goods, the DRP estimates for human capital-intensive goods demonstrate that China had a clear comparative disadvantage in these goods. This group consists of various engineering products requiring not only physical capital equipment but, more importantly, human capital or skills and sophisticated and rapidly changing technologies that are usually the fruit of long-term research and development (R&D).

1986	1987	1988	1989	1990	1991	1992	1993	1994	1995
23	33	40	36	39	46	49	39	34	35
38	28	16	5	4	6	13	16	17	11
57	58	53	47	50	51	47	44	45	47
30	31	41	46	54	56	58	54	55	54
48	42	47	52	49	43	48	50	43	45
54	51	55	55	57	54	51	48	50	57
59	59	57	57	55	57	56	59	59	60
40	40	44	44	41	37	35	37	23	22
34	25	24	18	21	21	23	17	26	26
18	20	22	14	19	20	22	21	25	32
10	7	11	21	25	29	40	43	33	25
21	18	10	11	9	18	18	38	24	12
39	38	34	30	29	38	45	53	47	40
53	53	35	33	42	50	53	55	56	50
49	49	48	50	44	44	39	41	39	46

Table 8.12   DRP ranking order for human capital-intensive products,1978–95

Product	1978	1979	1980	1981	1982	1983	1984	1985
37. Household chemicals	56	56	59	59	58	57	58	60
39. Medicines	60	61	60	61	60	61	61	58
51. Agri.machinery	47	47	47	48	49	49	49	45
52. Industrial equipment	48	48	48	49	48	50	52	54
53. Power equipment	40	39	39	37	34	32	29	32
54. Hshd. mech./elect.gds	30	34	37	40	40	41	41	40
55. Railway equipment	35	35	33	33	35	39	43	36
56. Motor vehicles	49	49	50	50	52	53	54	57
57. Ships	31	33	38	34	33	37	37	42
58. Oth transp. equipment	53	54	54	57	57	60	60	61
59. Other enging. prods.	45	45	43	44	41	42	50	48
60. Electronic products	43	43	42	46	46	47	48	50
61. Hshd.electronics	44	44	45	45	44	48	53	55

Source: Author's own calculations.

The situation changed during the reform period, especially in the 1990s (Table 8.12). Although many products in this group remain comparatively disadvantaged, a number of products have moved quickly up the ladder of DRP rankings. These include Medicines (39), Power Station Equipment (53), Household Mechanical and Electrical Goods (54), Railway Equipment (55), Other Engineering Products (58) and Household Electronics (61). Among them, Power Equipment (53), Household Mechanical and Electrical Goods (54) and Railway Equipment (56) are found to have a DRP estimate above unity by 1995 and Other Engineering Products (82) and Household Electronics (61) a DRP estimate very close to unity.

Also found in this group are those products in which China has least comparative advantage. Among them are Other Transport Equipment (58), Motor Vehicles (56), Household Chemicals (37) and Industrial Equipment (52). In these industries, China certainly has a long way to go in catching up with the developed world. As far as comparative advantage is concerned, there have been little changes in these industries as revealed in their DRP ranking results.

Unskilled Labour-intensive Goods

The DRP estimates of comparative advantage for unskilled labour-intensive products are mixed, as shown in Table 8.13. In the early years of the reform period, most products in this group had a DRP estimate below unity and some even had a negative value-added. This was apparently brought about by distortions in the domestic goods and factors markets. Many labour-intensive

1986	1987	1988	1989	1990	1991	1992	1993	1994	1995
61	61	60	59	58	60	59	60	60	58
55	56	59	60	60	55	52	49	48	49
43	43	46	48	45	48	46	45	44	43
52	52	52	54	53	53	55	52	53	56
31	30	28	32	27	25	24	20	16	18
44	44	45	42	36	33	32	28	18	17
45	48	38	35	32	31	28	26	20	23
58	57	58	56	56	58	60	58	58	59
46	47	50	49	48	52	50	47	46	41
60	60	61	61	61	61	61	61	61	61
41	41	42	39	38	35	30	24	32	37
47	46	49	51	52	45	44	42	42	42
56	55	54	53	51	42	43	40	36	33

products use agricultural products as their major intermediate inputs. The relatively high price for the final products and low price for the intermediate inputs encouraged inefficient use of intermediate inputs in many manufacturing industries. So if estimated at border prices, the added value for some labour-intensive manufactured products was very low or even negative, which led to negative DRP estimates. On the other hand, distortions in domestic factors markets also contributed to the low DRP estimates for this group of products because the wage rate for unskilled labour in the state industries was above its marginal product, as indicated in Chapter 7.

The situation has gradually changed as reforms proceed. Price reforms and market competition have substantially reduced domestic distortions in the factors and goods markets. The introduction of new technologies, especially those embodied in the imports of capital equipment or foreign direct investment (FDI), have also played an important role in increasing productivity in these labour-intensive sectors. The DRP estimates have shown that many unskilled labour-intensive goods have gained comparative advantage over the past two decades. These include some processed food, various textiles, knitted goods, clothing, cultural goods and rubber products. By 1995, China had a comparative advantage in most labour-intensive manufactured goods. However, there are some exceptions. For instance, the results show that China never had any comparative advantage in Paper (30). It also seems to have been losing comparative advantage in such goods as Furniture (29). These goods are all related to timber, one of the scarcest natural resources in China. As mentioned earlier, China has lost comparative advantage in timber production, and this has certainly contributed to the fall in DRP estimates for downstream industries such as paper and furniture-making. It seems feasible to expect that, as China's comparative advantage in

Table 8.13   DRP ranking order for unskilled labour-intensive products, 1978–95

Product	1978	1979	1980	1981	1982	1983	1984	1985
20. Sugar, tobacco, spirit	27	28	28	28	29	30	19	21
21. Other processed food	61	60	61	60	61	56	38	31
22. Cotton textiles	17	18	18	18	17	25	20	20
23. Wool textiles	46	46	49	47	42	31	30	25
24. Hemp textiles	58	57	58	58	56	59	47	43
25. Silk textiles	12	10	11	10	9	6	7	2
26. Knitted goods	28	29	31	31	31	28	27	17
27. Other textiles	57	30	26	26	23	51	39	28
28. Clothing	50	51	46	39	27	14	14	9
29. Furniture	2	1	1	8	13	23	26	26
30. Paper	59	59	57	54	50	46	35	44
31. Cultural goods	39	42	44	43	47	45	51	35
41. Rubber products	54	53	52	53	54	54	55	51
46. Other bldg materials	33	31	32	30	36	33	34	34

Source: Author's own calculations.

agricultural and natural resource products diminishes, those labour-intensive industries using agricultural and other natural resources as major inputs may also face the prospect of falling comparative advantage: Table 8.13 show the DRP ranking for processed foods, cotton and wool textiles all declining after dramatic rises in the 1980s. Unless a rapid rise in productivity occurs, brought about possibly by upgrading technologies in these industries, the declining trend of comparative advantage is likely to continue. However, for other labour-intensive manufacturing industries, China is expected to maintain its comparative advantage for a long time.

SOURCES OF CHANGES IN DRP MEASURES

Changes in DRP estimates over time are caused by four factors: changes in border–domestic price ratios, the use of intermediate inputs, factor prices and the use of factors. In this section, we propose a decomposition to trace the sources of changing comparative advantage in China's tradable goods over the reform period.

Suppose that the DRP estimate for tradable good j for time period t is expressed as

$$DRP_{jt} = \frac{p_{jt}^B - \sum_i a_{ijt}^D \, p_{it}^B}{\sum_s a_{sjt}^F \, p_{st}^s} = \frac{A_{jt}}{B_{jt}} \qquad (8.3)$$

1986	1987	1988	1989	1990	1991	1992	1993	1994	1995
15	19	39	43	35	32	37	36	31	28
28	24	14	10	14	11	10	10	10	20
17	14	17	22	24	27	26	23	28	24
19	23	7	8	7	7	8	8	9	15
22	26	21	23	46	40	34	18	7	4
3	2	2	1	1	1	1	1	1	1
13	8	12	16	18	17	15	7	5	6
6	12	9	26	28	39	41	31	35	21
7	5	5	6	10	10	5	4	2	2
36	45	51	45	47	47	36	27	41	48
51	54	56	58	59	59	57	56	49	55
24	16	18	9	6	8	4	12	8	7
42	35	25	27	37	28	33	30	21	29
27	22	23	24	13	16	16	32	27	31

where a_{ijt}^D is the share of intermediate input i directly and indirectly used to produce tradable good j in time period t; a_{sjt}^F is the share of primary factor s directly or indirectly used in producing tradable good j in time period t.[11]

The rate of change for DRP over a certain period of time can be obtained by taking logarithms of the variables and differentiating with respect to time, which gives

$$\frac{d\ln(A_{jt}/B_{jt})}{dt} = \frac{p_{jt}^B}{A_{jt}}\frac{d\ln p_{jt}^B}{dt} - \sum_i \frac{a_{ijt}^D \, p_{it}^B}{A_{jt}}\frac{d\ln p_{it}^B}{dt} - \sum_i \frac{a_{ijt}^D \, p_{it}^B}{A_{jt}}\frac{d\ln a_{ijt}^D}{dt}$$
$$- \sum_s \frac{a_{sjt}^F \, p_{st}^S}{B_{jt}}\frac{d\ln p_{st}^S}{dt} - \sum_s \frac{a_{sjt}^F \, p_{st}^S}{B_{jt}}\frac{d\ln a_{sjt}^F}{dt} \tag{8.4}$$

The above equation is in continuous time. The discrete approximation, taking the rates of change over a given period of the variables, indicated by a dot over the variable may be written as

$$d\dot{r}p_{jt} = a_{jt}\,\dot{p}_{jt}^B + \sum_i b_{ijt}\,\dot{p}_{it}^B + \sum_i b_{ijt}\,\dot{a}_{ijt}^D + \sum_s c_{sjt}\,\dot{p}_{st}^S + \sum_s c_{sjt}\,\dot{a}_{sjt}^F$$

where

$$a_{jt} = \frac{p_{jt}^B}{A_{jt}}; b_{ijt} = -\frac{a_{ijt}^D \, p_{it}^B}{A_{jt}}; c_{sjt} = -\frac{a_{sjt}^F \, p_{st}^S}{B_{jt}} \tag{8.5}$$

Equation (8.5) shows that the growth rate of DRP for a given tradable good per time period is equal to the sum of the rate of growth of the price ratio for tradable good, p_{jt}^B, *minus* the rate of growth of the tradable intermediate input coefficient, a_{ijt}^D; *minus* the rate of growth of the shadow-price conversion factor for primary factor, p_{st}^S, and *minus* the rate of growth of the primary factor coefficient, a_{sjt}^F. As the information on the growth rates of these variables and the coefficients are known, we can actually derive the contribution of each of these four factors to the overall DRP changes over time.

We now apply (8.5) to the DRP estimates for 1978 and 1995, to reveal the sources of changes in comparative advantage in China's tradable

Table 8.14   Sources of changes in DRP estimates for tradable goods 1978–95
(%)

Product	Goods price (1)	Goods input (2)	Factor price (3)	Factor input (4)	DRP changes (5)
1. Paddy rice	36.8	11.0	57.3	-5.1	–
2. Wheat	9.0	-2.8	44.7	49	–
3. Other grains	3.7	13.2	50.7	32.4	–
4. Oil-bearing crops	-333.8	28.2	229.1	176.5	–
5. Cotton	-17.4	18.1	91.2	8.1	–
6. Other industrial crops	39.7	1.1	39.3	19.9	–
7. Vegetables	64.4	-1.3	62.1	-25.2	–
8. Fruits	86.8	28.4	45.7	-60.9	–
9. Forest products	109.7	-15.7	-4.7	10.7	+
10. Wool and hides	56.8	49.1	32.7	-38.6	–
11. Meat, etc.	61.9	8.4	17.3	12.3	–
12. Fish	75.2	4	24.6	-3.7	–
13. Other agri. products	5.2	-6.2	61.4	39.6	+
14. Coal	65.6	22.2	11.7	0.5	–
15. Crude petroleum	92.9	9.8	12.7	-15.3	–
16. Ferrous minerals	81.6	39.3	12.8	-33.7	–
17. Non-ferrous minerals	273.5	-206.8	9.0	24.3	+
18. Non-metal minerals	134.7	-36.7	-32.4	-34.3	+
19. Timber	98.5	8.9	9.4	-16.7	–
20. Sugar, tobacco, alcohol	130.7	-35.5	-17.8	22.6	+
21. Other processed food	70.5	11.8	2.9	14.8	+
22. Cotton textiles	-86.5	114.4	138	-65.8	+
23. Wool textiles	102.2	-1.8	-0.7	0.3	+
24. Hemp textiles	102.9	-3.6	2.6	-1.9	+
25. Silk textiles	139.3	-19.5	-49.4	29.7	+
26. Knitted goods	111.1	-9.9	-5.5	4.3	+
27. Other textiles	57.1	38.2	2.3	2.4	+
28. Clothing	92.1	7.8	0.1	0	+
29. Furniture	92.0	18.0	6.7	-16.7	–
30. Paper	69.8	27.1	5.5	-2.4	+
31. Cultural goods	97.5	-0.4	-0.6	3.5	+
32. Petrol products	124.4	-20.7	-6.9	3.2	+
33. Coal products	60.7	69.8	-3.3	-27.2	+
34. Inorganic chemicals	153.8	-67.4	-16.2	29.7	+

Table 8.14 (Continued)

Product	Goods price (1)	Goods input (2)	Factor price (3)	Factor input (4)	DRP changes (5)
35. Chem. fertilizers	50.1	46.6	61.9	-58.6	–
36. Organic chemicals	105.5	-3.1	2.1	-4.5	+
37. Household chemicals	40.3	51.9	3.1	4.7	+
38. Other chemicals	88.2	19.9	3.6	-11.7	+
39. Medicines	60.8	32.4	5.4	1.3	+
40. Chemical fibres	111.9	-12.4	13.5	-13.0	–
41. Rubber manufactures	118.8	-18.8	2.1	-2.1	+
42. Plastic articles	107.5	-9.0	-1.9	3.4	+
43. Cement	2.2	73.1	115.5	-90.8	–
44. Glass	152.8	-49.8	-24.9	21.8	+
45. Ceramic products	145.2	-30.6	-22.8	8.2	+
46. Other bldg materials	118.1	-14.7	-7.8	4.5	+
47. Iron	253.1	371.5	-22.9	-501.8	+
48. Steel	125.4	-18.2	-16.6	9.4	+
49. Non-ferrous metals	157.0	-55.0	-22.8	20.8	+
50. Metal products	196.4	-125.2	-27.4	56.2	+
51. Agri. Machinery	114.6	-16.1	0.3	1.3	+
52. Industrial equipment	130.6	-32.9	-0.1	2.4	+
53. Power equipment	106.6	-10.4	-0.9	4.8	+
54. Hshd. mech./elect.gds	116.8	-25.8	-7.7	16.6	+
55. Railway equipment	107.1	-6.9	0.1	-0.3	+
56. Motor vehicles	150.4	-49.9	0.1	-0.5	–
57. Ships	116.4	-30.6	7.8	6.4	+
58. Both transp. equipment	301.5	-106.2	-36.2	-59.1	+
59. Other enging. prods.	114.4	-17.0	-0.6	3.2	+
60. Electronic products	109.3	-24.7	2.3	13.1	+
61. Hshd electronics	98.5	-2.8	2.6	1.7	+

Note: Column(5) shows the direction of DRP changes: + increase; - decrease.
Source: Author's own calculations.

goods-producing sectors. The results are reported in Table 8.14. Column (1) shows the percentage contribution of relative price changes to the DRP variation over the period 1978–95, Column (2) shows the contribution of the tradable intermediate inputs, Column (3) the contribution of primary-factor shadow-price conversion factors and Column (4) the contribution of primary-factor inputs. The sum of the contributions of the four factors is 100 per cent. Column (5) shows the direction in which the DRP estimates changed over the entire period.

Taking Paddy Rice (1) as an example, the DRP estimate is 2.15 for 1978 and 1.55 for 1995, implying a negative growth rate. Table 8.14 shows that factor-price changes were responsible for 57 per cent of the variations in the DRP estimates and the changes in the relative prices of tradable goods were responsible for 36.8 per cent. The changes in tradable intermediate inputs also contributed to 11 per cent of the DRP downfall. However, the changes in factor inputs increased the DRP by 5 per cent. This may indicates some factor-saving technical progress occurring in rice production during the period. Overall, the factor shadow-price changes contributed the most to the decline in the DRP estimates.

It can be seen in Table 8.14 that, for most tradable goods, changes in the relative prices dominate the variations in the DRP estimates over the period. Except a few, they all contribute positively to the DRP changes. The changes in the shadow prices of primary factors contribute also to the changes in the DRP estimates. In the case of many agricultural products, it contributes to the fall in their comparative advantage as shown in the fall in their DRP estimates, whereas for many capital-intensive manufactured products–such as iron, steel and metal products – it contributes negatively to their DRP rises. Compared with the relative price changes, the intermediate inputs of tradable goods and factors contribute less to the changes in the DRP estimates for most tradable goods. The decomposition results seem to indicate that the domestic economic reforms in tradable goods prices and factor markets are most responsible for the changes in China's comparative structure over the past two decades. The changes in the domestic production structure–especially technical progress in the use of intermediate input and primary factors–have also helped to shape China's comparative advantage structure, but their role varies considerably across the tradable industries. Some industries recorded high productivity gains that led to an increase in DRP ranking positions while other industries recorded increased use of intermediate inputs or factors which contributed to a fall in their ranking positions.

CONCLUSION

The DRP estimation of China's comparative advantage indicates a significant improvement in the international competitiveness of Chinese tradable goods producing industries during the period 1978–95. Structural changes in China's comparative advantage were mainly brought about by economic reforms and the realignment of a previously irrational domestic price structures with that of the international market place. Compared with 1978, the structure of China's comparative advantage in 1995 seemed to be more in line with its factor endowments. Economic reforms have provided a fertile environment for Chinese industries to explore fully and more efficiently all of the country's available resources.

APPENDIX

Table 8A.1 Concordance between the 69-sector input–output table and the 117-sector input–output table of China

Code Sector	117 sector code
Tradables (61)	
1. Paddy rice	1101
2. Wheat	1101
3. Other grains	1101
4. Oil-bearing crops	1109
5. Cotton	1109
6. Other industrial crops	1109
7. Vegetables	1109
8. Fruits	1109
9. Forest products	1200
10. Wool and hides	1300
11. Meat, eggs and milk	1300
12. Fish	1500
13. Other agri. products	1400
14. Coal	02100 022 00
15. Crude petroleum	03100 032 00
16. Ferrous minerals	4100
17. Non-ferrous minerals	4200
18. Non-metallic minerals	05100, 05200
19. Timber	5300
20. Sugar, tobacco and alcohol	06105, 06201, 06300
21. Other Processed food	06101, 06102, 06103, 06104, 06109, 06209, 06400
22. Cotton textiles	7001
23. Wool textiles	7200
24. Hemp textiles	7003
25. Silk textiles	7004
26. Knitted goods	7005
27. Other textiles	7009
28. Clothing	08100, 08200
29. Furniture	09100, 09200
30. Paper	10100
31. Cultural goods	10200, 10300
32. Petroleum products	12000
33. Coal products	13001, 13002
34. Inorganic chemicals	14101
35. Chemical fertilizers	14102, 14103
36. Organic chemicals	14104
37. Household chemicals	14105
38. Other chemicals	14106, 14109
39. Medicines	14200
40. Chemical fibres	14300
41. Rubber manufactures	14401, 14402

Table 8A.1 (Continued)

Code Sector	117 sector code
42. Plastic articles	14501, 14502
43. Cement	15001 ,15002
44. Glass	15004
45. Ceramic products	15005, 15006
46. Other bldg. materials	15003, 15009
47. Iron	16100
48. Steel	16100
49. Non-ferrous metals	16200
50. Metal products	17001, 17002
51. Agricultural machinery	18004
52. Industrial equipment	18002, 18003, 18006
53. Power station equipment	18001, 20001
54. Household mech. and elec. goods	18005, 20002, 24002
55. Railway equipment	19001
56. Motor vehicles	19002
57. Ships	19003
58. Other trans. equipment	19004, 19009
59. Other enging. products	18009, 20009, 22000, 24001
60. Electronic products	21001, 21009
61. Household electronics	21002
Non-tradables (8)	
62. Electricity and water	05400, 11000
63. Repair	23000
64. Construction	25000
65. Transport	26101, 26102, 26103, 26104
	26105, 26200, 29001, 29002
	29003, 29004
66. Commerce	27101, 27102, 27200, 28000
67. Public utilities	30100, 30200, 30300
68. Finance	32001, 32002
69. Other services	31101, 31102, 31103, 31201,
	31202, 31301, 31302, 33000

Source: State Statistical Bureau, Department of Balances of National Economy and Office of National Input–Output Survey (1991).

9 China's Trade Patterns and Comparative Advantage

Was China's foreign trade consistent with its comparative advantage in the late 1970s before the economic reform process began? Has the reform process led to a convergence between China's trade patterns and its underlying comparative advantage? The net export performance ratio (NEPR) and the domestic resource productivity (DRP) measures estimated in the previous chapters allow a further investigation into the relationships between China's trade patterns and comparative advantage. This analysis will reveal the impact of China's economic reforms on allocative efficiency in the tradable goods producing sectors.

COMPARATIVE ADVANTAGE AND TRADE PATTERNS: THE DRP AND THE NEPR

Trade theory suggests that if a country employs neutral trade policies its trade will follow its comparative advantage. In so doing, the country will be able to maximize the gains from trade. This also implies that domestic resources will be allocated across industries according to the country's comparative advantage. The relationship between a country's comparative advantage, trade patterns and production structure can be illustrated using Figure 9.1. This is a simple two-sector Heckscher–Ohlin model of a small economy. In isolation, the economy produces and consumes two goods X_1 and X_2 at point Y_a of the production possibility frontier on the domestic relative price line P_a. Suppose that the opportunity cost of producing X_1 is higher in the country than in the world, implying that the international relative price line P_f is flatter than P_a. The country, therefore, has a comparative advantage in X_2 and a disadvantage in X_1. Given the existing production structure, if the country begins to trade with the rest of the world according to its comparative advantage– that is exports X_2 and imports X_1– it could increase its welfare by consuming at C_t, and moving from the social indifference curve U_a to a higher curve U_t. This gain, however, is limited and obtained only when the domestic resources are immobile between the sectors and hence production remains at Y_a.

Assuming all prices are competitive, comparative advantage in this model is determined by the difference in the relative commodity prices between the

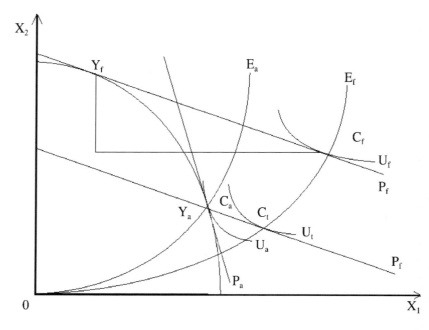

Figure 9.1 Relationship between comparative advantage, trade patterns and the structure of production

home country in its pre-trade equilibrium and the rest of the world. It is this difference that shapes the optimum pattern of trade.

Although the home country can still gain from trade whilst keeping its production structure intact, to maximize the gains from trade, domestic resources must be reallocated in accordance with comparative advantage. It requires the trade to expand. Without adjusting its domestic production, a country has a limited capacity to expand trade. This is illustrated in Figure 9.1. As the export of X_2 in exchange for X_1 is beneficial for the country, the production structure should be rearranged so that the production of X_2 increases. This is shown in the movement of the production point from Y_a along the production possibility frontier toward Y_f. The change in the structure of production enables the home country to export more X_2 in exchange for more imports of X_1 and further increase its welfare. As trade expands and domestic resources are continuously reallocated between the sectors in the way described above, the country's welfare improves. The maximum gain is achieved when the country produces at point Y_f and consumes at C_f on the international relative price line P_f.

The maximization of gains from trade is associated with efficient resource allocation among sectors. Resource-allocation efficiency in production may be detected by changes in a country's trade patterns in relation to its underlying comparative advantage structure.

When an economy moves from isolation to open trade or from a system of central planning to free markets, trade patterns are expected to move toward those which are in line with its comparative advantage. As shown in the previous chapter, policy changes may also alter a country's domestic production and, therefore, its underlying international comparative advantage structure. In the process of significant policy shifts, a growing correlation between the patterns of trade and the structures of comparative advantage can be seen as a sign of positive gains from trade; changes in production structure may follow later. As induced by trade, these changes can be detected by variations in the trade patterns: a comparison of trade patterns and comparative advantage reveals the impact of policy shifts.

In this study, the NEPR is descriptive of actual trade patterns and the DRP is a proxy for comparative advantage. It is expected that the NEPR estimates will correlate with the DRP if domestic resources are allowed to be allocated efficiently under the emerging market condition. Other things being equal, the NEPR estimates may be expressed as a function of the DRP estimates for tradable goods, that is,

$$NEPR = f(DRP) \tag{9.1}$$

This relationship between the DRP and the NEPR estimates is valid in an economy which is in the process of transition from a non-free trade equilibrium, characterized by various distortions in the domestic market, to a free trade equilibrium. In a non-free trade situation, the domestic factor shadow costs of producing a given good are usually not identical to its value-added measured at the border prices. A DRP estimate above (below) unity for a tradable good indicates a low (high) opportunity cost of domestic production relative to its corresponding international value-added price. It implies that this tradable good should be encouraged for export (import) if domestic resources are to be utilized more efficiently. The degree of correlation between the DRP and the NEPR can thus be viewed as an indication of resource allocation efficiency in tradable goods producing industries.

The relationship between the DRP and NEPR may be illustrated in Figure 9.2. The horizontal axis refers to the DRP and the vertical axis refers to the NEPR. The upward sloping line illustrates the convergence of the DRP and the NEPR estimates, which implies a perfect correlation. As we know, a DRP measure larger than unity implies a comparative advantage and a DRP measure below unity indicates a disadvantage. On the other hand, a NEPR estimate greater than zero implies that the country is a net exporter in the world market for the good concerned and, otherwise, it is a net importer. The figure could thus be divided into four quadrants. Commodities with a DRP measure above unity have an international comparative advantage and are,

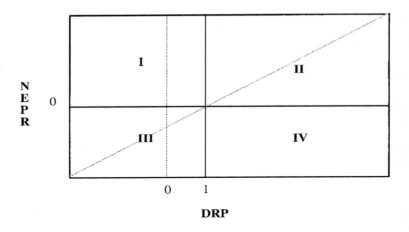

Figure 9.2 Relationship between DRP and NEPR

accordingly, expected to be net exporters; so positive NEPR measures are expected. These commodities should be located in Quadrant II. Commodities with a DRP measure below unity have a comparative disadvantage and should be net importers. The negative NEPR estimates should lie in Quadrant III. A convergence line could be fitted in the figure to show the expected correlation between the DRP and NEPR estimates. Formally, the relationship between them for a particular period of time may be expressed as a linear function, that is,

$$NEPR = a + b(DRP) \qquad (9.2)$$

where a is the intercept and b is the slope of the convergence line.

In general, a high DRP estimate should be associated with a high value of NEPR estimate, and a low DRP with a low NEPR if domestic resources are allocated efficiently across tradable goods-producing industries. In a competitive market environment, the high DRP estimate for a good will eventually lead to a high NEPR record for it. In the case of efficient resource allocation, the measures of DRP and NEPR for all tradable goods should be found close to the upward-sloped convergence line in Figure 9.2.

In the real world, however, various distortions may prevent countries from trading with each other in a manner that accords with their respective potential comparative advantages. As a result, the observed trade patterns may not follow exactly a country's comparative advantage as indicated by the convergence line in Figure 9.2. The deviation of trade patterns from comparative advantage could be used in detecting the degree of resource-allocation inefficiency in the tradable goods-producing industries.

In a distorted economy, the domestic and international prices for tradable goods could diverge so greatly that the DRP estimates for some tradable goods might be a long way from unity. In the extreme cases, value-added for certain tradables may even be negative if their distorted domestic production were conducted under free trade prices. This may result in a negative DRP estimate for certain tradable commodities. With the distorted market signals, domestic firms are unlikely to make correct decisions about their foreign trade transactions. In addition, trade flows may be even more irregular and diverted from underlying comparative advantage if the government intervened in enterprises' trade decisions or sought direct control over foreign trade business, as used to be the case in China. In such circumstances, commodities could be either over-traded (excessively exported or imported) or under-traded (heavily protected domestic production). As a result, it is unlikely for the DRP and NEPR estimates to be correlated closely with each other. One expected outcome of economic reforms is that domestic relative prices tend to gradually fall in line with international prices and recorded NEPR estimates are more likely to correlate with DRP estimates.

As mentioned in Chapter 5, in the presence of serious distortions, the DRP estimates may vary widely across tradable goods. As a country moves from distortion to a free trade equilibrium, on the other hand, the DRP estimates will move toward unity. This will have the impact of rotating the convergence line in Figure 9.2 back toward the vertical line through the horizontal axis at unity. The slope of the convergence line in Figure 9.2 could therefore be used as an indicator of the seriousness of domestic distortions as well as how closely an economy is moving toward a free trade equilibrium. The ideal convergence line should be vertical and coincide with the vertical line which goes through unity on the horizontal axis in Figure 9.2. However, this would require some rigid conditions, such as identical technologies across countries and full factor-price equalization, which are unlikely to be satisfied in the real world. The observed convergence line is therefore expected to lie somewhere outside the vertical line.

The movement of DRP estimates towards unity over time as an economy moves toward free trade may also be accompanied by an increase in the correlation between DRP and NEPR estimates. On the one hand, as the DRP measures for all tradable goods move closer to unity the NEPR estimates tend to converge towards the DRP estimates. On the other hand, in the process of moving toward free market and open trade, the comparative advantage structure will change, too. This change may point to the direction of fuller and more efficient utilization of a country's most abundant resources. The two measures may converge toward each other. In other words, the degree of correlation between the two estimates will rise as the economy opens up because domestic prices will gradually reflect the true social costs so that foreign trade decisions are made more closely in accordance with a country's underlying comparative advantage. Domestic tradable goods producers also respond to the changing price signals by moving resources toward the industries with the lowest opportunity costs and expand their exports. The two processes reinforce each other and push the trade pattern and comparative advantage structures to converge over time. In the optimal case of perfect correlation, the NEPR estimates for tradable goods will all lie on the convergence line and their correlation coefficient will equal one. In the real world, however, recorded NEPR estimates are expected to lie somewhere around the convergence line because not all goods have equally high elasticity of supplies.

In the next section, we will apply the above analysis to China. The correlation coefficients between the estimates of China's DRP and NEPR over the period 1978–95 will be examined in an attempt to find out whether, after two decades of intensive economic reforms, resource-allocation efficiency in China's tradable goods-producing industries has indeed improved as indicated by its increasing trade specialization.

CHINA'S TRADE PATTERNS AND COMPARATIVE ADVANTAGE

If the efficiency of resource allocation in China's trade sector has improved through the process of economic reforms, two changes in the DRP and NEPR estimates should be visible over time:

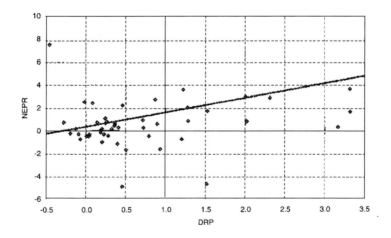

Figure 9.3 DRP and NEPR estimates for China's tradable goods, 1978
Sources : Tables 4A.2 and 8.1.

- NEPR estimates should become more closely correlated with DRP estimates as firms increasingly based their trade decisions on market signals instead of central plans.
- The dispersion of DRP estimates should have fallen as the economy opened up to free trade and the domestic and the world relative price differentials fell. The observed convergence line should have rotated toward the vertical line in terms of Figure.9.2.

We start our analysis with a visual comparison of the relationship between the DRP and NEPR measures for three representative years, 1978, 1987 and 1995. Each of these years represents a different period: 1978 represents the pre-reform era, 1987 the first 10 years of economic reforms and 1995 the latest developments of economic reforms.

The first expected change, correlation between the DRP and NEPR estimates, could be analyzed by plotting the DRP and NEPR estimates for all tradable goods for 1978 (Figure 9.3). A glance reveals that tradable goods are spread so widely that little correlation can be found between the DRP and NEPR estimates. More specifically, China exported 22 categories of goods for which it did not have comparative advantage (*DRP* < 1) and imported four groups of goods which it had comparative advantage (*DRP* > 1): these goods can be seen in Quadrants I and IV of Figure 9.3.[1] As a DRP measure of unity delineates comparative advantage and disadvantage, these 26 groups of commodities were traded against China's comparative advantage. At the 1978 price, the 22 exports accounted for 45 per cent of China's total exports while the four imports accounted for 18 per cent of total imports.

These results are not surprising because, at that time, the centrally planned trade system was firmly in place. Production and trade decisions were almost exclusively made through plans and, as a result, resource flows between industries were not guided by market signals or profitability.

Since the early 1980s, foreign trade corporations and tradable goods producers have had more freedom in the decision-making process.[2] Foreign direct investments (FDI) in production for exports have also had a substantial impact on the economy, greatly stimulating the growth of exports in recent years. However we need to determine whether China's trade patterns have changed in the direction of converging towards or diverging away from its comparative advantage in order to evaluate the real impact of economic reforms on resource allocation efficiency in China's tradable industries.

To seek an answer to this question, we compare China's trade pattern with its comparative advantage for 1987 and 1995, respectively, in the same manner as for 1978. The DRP measures of comparative advantage and the NEPR measures of trade patterns for 1987 and 1995 are plotted in Figures 9.4 and 9.5, respectively. The difference between Figure 9.4 and Figure 9.3 is impressive. The spread of tradable goods has narrowed substantially and

China's Trade Patterns

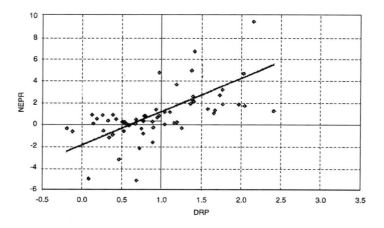

Figure 9.4   DRP and NEPR estimates for China's tradable goods, 1987
Sources: Tables 4A.2 and 8.1.

most goods have moved closer to the regression line. A clear correlation between the estimates of DRP and NEPR for tradable goods emerged over this period.

Figure 9.4 indicates that the number of goods or groups of goods traded against comparative advantage fell from 26 to 17. The number of imported goods with a DRP estimate above unity remained four.[3] But, the number of exported goods with a DRP estimate below unity declined from 22 to 13.[4]

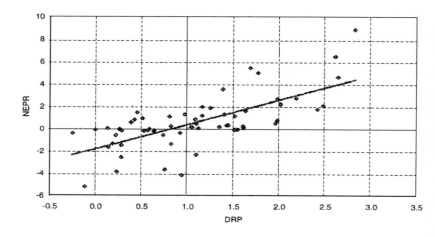

Figure 9.5 DRP and NEPR estimates for China's tradable goods, 1995
Sources: Tables 4A.2 and 8.1.

This suggests that improvements in efficiency were much greater in the export than in the import sector. Despite the number of imports traded against advantage remaining constant, the share of these goods in total imports fell to just 2 per cent while the proportion of the exports traded against comparative advantage in total exports declined to 24 per cent.

The convergence trend is further confirmed by our results for 1995 in Figure 9.5. The number of tradable goods traded against comparative advantage fell further from 17 to 10. The number of exported goods with DRP estimates lower than unity declined from 13 to just seven[5] while the number of the imported goods with DRP estimates higher than unity was reduced to three.[6] The former accounted for 13 per cent of the total exports, the latter for 4.6 per cent of the total imports.

The improvement in resource allocation in the trade sector can be verified more formally by examining the changes in the correlation coefficients between the DRP and NEPR measures for the whole period concerned. The normal correlation coefficient will be calculated for every year of this period. It should be noted, however, that the extent to which the two measures are correlated depends, to a considerable extent, on the classification of industries. If an industry in which these two measures are closely correlated is further divided into a number of sub-industries or commodity groups, the number of correlated observations could be arbitrarily increased and thus also the level of correlation coefficient. As the industries in this study are not divided evenly by size, a simple ordinary least squares (OLS) regression may bias the actual correlation between the DRP and NEPR estimates. To tackle this problem, the weighted least squares (WLS) estimation is also used in calculating correlation coefficients with the sectoral gross and net output values (value-added) as the weights. The correlation coefficients are derived from the regression of (9.2). The estimated results for weighted and unweighted correlation coefficients between the DRP and NEPR estimates for the whole period from the OLS and WLS regressions are reported in Table 9.1.

The three estimated correlation coefficients are quite similar for most of the years concerned. The correlation coefficients between the DRP and NEPR estimates are between 0.199 and 0.272 in 1978, indicating very little correlation between the two sets. This result implies that, at that time, China's trade specialization was not based on its international comparative advantage. As shown in Table 9.1, all three sets of estimates after 1978 indicate a steady convergence between China's patterns of trade and its comparative advantage. During the period from 1978 to 1995, the correlation coefficient between estimates of the DRP and NEPR rose from 0.23 to 0.66 (Table 9.1).[7] The increase in correlation between the DRP and NEPR measures indicates a movement toward a more optimal pattern of trade. It also implies that domestic resources have been allocated more efficiently among tradable goods producing sectors in 1995 than in 1978.

Table 9.1 Correlation coefficients between DRP and NEPR, 1978–95

Year	Unweighted	Value-added weighted	Output weighted
1978	0.199	0.272	0.225
1979	0.248	0.317	0.277
1980	0.267	0.293	0.266
1981	0.240	0.243	0.225
1982	0.276	0.323	0.291
1983	0.290	0.350	0.310
1984	0.411	0.454	0.416
1985	0.519	0.520	0.518
1986	0.560	0.591	0.572
1987	0.575	0.584	0.573
1988	0.578	0.578	0.571
1989	0.567	0.559	0.567
1990	0.544	0.530	0.524
1991	0.584	0.549	0.568
1992	0.650	0.619	0.660
1993	0.710	0.683	0.724
1994	0.731	0.685	0.735
1995	0.699	0.615	0.659

Source: Author's own calculations.

It is conventional to regard a correlation coefficient between 0.2 and 0.5 as indicative of weak correlation, between 0.5 and 0.8 as mild correlation and above 0.8 as strong correlation. In terms of the level of correlation coefficients, the reform period could be divided into three phases. From 1978 to 1983, trade patterns were slightly correlated with comparative advantage while from 1983 to 1991 China's trade patterns became mildly correlated with comparative advantage. During the first phase, the correlation coefficient was relatively stable and fluctuated between 0.20 and 0.35. Major jumps occurred in the second phase when the correlation coefficient climbed to above 0.4 in 1984. In the second phase from 1984–91, the correlation coefficients varied between 0.41 and 0.59. The highest point was recorded around 1987–8. It then declined in the following years until 1992, apparently due to domestic austerity policies. The third phase, from 1992 to 1995, saw China's trade patterns further converging toward its comparative advantage. (chapter 9). The correlation coefficient between the DRP and NEPR estimates reached to a new high of above 0.61–0.73. This is consistent with the findings of a favourable impact of economic reform from the mid-1980s onward on the structural changes in the patterns of trade (Chapter 5) and comparative advantage. It provides further evidence that resource allocation in China's trade sector has improved significantly over the past two decades.

The correlation coefficients could be decomposed into those for individual commodity groups to reveal the extent to which each group has contributed to the overall convergence between China's trade pattern and comparative advantage. These decompositions could also indicate where resource allocation has become more efficient. The individual correlation coefficients for five categories of tradable goods are provided in Table 9.2. The table shows that, in 1978, agricultural products as a group contributed 94 per cent of the total correlation coefficient, implying a relatively strong correlation between trade in agricultural products and the underlying comparative advantage in agriculture. However, other commodities accounted for only 6 per cent of the already weak total correlation coefficient of 0.225. This means that the trade inefficiency at the time came mainly from non-agricultural sectors. In particular, a negative correlation was recorded in human capital-intensive and unskilled labour-intensive goods, implying that these groups were traded, on average, against the underlying comparative advantage.

This situation began to change rapidly after 1978. The patterns of non-agricultural trade were increasingly correlated with comparative advantage. This growing correlation is most notably reflected in the coefficients for unskilled labour-intensive goods. In the early 1980s, unskilled labour-intensive goods contributed about 10 per cent of the total correlation between the DRP and NEPR measures for China's total tradable goods; by 1994, more than 57 per cent of the overall correlation could be explained by this group of tradables. Table 9.2 shows that, from 1978 to 1995, the correlation coefficient for agricultural products was relatively stable until 1988. The coefficients for other goods, except unskilled labour-intensive ones, rose slightly. During this period, the total correlation coefficient rose from 0.23 to 0.66 while the correlation coefficient for unskilled labour-intensive goods increased from -0.014 to 0.34. This implies that unskilled labour-intensive goods alone contributed the most to the total increment in the convergence between the DRP and NEPR estimates. In other words, improvement in resource-allocation efficiency was concentrated largely in the trade and production of unskilled labour-intensive goods.

The total correlation coefficients could also be decomposed into those for importables and exportables, or import-competing and export-producing industries. A commodity category is defined as 'exportable' if it is a net exporter, otherwise 'importable'. Correlation coefficients are calculated for these two groups of goods, respectively, for the period 1978–95. The results are reported in Table 9.3.

Table 9.3 shows that there was very little (and even negative) correlation between import patterns and comparative advantage during the period 1978–84. This implies that commodities were imported largely without consideration of their social benefits and costs. Improvements in import patterns began subsequently. By the 1990s, there had been a marked rise in the correlation between the NEPR estimates for the importables and their comparative

Table 9.2 Decomposition of correlation coefficients: five tradable groups, 1978–95

Good	1978	1979	1980	1981	1982	1983	1984
Decomposition							
Agricultural	0.211	0.221	0.187	0.142	0.205	0.214	0.239
Natural resources	0.002	0.004	0.003	0.005	0.010	0.011	0.016
Physical capital	0.030	0.025	0.035	0.042	0.039	0.031	0.065
Human capital	-0.004	0.003	0.007	0.005	0.002	0.007	0.029
Unskilled labour	-0.014	0.024	0.034	0.032	0.035	0.047	0.068
	0.225	0.277	0.266	0.225	0.291	0.310	0.416
Contribution							
Agricultural	0.938	0.798	0.704	0.629	0.706	0.690	0.574
Natural resources	0.008	0.014	0.010	0.021	0.035	0.036	0.038
Physical capital	0.134	0.092	0.132	0.187	0.135	0.100	0.157
Human capital	-0.016	0.011	0.026	0.020	0.005	0.021	0.069
Unskilled labour	-0.064	0.086	0.128	0.142	0.119	0.152	0.162
	1.000	1.000	1.000	1.000	1.000	1.000	1.000

Note: Weighted by gross output value.
Source: Author's own calculations.

advantage. On the other hand, there was a sharp increase (0.34) in the correlation coefficient for the exportable goods, which nearly tripled over the reform period. This increase accounted for more than 79 per cent of the incremental of correlation coefficient (0.43) for China's total tradable goods.

The commodity pattern of exports seems to be more consistent with comparative advantage than the pattern of imports does. As indicated above, unskilled labour-intensive goods were major contributors to the overall improvement in the pattern of trade. They were also the single most important commodity group in China's exports. Certainly it was unskilled labour-intensive exports that brought about the rise in the correlation between trade and comparative advantage for exportables.

These estimates confirm the earlier finding that efficiency improved more in the export sector than in the import sector. As mentioned above, after 1985, China gained comparative advantage in most unskilled labour-intensive products and some capital-intensive manufactured goods. However, the domestic import-substituting industries seemed to have been slow in responding, effectively, to these changes in China's comparative advantage structure. As a result, the domestic supply of these products fell short of their demand while the imports for the same products increased sharply. The imports of textile materials, for instance, increased rapidly.[8]

In addition, the rapid growth of exports has also changed import patterns. This is particularly so in the coastal areas where spiralling numbers of enterprises are involved in export-processing and assembling activities, which

1985	1986	1987	1988	1989	1990	1991	1992	1993	1994	1995
0.181	0.251	0.221	0.201	0.176	0.171	0.133	0.123	0.147	0.153	0.139
0.014	0.010	0.014	0.017	0.021	0.025	0.026	0.030	0.029	0.024	0.028
0.085	0.053	0.048	0.065	0.047	0.088	0.121	0.131	0.135	0.102	0.125
0.075	0.044	0.033	0.019	0.002	0.008	0.010	0.021	0.039	0.035	0.026
0.163	0.214	0.257	0.270	0.320	0.232	0.278	0.355	0.375	0.421	0.341
0.518	0.572	0.573	0.571	0.567	0.542	0.568	0.660	0.724	0.735	0.659
0.350	0.439	0.386	0.352	0.311	0.327	0.235	0.186	0.203	0.208	0.210
0.027	0.017	0.024	0.029	0.037	0.048	0.046	0.045	0.040	0.033	0.042
0.164	0.093	0.085	0.113	0.083	0.167	0.213	0.198	0.186	0.138	0.190
0.144	0.077	0.058	0.034	0.003	0.015	0.017	0.032	0.053	0.048	0.040
0.315	0.373	0.448	0.472	0.565	0.443	0.489	0.538	0.518	0.573	0.517
1.000	1.000	1.000	1.000	1.000	1.000	1.000	1.000	1.000	1.000	1.000

rely heavily on imported intermediate inputs and materials. To assess this intra-industry trade or international production integration, however, requires an analysis at a more disaggregated level than the data of this study allow.

The above results show that, in the 1980s, despite the continuing large-scale price adjustments and liberalization, the divergence between domestic and international prices remained for the imports of some key industrial raw materials and intermediate goods, whose importation and prices were, to various extents, controlled by the government. Consequently, import subsidies for state-owned enterprises had not been completely removed. These remaining administrative controls and subsidies encouraged the domestic producers to use excessive amounts of imported materials, which distorted import patterns. In China's partially reformed trade system, the decentralization of import decision-making combined with a centrally subsidized financial arrangement became the major source of import inefficiency and resulted in a sustained trade deficit in the mid-1980s.

Even in 1987, the correlation between China's trade patterns and comparative advantage remained moderate. The correlation coefficient of 0.57 implies that only 33 per cent of the variation in the total sum of squares of deviations in the NEPR estimates could be explained by changes in the DRP estimates. In other words, only one-third of the variations in China's commodity patterns of trade could be explained by changes in the estimated comparative advantage. This mild correlation indicates that inefficiency remained in China's foreign trade sectors and that further reforms in the trade sector and other related areas were required. The acceleration of economic reforms since 1992 has had a significant impact on the tradable

Table 9.3 Decomposition of correlation coefficients: importables and exportables, 1978–95

Good	1978	1979	1980	1981	1982	1983	1984
Decomposition							
Importables	0.034	0.040	0.047	0.046	0.045	0.049	0.094
Exportables	0.191	0.237	0.219	0.179	0.246	0.261	0.322
	0.225	0.277	0.266	0.225	0.291	0.310	0.416
Contribution							
Importables	0.149	0.145	0.177	0.205	0.156	0.157	0.227
Exportables	0.851	0.855	0.823	0.795	0.844	0.843	0.773
	1.000	1.000	1.000	1.000	1.000	1.000	1.000

Source: Author's own calculations.

sector, reflected in a jump in the correlation coefficient of the DRP and NEPR estimates to as high as 0.73. This shows that over 53 per cent of the changes in China's foreign trade patterns can be explained by its underlying comparative advantage. The resource-allocative efficiency in China's tradable sector has improved substantially, even compared with 10 years ago.

When the Chinese economy moved to opening up further to the outside world, the level of distortions in terms of domestic price deviations from the international market was reduced markedly. World market price signals had been increasingly channelled through the domestic economy and reflected in the domestic market. As a result, the domestic relative price structure exhibited a converging trend toward that of the world. This can be seen in the increase in the coefficients for the DRP estimates, b, in the regressions of (9.2) (Table 9.4). As mentioned above, b represents the slope of the convergence line. A high level of coefficient implies that the economy is moving to a free trade equilibrium. It can be seen in Table 9.4 that in the first five years of reform, the slope of the convergence varied in size between 1.2 and 1.7 (based on the gross output weighted least square regression) and by 1986–7 it had peaked at 3.1. In other words, the regression line rotated considerably toward the vertical line. This rotation indicates a significant realignment between Chinese domestic prices and world prices for tradable goods after the introduction of the two-tier price system. This process seems to have slowed down by the mounting inflation in the late 1980s and the austerity policies that followed. During those years, domestic markets were again distorted by high inflation and the reintroduction of many anti-inflation price control measures. As a result, the process of realigning the domestic price structure with the world was disrupted. All these are indicated in the decline in the coefficient for the DRP after 1987 in Table 9.4. Since 1992–3, however, this downward trend has been gradually reversed. In 1994–5, there was a slow

1985	1986	1987	1988	1989	1990	1991	1992	1993	1994	1995
0.138	0.102	0.116	0.108	0.093	0.122	0.144	0.169	0.183	0.144	0.130
0.380	0.470	0.457	0.463	0.474	0.402	0.424	0.491	0.541	0.591	0.530
0.518	0.572	0.573	0.571	0.567	0.524	0.568	0.660	0.724	0.735	0.659
0.267	0.178	0.203	0.188	0.164	0.233	0.253	0.256	0.252	0.196	0.197
0.733	0.822	0.797	0.812	0.836	0.767	0.747	0.744	0.748	0.804	0.803
1.000	1.000	1.000	1.000	1.000	1.000	1.000	1.000	1.000	1.000	1.000

Table 9.4 Coefficient for DRP in the regressions, 1978–95

Year	Unweighted	Value-added weighted	Output weighted
1978	1.194	1.710	1.276
1979	1.659	2.123	1.745
1980	1.956	1.882	1.560
1981	1.820	1.173	1.064
1982	1.750	1.426	1.258
1983	1.790	1.491	1.468
1984	2.354	1.884	2.003
1985	3.065	2.741	3.074
1986	3.445	2.929	3.069
1987	3.032	3.007	3.030
1988	2.823	3.058	2.882
1989	2.232	2.290	2.299
1990	2.451	2.696	2.571
1991	2.389	2.302	2.351
1992	1.987	1.853	1.967
1993	1.899	1.894	2.068
1994	2.126	1.940	2.083
1995	2.192	2.015	2.100

Source: Author's own calculations.

increase in the coefficient for the DRP variable which implies a fall in domestic distortions. As domestic inflation is brought under control and further deep reform measures are introduced, it is expected that the realignment of domestic and world prices will resume and DRP estimates for tradable goods are likely to resume convergence toward unity.

CONCLUSION

The findings of this chapter can be summed up as follows:

- During the pre-reform period, China's foreign trade was not related to its structure of comparative advantage. By 1995 after nearly two decades of economic reforms, China's patterns of both commodity trade and comparative advantage have changed dramatically and moved towards convergence. This is evidence of an improvement of resource allocation brought about by the economic reform.
- The pattern of exports improved more than that of imports, indicated by their correlation with comparative advantage. The changes in exports resulted from the fact that exporting firms have enjoyed much more autonomy than importing firms. Informal FDI in exports has also played an important role in export expansion. Inefficiency in the import sector was largely due to the incomplete nature of the reforms. But, despite inefficiency in imports in the 1980s, the overall improvement in China's foreign trade patterns is evident and gradually increasing.
- The improvement in the trade patterns also reflects the increased efficiency of resource allocation in the tradable goods production industries. The above results seem to indicate that resource allocation in export production improved considerably while the import-competing industries responded relatively slowly. Domestic production changed at a much slower pace than did the structure of the trade sector over the same period, China's domestic economy has not yet been fully integrated into the international economy and, therefore, the influence of foreign trade on the structure of domestic production remains modest. This also demonstrates the rigidity and sluggishness associated with the structural adjustment for the economy as a whole. However, as the current economic reforms and the open-door policies are set to be pursued even further, the Chinese economy will be more closely linked with the outside world. Its domestic resource allocation is expected to be affected increasingly by its foreign trade and inward foreign investment. The benefits from trade and investment will eventually flow through the tradable goods-production sectors and, through these sectors, to the rest of the economy.

10 Summary and Conclusion

This study has analyzed the impacts of economic reforms and the open-door policies on China's foreign trade. The efficiency of China's trade and production has been examined by a detailed investigation into the changes in the commodity patterns of trade and production structure which have taken place over the reform period and their relationship with comparative advantage. This chapter summarizes the main conclusions of the study, links the findings of various chapters together and draws policy implications from these findings.

TRADE REFORMS

One of the major empirical findings of this study is that China's commodity patterns of trade and comparative advantage have been, and are, converging. This improvement in trade patterns can be attributed largely to economic reforms in the trade sector as well as in other related areas such as price reforms. The most notable consequence of the reform measures was the establishment of functioning markets for tradable goods, particularly exportables. Flexible prices, more freedom in trade decision-making, and increasing competition among companies fuelled trade-pattern optimization. FDI in exporting firms, particularly those in the coastal regions, has also played an important role in the remarkable growth of labour-intensive exports in recent years.

In the pre-reform era, the central government had controlled or manipulated every aspect of foreign trade, from the daily operation of foreign trade corporations (FTCs) to the allocation of foreign exchange. This rigid system was intended to ensure a safe environment for the development of domestic industries but it also effectively isolated China's economy.

The economic reform and open-door policies launched in the late 1970s have brought dramatic changes to China's trade system. An increasing proportion of trade is now handled by the decentralized FTCs, export producers and firms with foreign investment. Centralized trade plans have been abolished along with the subsidies to the FTCs.

The role of the central government in foreign trade management has shifted from direct plan control to indirect regulation and monitoring through instruments such as licensing, tariffs and taxation. This allows trading companies and enterprises, notably those with FDI, to make their own trade decisions in response to market signals: one result has been the unprecedented growth in China's foreign trade. This has also been accompanied by substantial shifts in the commodity composition of trade—most noticeably, the rising proportion of manufactured goods as a percentage of total exports. The most rapid growth in this sector occurred in unskilled labour-intensive products.

China's foreign trade patterns have been analysed in this study with the aid of the net export performance ratio (NEPR). This index allows for a comparison of China's trade position not only with its own previous records but also with global commodity markets. The measurement of comparative advantage in this study supports the observation that the competitiveness of the Chinese economy in general, and the tradable goods producing industries in particular, has been enhanced since 1978.

These changes are the result of various factors. Among them, domestic-price reforms need to be particularly emphasized. China's domestic relative pricing system was developed in isolation and kept relatively stable for decades in the pre-reform era. At the onset of the reform period, China's domestic relative prices for tradable goods were very different from those in international markets. The prices of most primary products, key industrial raw materials and intermediate inputs were lower, while the prices of most manufactured goods were higher, than their equivalent international levels. The bias in relative prices resulted in an inefficient use of resources in many manufacturing industries, which precluded these goods from competing with foreign products in a free trade environment. Price reform was, thus, given high priority from the onset, and was aimed at removing price biases, opening up the domestic market and linking domestic and world markets.

One of the major findings of this study is that after the sustained price adjustments and liberalization, China's domestic price bias has been substantially reduced. The prices of many primary products are significantly increased relative to those of manufactured goods. As state monopoly in many industries is relaxed, domestic manufacturing enterprises are forced to reduce their production costs in order to compete with each other in the newly emerging markets.

Reforms in the domestic factors markets have also contributed to the general improvement in China's comparative advantage. This can be seen in the reduction of distortions in factors markets, particularly in the labour market. As discussed in Chapter 7, the gap between wage rates and the marginal product of labour has also narrowed considerably since 1978: returns to skilled and unskilled labour are now more closely related to China's actual endowments of these factors. This has enabled enterprises to base their decisions on less distorted factor prices and make more efficient use of these resources.

Township and village enterprises have been the major beneficiaries of factor market liberalization. Their increased autonomy allowed them to take advantage of unskilled labour in the rural area. The advantage of low labour costs is most notable in the coastal area where, combined with foreign investment (especially from Hong Kong and Taiwan), it has become the driving force behind the rapid increase in the exports of unskilled labour-intensive manufactures.

TRADE EFFICIENCY

The prerequisite for a country to maximize the gains from trade is to export the goods in which it has a comparative advantage and import those in which it does not. This is equivalent to saying that an optimal pattern of trade should be consistent with a country's underlying comparative advantage. In a transitional economy with distorted relative prices, however, trade efficiency could not be judged simply by financial profits or losses. As an alternative, the estimation of underlying comparative advantage becomes essential for trade efficiency analysis.

The central part of this study is a domestic resource productivity (DRP) measure of China's international comparative advantage. The results show that, in 1978, DRP estimates were higher than unity for most agricultural and natural resource products but lower than unity for most manufactured goods. This implied that China's comparative advantage was confined mainly to primary products and China's manufactured goods on average were not competitive internationally.

During the economic reform period since then, the ranking of the DRP estimates of China's comparative advantage for agricultural and natural resource products has consistently declined. Meanwhile, the ranking of the DRP measures for manufactured goods in general and the unskilled labour-intensive manufactures in particular increased rapidly. The results show that by the mid-1990s most labour-intensive manufactured goods had a DRP estimate greater than unity. This implied that China had gained a comparative advantage in this group of tradable goods. Despite the decline in the DRP measures for some primary products, the range of commodities with a DRP measure above unity had widened. This indicates that the competitiveness of the Chinese economy in general, and the tradable goods-producing industries in particular, has been enhanced since 1978.

The DRP estimates can be used as a guideline to assess the performance of China's foreign trade during the reform period. China's commodity patterns of trade are compared with the DRP estimates of comparative advantage. A clear trend of convergence between these two sets of measures emerges from the empirical analysis. The results also show that, at the beginning of the economic reforms in the late 1970s, China's trade patterns were substantially different from the estimated structure of comparative advantage. During the 1980s, however, the trade patterns and comparative advantage gradually converged. By 1987, a modest correlation had emerged between China's trade pattern and its estimated comparative advantage structure. The high inflation and the subsequent austerity policies in the late 1980s and early 1990s had a detrimental effect on the process of convergence. It is not until 1993 that the convergence between the trade patterns and comparative advantage had renewed and further increased.

Although this correlation is still moderate, the underlying trend of growing convergence is important and indicates the increased optimization of China's trade patterns and the improvement in allocative efficiency in Chinese tradable goods producing sectors. As also discussed in the study, the commodity pattern of exports seemed to be more in line with comparative advantage than that of imports. Changes in the structure of imports were less encouraging, mainly because import controls were relaxed relatively more slowly during the period studied. Remaining price controls and national FTCs' exclusive handling of important imported goods, such as key raw materials and intermediate inputs, contributed greatly to the less desirable performance of imports.

POLICY IMPLICATIONS

The increasing correlation between China's trade patterns and comparative advantage implies that the economic reforms since 1978 have indeed generated positive impacts on resource allocation in China's foreign trade. Commodity compositions of trade are converging toward China's underlying comparative advantage to a greater degree than before. The large-scale price adjustments and opening up of domestic markets have also brought domestic relative prices closer to those of their international counterparts, improving the allocative efficiency of enterprises.

This does not necessarily mean, however, that China's trade pattern and production structure has become optimal. To maximize the potential gains from trade, the production structure must also be adjusted in a way that allows resources to be reallocated more freely from industries in which China has less or no comparative advantage to those in which it has high comparative advantage. Such structural changes require further reform measures to remove remaining distortions in the economy and allow markets to play a even greater role in guiding resource allocation.

Market-oriented reforms can improve the allocation of resources in trade and production. In a transitional economy where market distortions remain, the empirical study of comparative advantage by DRP measures could play an important part in guiding government policies and firm decision-making. To transform China's heavy industry-biased economic structure, for instance, the government and enterprises need to know in which industries investment would be of greatest benefit to the society. The DRP estimates can serve as a basis for such deliberations.

The DRP analysis is static in nature but in this study the analysis was applied to a multiyear period in an attempt to shed some light on the dynamics of China's comparative advantage. The study shows that, although China still has DRP estimates above unity in agricultural and natural resource products, comparative advantage is moving away from these primary products and toward manufactured goods. Unskilled labour-intensive goods account for a large proportion of Chinese exports and are the main source of the benefits from trade. The DRP measures, however, show that the level of comparative advantage in this commodity group is decreasing. As also indicated in the study, in the future, some fast growing capital-intensive industries are likely to become internationally competitive. Despite that the reform years might be too short a period from which to draw any long-term projections, the DRP estimates presented in this study can still signal possible directions in which future changes in China's comparative advantage, and therefore its trade patterns, may occur.

China consists of diverse regions, each of which is unique and distinctive. Factor mobility across the regions is still restricted by geographical or economic barriers. Factor prices are not equal across regions, nor are factor concentrations or distributions. Regional disparities give rise to a situation in which different areas may have comparative advantages in different productive activities. Even intra-regional or intra-provincial divergences can be so substantial as to justify a variety of productive activities. For instance, Guangdong province has been trying to encourage some labour-intensive manufacturing industries to move from the coastal areas adjacent to Hong Kong and Macao to the relatively poor inland mountain counties where labour cost is still low. The more affluent coastal areas could then specialize in more skill-intensive production. As a large and diverse country, China as a whole could be competitive in a wide range of products.

This study provides a method of assessing resource-allocation efficiency in the trade sector of a national economy, the application of this method to a specific region requires incorporation of regional characteristics into the analysis. Such studies would further enhance our understanding of China as a major trading nation in the world and its potential in a rapid changing global economy.

Notes and References

1. Introduction

1. The DRC in this study is presented as its inverse, or domestic resource productivity (DRP). See Chapter 5 for details.

2. Reforming a Centrally Planned Foreign Trade System

1. In 1982, the MOFT became the Ministry of Foreign Economic Relations and Trade (MOFERT) after an amalgamation with the State Import Commission, the State Foreign Investment Commission and the Ministry of Foreign Economic Relations. In 1993, it was renamed the Ministry of Foreign Trade and Economic Cooperation (MOFTEC).
2. For an example of China's tradable commodity wars, see Findlay (1992).
3. They are (1) minerals, metals and chemicals, (2) light industrial, art and crafts, (3) agricultural products, (4) textiles, garments and silk, (5) machinery and electronics and (6) health care and medical products.
4. They were (1) cereals and vegetable oils, (2) silk, (3) textiles, (4) animal products, (5) light industry products, (6) arts and crafts, (7) metal and minerals, (8) chemicals, (9) machinery, (10) engineering equipment.
5. Include also electric and electronic products.
6. According to the licence code numbers, these 114 exports can be categorized into 143 exportables as reported in Table 2.4.
7. For a discussion on the tradable goods pricing policies, see Lardy (1992).
8. Only in the following two circumstances, could procurement prices diverge from their domestic levels:
   - For industrial products with high domestic prices and profits which could potentially cause export losses and the prices of which, for some reason, could not be lowered, the export procurement prices were allowed to be reduced accordingly.
   - For industrial products with domestic prices so low that firms were unable to secure normal returns or even suffered losses, if the low prices could not be raised for some reason, the export purchasing prices could be raised separately to encourage firms to produce for export.
   In both circumstances, the impact of the biased domestic prices on exports required some readjustments of the pricing practice for some exports. However, the adjustments were partial and segmented. More importantly, they were not geared to world prices (State Council 1979b).
9. The mark-up rate was 30 per cent for this group of imports on top of the c.i.f. costs converted at the official exchange rate. It should be noted that the exchange rate used in converting these prices was the official rate not the internal settlement rate. After the 30 per cent mark-up, domestic prices were actually quite close to what they would have been if they had been converted at the internal settlement rate through agent pricing practices.

10. For details, see *Customs Import and Export Tariff Schedule of the People's Republic of China*, compiled by the Department of Customs Administration at the Ministry of Foreign Trade (1961).
11. The average tariff rate under the HCDCS was higher than that under the old customs classification system owing to an increase in the number of items in the HCDCS which attracts higher tariff rates.
12 . For details about this round of tariff reduction see *Import and Export Customs Tariff Regulation of the People's Republic of China*, compiled by the Office of Tariff Rate Committee of the State Council and the Tariff Department of the General Customs Administration (1996).
13. For details about the reduction see *Tabulation of Import and Export Tariff Rate Adjustments*, compiled by the Office of Tariff Rate Committee of the State Council and the Tariff Department of the General Customs Administration (1997).
14. Only foreign exchange quota certificates were allowed to be swapped. This is because domestic firms were not allowed to hold any foreign currencies and all the foreign currencies had to be sold to the Bank of China at the official rate.

3.   Factors Intensity of Chinese Tradable Commodities

1. The data on capital assets from Chinese statistics are based on the sum of the original values of investments at their completion. No adjustment has been made for possible changes in the prices of capital assets. However, the main concern here is the relative level of capital per worker across industries. The above problem with capital data is unlikely to seriously bias the ranking of industries.
2. The input–output coefficients are estimated from *Input–Output Table of China 1987* (State Statistical Bureau, Department of Balances of National Economy and Office of National Input–Output Survey 1991). For a detailed discussion of Chinese input–output tables, see Chapter 8.

4.   China's Foreign Trade Patterns and Performance

1. The discussion in this and the following sections is based on foreign trade statistics published by the United Nations and provided by the International Economic Data Bank of the Australian National University. China's trade statistics are estimated from its trade-partner's data because China did not report its foreign trade statistics to the United Nations until the late 1980s.
2. Export and import growth rates are estimated on the basis of current prices because the relevant price indices are not available.
3 . It should be noted that the increase in human capital-intensive exports is partially due to an increase in exports from processing or assembling operations using imported components. These operations could be labour-intensive. However, the present available information does not allow for further distinction between assembled and non-assembled exports.
4. The emerging export processing and assembling activities complicate the analysis of trade. The vertical division of labour in manufacturing exports between China and other economies blurs the distinction between different groups of tradables. For instance, the assembling of a human capital-intensive product can be very labour-intensive. Although China does not have the ability to manufacture many human capital-intensive goods itself, this does not prevent it from assembling them with imported components for export. It is likely that some of these human capital-intensive exports are composed of processed or assembled goods.

5. The NEPR measures for China's trade performance during the period 1978–96 at the commodity level are given in the Appendix (Table 4A.2) (p.000).

5. Measuring Comparative Advantage

1. For some multicountry studies, see Leamer (1984) and Song (1996).
2. For a discussion of some indices of 'revealed' comparative advantage, see Chapter 4.
3. For an application of 'revealed' comparative advantage to China, see Yeats (1991).
4. In reality, however, demand conditions must also be introduced to determine the dividing line between exports and imports in the commodity chain of comparative advantage (Jones 1956).
5. See Bruno (1962).
6. As Srinivasan and Bhagwati note (1978: 105), the DRC could also be expressed, equivalently, in the gross value terms, but such a formula has not been very popular among practitioners.
7. For a DRC measure with non-tradable goods, see Warr (1991).

6. Tradable Goods Price Structure in China, 1978–95

1. See, for instance, Naughton (1992).
2. For a recent example, see Ren and Chen (1994).
3. The EER for a tradable good is defined as the amount of the domestic currency that would accrue to a domestic firm when it produces and sells that good on the domestic market that would cost $1 to import if the good is importable, or when it exports that good on the international market that is worth $1 if the good is exportable. It should be noted that, in the trade literature, the term (EER) is sometime also used to mean the trade-weighted average of various bilateral exchange rates.
4. This discrepancy leads to the use of the customs duty collection ratios. It is based on the same principle but takes into account the possibility of tarrif reductions or exemptions.
5. In recent years, there have been increasing discrepancies between China's nominal tariff rates and the import duty collection rate. For instance, the trade-weighted average nominal tariff rate was estimated to be 20–30 per cent in 1992 while the ratio of import tariff revenue to the value of total imports was only 4.8 per cent (State Statistical Bureau 1997). It implies that, for variety of reasons, imports into China might not have been taxed at the same rates shown on the official tariff schedule. This indicates the danger of misleading if either nominal tariff rates or duty collection rates are used in measuring China's NRP.
6. For the foreign trade system reforms, see Chapter 2.
7. The term refers to the approach adopted by other formal centrally planned economies in East Europe and Russia.
8. They were sugar, iron wire, nails, chemical fertilizers, pesticides, iron and steel scrap, cotton piece-goods, cotton polyester blended fabrics, polyester–viscose blended fabrics, woollen piece-goods, selected wines and spirits, washing powder, rubber shoes and iron pans.

9. These included sewing machines, watches, radios, electric fans, bicycles, refrigerators, black and white television sets, radio-cassette recorders, washing machines, polyester–viscose blended fabrics, cotton yarn ($\geqslant 80$ count) and its products.
10. It was applicable only to collectively owned forests in South China.
11. For the information on the prices of producer goods, see Yang Songhao (1988); Zhang Zhuoyuan and Yang Shengming (1992).
12. These indices are available from the *Statistical Yearbook of China 1997*.
13. They include the various issues of the *Statistical Yearbook of China* and the *Statistical Yearbook of the Chinese Industrial Economy*.
14. China's domestic price for crude oil was close to the world price in the early 1970s. The world price of crude oil increased dramatically in 1973 while China's domestic price for crude oil remained unchanged. The domestic price of crude oil was still 100 yuan per ton in the early 1980s, which was about US\$4.86 per barrel at an exchange rate of 2.8.
15. It is unclear, however, whether or not all non-centrally distributed timber was actually traded in the market. A large proportion might have been handled by provincial governments. Unfortunately, information on the proportion of timber output traded in markets was not available.
16. See various issues of the *Statistical Yearbook of China's Commodity Prices*.
17. It was reported that, in some areas, the price of cotton yarn was even lower than that of raw cotton.
18. They were copper, lead, zinc, tin, nickel, aluminium, antimony, mercury and magnesium.
19. This includes the internal settlement rate for exports and imports over the period 1981–4.
20. The State Administration of Commodity Prices (SACP) is now affiliated to the State Planning Commission.

7.   Shadow Prices of Primary Factors of Production

1. For shadow pricing, see, for instance, Srinivasan and Bhagwati (1978); Tower (1985); Tower and Pursell (1986).
2. Note that $\sum_{j} \alpha_{sj} + \sum_{k} \beta_{sk} = 1$ for all s.
3. The construction and modification of China's input–output tables will be discussed in Chapter 8.
4. The shadow price of labour may be estimated by two methods: one uses the average product of labour and the other marginal product of labour. The World Bank adopts the first method in its project appraisal report on China. The marginal product of labour is estimated by shadow pricing the components of the average output of rural labour (World Bank, China Department 1988). But in the presence of surplus labour, the marginal product may be well below the average product. The average-product method could hence over-estimate the marginal product. To avoid this problem, we use the second method in which the marginal product of labour is directly estimated from production functions.
5. The data used were taken from China's statistical yearbooks.
6. The comparable data for 1978 were not available.
7. The similar data are also available from *China Regional Economy: A Profile of 17 Years of Reform and Opening-Up* (State Statistical Bureau 1996).

8. It should be noted that, if a linear homogeneous Cobb–Douglas function were used, and if each input were assumed to be paid its marginal product, the relative shares of total product accruing to labour and non-labour inputs should be equal to a_1 and a_2, respectively, the marginal product of labour could then be derived directly from labour's income share. This property, however, is based on the assumption of profit–maximization behaviour in production. In China, the market economy is under-developed and labour is unlikely to be paid its marginal product. It is therefore impossible to derive the marginal product of labour directly from its income share. Factor's marginal products could only be estimated from a production function.

9. See Naughton (1992) for a discussion of the reasons for declining capital returns.

10. The calculation of shadow prices for non-tradables and factors requires input–output coefficients as well. A discussion of China's input–output coefficients and the tradable and non-tradable division will be provided in Chapter 8.

11. Other cost items include, among other things, welfare payments to labour.

8. China's International Comparative Advantage, 1978–95 : DRP Results

1. For the use of a similar method, see Warr (1991).

2. Or, in non-matrix form, the DRP may be expressed as

$$DRP_j = \frac{(p_j^b/p_j^d) - \sum_i \bar{b}_{ij}(p_i^b/p_i^d)}{\sum_s \bar{g}_{sj}(p_s^s/p_s^f)}$$

Where $\bar{b}_{ij}$ and $\bar{g}_{sj}$ are total requirements of intermediate input i and s in production of one unit of commodity j, and p_j^b/p_j^d and p_s^s/p_s^f are the border and domestic price ratios of tradable goods and the shadow-price conversion factors for primary factors.

3. The input–output table was compiled for internal use in formulating price reform policies. It contains 58 commodities in which 13 are agricultural products.

4. The iron and steel industry in the Chinese input–output table is also decomposed into the iron and the steel groups.

5. For a concordance between the classifications of this modified 69-sector table and the 117-sector table see Appendix Table 8A.1 (p.205)

6. RAS is a technique of updating input–output coefficients. For description of the RAS procedure and its properties see, for example, Stone (1961); Stone and Brown (1962); Cambridge University, Department of Applied Economics (1963); Bacharach (1970); and MacGill (1977).

7. In the theoretical literature, it has been demonstrated that, in the presence of factor market distortions, almost anything can happen: the 'wrong' good may be exported or the 'right' good is exported with the 'wrong' factor intensities. For a discussion of impact of labour market distortions on trade, see Krueger (1988).

8. Except Sectors 20, 22 and 29.

9. For the levels of the DRP estimates, see Table 8.1.

10. For a similar argument, see Garnaut (1988).

11. The indirect use of intermediate inputs or primary factors refer to the goods and factors used in producing those non-traded goods that are used in producing tradable good j.

9. China's Trade Patterns and Comparative Advantage

1. The 22 categories of exports were Non-ferrous Minerals (17), Non-metal Minerals (18), Petrol Products (32), Coal Products (33), Plastic Articles (42), Glass (44), Metal Products (50), Household Chemicals (37), Medicines (39), Household Mechanical and Electrical Goods. (54), Railway Equipment (55), Other Engineering Products (59), Household Electronics (61), Other Processed Food (21), Wool Textiles (23), Hemp Textiles (24), Knitted Goods (26), Other Textiles (27), Clothing (28), Cultural and Sporting Goods (31), Rubber Manufactures (41) and Other Building Materials (46). The four groups of imports were Wheat (2), Other Grains (3), Cotton (5) and Iron (47).

2. For the detailed discussion of trade reforms, see Chapter 2.

3. The four groups of imports were Sugar, Tobacco and Alcohol (20), Cement (43), Glass (44) and Other Building Materials (46).

4. The 13 groups of exports were Other Grains (3), Fruits (8), Crude Petroleum (15) Non-ferrous Minerals (17), Hemp Textiles (24), Petrol Products (32), Coal Products (33), Inorganic Chemicals (34), Plastic Articles (42), Non-ferrous Metals (49), Metal Products (50), Medicines (39) and Household Electronics (61).

5. The seven groups of exports were Paddy Rice (1), Meat, etc. (11), Furniture (29), Inorganic Chemicals (34), Medicines (39), Metal Products (50) and Household Electronics (61).

6. The three groups of imports were Wool (10), Sugar, Tobacco and Alcohol (20) and Power Equipment (53).

7. The differences between the two correlation coefficients for 1978 and 1995 from OLS and gross output value WLS are significant at the 0.95 level. The difference between two coefficients from the net output value WLS regression was significant at the 0.90 level.

8. An important possible explanation for this is the rapid expansion of export-processing and assembling activities. A large proportion of textile imports may be related to these activities. Unfortunately, the available information does not allow for separation between normal imports and imports for export-processing activities.

Bibliography

Almanac of Anhui Economy Editoral Board (1987) *Almanac of Anhui Economy 1986* (*Anhui jingji nianjian 1986*) (Hefei: Anhui People Publishing House).

Almanac of China's Agriculture Editorial Board, 1982–6; (1981–97) *Almanac of China's Agriculture* (*Zhongguo nongye nianjian*) (Beijing: Agricultural Publishing House, various issues).

Almanac of China's Finance and Banking Editorial Department (1990) *Almanac of China's Finance and Banking 1989* (*Zhongguo jinrong nianjian 1989*) (Beijing).

Almanac of China's Transport Editorial Board (1987) *Almanac of China's Transport 1986* (*Zhongguo jiaotong nianjian 1986*) (Beijing: Almanac of China's Transport Editorial and Publishing House).

Bacharach, Michael (1970) *Biproportional Matrices and Input–Output Change* (Cambridge: Cambridge University Press).

Baharal, U. (1956) *The Real Rate of the Dollar in the Economy of Israel* (Jerusalem: Ministry of Commerce and Industry).

Balassa, Bela (1965) 'Trade liberalization and "revealed" comparative advantage', *The Manchester School of Economics and Social Studies*, 33, 99–123.

————— (1977) 'A "stage approach" to comparative advantage', *World Bank Staff Working Papers*, 156 (Washington, DC: World Bank).

————— (1979) 'The changing pattern of comparative advantage in manufactured goods', *The Review of Economics and Statistics*, 61 (1979), 259–66.

————— (1986) 'Comparative advantage in manufactured goods: a reappraisal', *The Review of Economics and Statistics*, 68, 315–19.

Balassa, Bela and Bauwens, Lac (1988) *Changing Trade Patterns in Manufactured Goods: An Econometric Investigation* (Amsterdam: North-Holland).

Balassa, Bela and Schydlowsky, Daniel (1972) 'Domestic resource cost and effective protection once again', *Journal of Political Economy*, 80, 61–9.

Balassa, Bela and associates (1982) *Development Strategies in Semi-Industrial Countries* (Baltimore: Johns Hopkins University Press).

Balassa, Bela *et al.* (1984) *Morocco: Industrial Incentives and Export Promotion*, A World Bank Country Study (Washington, DC: World Bank).

Barkai, H. (1956) 'Consumption of edible oil in Israel and supply of local materials for their production', *Studies in Economics*, *No*.1 (Jerusalem: Hebrew University).

Behrman, Jere (1997) 'Foreign trade and economic development: Chile', NBER (New York: Columbia University Press).

Beijing Statistical Bureau (1987) *Beijing Social and Economic Statistical Yearbook 1986* (*Beijing shehui jingji tongji nianjian 1986*) (Beijing: China Statistical Publishing House).

Bertrand, Trent J (1979) 'Shadow pricing in distorted economies', *American Economic Review*, 69, 902–14.

Branson, W. H. and Junz, H. (1971) 'Trends in US comparative advantage', *Brookings Papers on Economic Activity*, 2.

Bruno, Michael (1962) *Interdependence, Resource Use and Structural Change in Israel* (Jerusalem: Bank of Israel).

————— (1965) 'The optimal selection of export-promoting and import-substituting projects', *in United Nations, Planning the External Sector: Techniques, Problems and Policies* (New York: United Nations).

————— (1972) 'Domestic resource cost and effective protection: clarification and synthesis', *Journal of Political Economy*, 80, 16–33.

Cambridge University, Department of Applied Economics (1963) *Input–Output Relationships, 1954-1966*, 3, *A Programme for Growth* (London: Chapman & Hall).

Chao, Kang (1964) 'Pitfalls in the use of China's foreign trade statistics', *China Quarterly*, 47–65.

Chen Jiaqin and Jiang Wai (1984) 'Macroeconomic efficiency of foreign trade and its analysis' (Waimao hongguan jingji xiaoyi jiqi fenxi), *Financial and Economic Studies (Caijing wenti yanjiu)*, 4, 19–24.

Chen, Nai-Ruenn (1975) 'China's foreign trade 1950–1974', Joint Economic Committee, US Congress (Washington, DC: Government Printing Office).

Chen Yiyun (1991) *Introduction to China's Foreign Economic and Trade Laws and Regulations (Zhonggou duiwai jingji maoyi fagui zhishi)* (Chengdu: Sichun People's Publishing House).

Chen, Yuanzhong, Lin, Xiaomao, Yuan, Chaoshen and Du, Bocheng (1993) *The GATT and the Chinese Market (Guanmao zongxieding yu zhongguo shichang)* (Beijing: Haichao Publishing House).

Chenery, H. B. (1961) 'Comparative advantage and development policy', *American Economic Review*, 18–57.

Chinese Communist Party (1984) 'Decision of the Central Committee of the Chinese Communist Party on Reform of the Economic Structure' (20 October), *Beijing Review* (29 October) centre fold; i–xvi.

Chinese Student's Society for Economic Studies (1991) *China: Trade and Reform* (The Australian National University, Canberra: National Centre for Development Studies).

Customs General Administration (1981–90) *Annual Customs Statistics of the People's Republic of China (Zhonghua renmin gongheguo haiguan tongji nianbao)* Annual 1980–9 (Beijing).

————— (1991–7) *Customs Statistical Yearbook of the People's Republic of China (Zhonghua renmin gongheguo haiguan tongji nianjian)* Annual 1990–6 (Beijing).

Deardorff, Alan V. (1982) 'The general validity of the Heckscher–Ohlin theorem', *American Economic Review*, 72, 683–94.

————— (1984) 'Testing trade theories and predicting trade flows', in Jones and Kenen (eds), 1, 467–517.

Dervis, Kemal, de Melo, Jaime and Robinson, Sherman (1982) *General Equilibrium Models of Development Policy*, A World Bank Research Publication (Cambridge: Cambridge University Press).

Diamond, Peter A. and Mirrlees, James A. (1976) 'Private constant return and public shadow prices', *Review of Economics and Statistics*, 43, 41–8.

Eckstein, Alexander (1996) *Communist China's Economic Growth and Foreign Trade* (New York: McGraw-Hill).

Economic Daily (Jingji ribao) A daily newspaper published in Beijing.

Economic Information (Jingji cankao) A daily newspaper published in Beijing.

Economic Information Centre for the Northeast Economic Zone (1988) *Statistical Yearbook of the Northeast Economic Zone 1987 (Dongbei jingjiqu tongji nianjian 1987)* (Beijing: China Statistical Publishing House).

Editorial Board (1993) *The GATT Manual (Guanmao Zongxieding shiyong yewu quanshu)* (Beijing: Qiye Guanli Publishing House).

Editorial Board of the Almanac of China's Finance and Banking (ACFB) (1989) *Almanac of China's Finance and Banking 1989 (Zhongguo jinrong nianjian)* (Beijing).

Editorial Board of the Almanac of China's Foreign Economic Relations and Trade (ACFERT) (various issues 1984–6) *Almanac of China's Foreign Economic Relations and Trade*, China Resources Trade Consultancy Co., Ltd. (Hong Kong).

————— (various issues 1988–96/7) *Almanac of China's Foreign Economic Relations and Trade 1987–96/7* (Beijing: China Prospect Publishing House).

Editorial Board of *Price: Theory and Practice* (ed.) (1986) *Chronology of Major Events in Price Reforms 1978–1985* (*Wujia dashiji 1978–1985*) (Beijing: China Fiscal and Economic Publishing House).

Editorial Board of the *PYC* (1989–95) *Price Yearbook of China* (*Zhongguo wujia nianjian*) (Beijing: Chinese Price Publishing House).

Ellis, H. S. and Metzler, L. A. (eds) (1949) *Readings in the Theory of International Trade* (Irwin, Homewood).

Ethier, Wilfred (1983) *Modern International Economy* (New York: W.W.Norton).

Fang Xiangdong (1992) 'China's foreign trade system' (Zhongguo duiwai maoyi tizhi), in Zhou Zexi and Hu Jingen (eds), *Foreign Trade in the Process of China's Industrialization* (*Zhongguo gongyehua jincheng zhongde duiwai maoyi*) (Beijing: China's Price Publishing House), 41–74.

Findlay, Christopher (1992) *Challenges of Economic Reform and Industrial Growth: China's Wool War* (St Leonards: Allen & Unwin)

Findlay, Christopher, Phillips, Prue and Tyers, Rodney (1985) 'China's Merchandise Trade: Composition and Export Growth in the 1980s', *ASEAN–Australia Economic Paper*, 19 (Canberra).

Fujian Statistical Bureau (1988) *Fujian Statistical Yearbook 1987* (*Fujian tongji nianjian 1987*) (Beijing: China Statistical Publishing House).

Gansu Statistical Bureau (1989) *Gansu Statistical Yearbook 1988* (*Gansu tongji nianjian 1988*) (Beijing: China Statistical Publishing House).

Garnaut, Ross (1988) 'Asia's giant', *Australian Economic Papers* (December), 173–86.

Greenaway, David and Milner, Chris (1990) 'Industrial incentives, domestic resource costs and resource allocation in Madagascar', *Applied Economics*, 22, 805–21.

Guangdong Finance Society and Guangdong Provincial Branch of the People's Bank of China, Research Institute of Finance (1984) *Chronology of Major Events in Economic and Finance Laws and Regulations Since the Founding of the Nation* (*Jianguo yilai jingji jinrong falü zhidu da shi yiaolue*) (Guangzhou: Editorial Board of Guangdong Finance).

Guangdong Statistical Bureau (1989) *Guangdong Statistical Yearbook 1988* (*Guangdong tongji nianjian 1988*) (Beijing: China Statistical Publishing House).

Guangxi Statistical Bureau (1988) *Guangxi Statistical Yearbook 1987* (*Guangxi tongji nianjian 1987*) (Beijing: China Statistical Publishing House).

Guangzhou Municipal Industrial and Commercial Administration and Management Society (1985) *Compendium of Economic Laws and Regulations 1978–1984* (*Jingji fagui xuanbian 1978–1984*) (Guangzhou: Zhongshan Economic and Technical Consultative Centre).

Guizhou Reginal Annals Compilatory Committee (1987) *Almanac of Guizhou 1986* (*Guizhou nianjian 1986*) (Guiyang: Guizhou People's Publishing House).

Guo, Jinwu *et al.* (eds) (1987) *China Today: Commerce* (*Dangdai zhongguo de shangye*) (Beijing: Chinese Social Science Publishing House).

Han Jiyun (1991) 'Reflection on "two-tier system" of Renminbi exchange rate' (Dui renminbi huilü 'shuangguizhi' de sikao), *International Trade Journal* (*Guoji maoyi wenti*), 6, 35–37, 63.

Handbook of Agricultural Technology and Economics Editorial Board (1983) *Handbook of Agricultural Technology and Economics* (*Nongye jingji jishu shouce*) (Beijing: Agriculture Publishing House).

Hebei Statistical Bureau (1988) *Hebei Economic Statistical Yearbook 1987* (*Hebei jingji tongji nianjian 1987*) (Beijing: China Statistical Publishing House).

Heckscher, E. F. (1949) 'The effect of foreign trade on the distribution of income', in Ellis and Metzler (The original article in English translation, 1919).

Heilongjiang Statistical Bureau (1988) *Heilongjiang Statistical Yearbook 1987* (*Heilongjiang tongji nianjian 1987*) (Beijing: China Statistical Publishing House).

Helpman, Elhanan, and Krugman, Paul R. (1985) *Market Structure and Foreign Trade: Increasing Returns, Imperfect Competition, and the International Economy* (Cambridge, Mass.: MIT Press).

Henan Statistical Bureau (1990) *Henan Economic Statistical Yearbook 1989* (*Henan jingji tongji nianjian 1989*) (Beijing: Henan People Publishing House).

Hsiao, Gene T. (1977) *The Foreign Trade of China: Policy, Law and Practices* (Berkeley: University of California Press).

Hsu, John C. (1989) *China's Foreign Trade Reform: Impact on Growth and Stability* (Cambridge: Cambridge University Press).

Hu Bangding *et al.* (eds.) (1989) *China Today: Prices* (*Dangdai zhongguo de wujia*) (Beijing: Chinese Social Science Publishing House).

Huang Yaohua and Wang Zhengxiao (1991) 'Reflection on current commodity imports of our country' (Dui dangqian woguo shangpin jinkou de sikao), *Finance and Trade Economics* (*Caimao jingji*), 7, 58–62.

Hubei Statistical Bureau (1988), *Hubei Statistical Yearbook 1987* (*Hubei tongji nianjian 1987*) (Beijing: China Statistical Publishing House).

Hughes, Helen (ed.) (1992) *The Dangers of Export Pessimism* (San Francisco: ICS Press).

Hunan Statistical Bureau (1989) *Hunan Statistical Yearbook 1988* (*Hunan tongji nianjian 1988*) (Beijing: China Statistical Publishing House).

Industrial Classification and Codes for National Economic Activities (1985) (Guomin jingji hangye fenlei yu daima), GB 4754-84.

Inner Mongolia Statistical Bureau (1989) *Inner Mongolia Statistical Yearbook 1988* (*Neimenggu tongji nianjian 1988*) (Beijing: China Statistical Publishing House).

International Business (*Guoji shangbao*) A newspaper published by the MOFERT in Beijing.

International Economic Data Bank (IEDB) *The International Trade System, compiled from United Nations' International Trade Statistics* Canberra: The Australian National University.

International Monetary Fund (IMF) (1988–96) *International Financial Statistics*, yearbook (Washington, DC).

Jiangsu Statistical Bureau (1989) *Jiangsu Statistical Yearbook 1988* (*Jiangsu tongji nianjian 1988*) (Beijing: China Statistical Publishing House).

Jiangxi Statistical Bureau (1989) *Jiangxi Statistical Yearbook 1988* (*Jiangxi tongji nianjian 1988*) (Beijing: China Statistical Publishing House).

Jiang Zemin (1992) 'Report to the 14th National Congress of the Chinese Communist Party', *Documents of the 14th National Congress of the Chinese Communist Party* (Beijing: People's Publishing House).

Jilin Regional Annals Compilatory Committee (1988) *Almanac of Jilin 1987* (*Jilin nianjian 1987*) (Changchun).

Joint Economic Committee, US Congress, (ed) (1975) *China: A Reassessment of the Economy* (Washington, DC: US Government Printing Office).

Jones, R.W. (1956) 'Factor proportions and the Heckscher–Ohlin theorem', *Review of Economic Studies*, 24, 1–10.

Jones, R. W. and Kenen, P. B. (eds) (1984) *Handbook of International Economics, 1* (Amsterdam: Elsevier).

Jones, R. W. and Neary, J. Peter (1984) 'The positive theory of international trade', in Jones and Kenen (eds) 1, 1–62.

Ju, Jinwen and Wu, Li (eds) (1993) *A Practical Guide to the GATT* (*Guanmao Zongxieding shiyong zhishi quanshu*) (Beijing: Zhongguo Wuzi Publishing House).

Kenen, P. B. (1965) 'Nature, capital and trade', *Journal of Political Economy*, 73.

Kenen, P.B. and Lawrence, Roger (eds) (1968) 'The open economy: essays on international trade and finance', *Columbia Studies in Economics*, 1 (New York: Columbia University).

Kenen, P.B. and Yudin, E. B. (1965) 'Skills, human capital and US foreign trade' (New York: Columbia University, International Economic Workshop).

Kim, Chungsoo (1983) *Evolution of Comparative Advantage: The Factor Proportions Theory in a Dynamic Perspective* (Kiel: Kieler Studien).

Krause, B. L. (1982) *US Economic Policy Toward the Association of Southeast Asian Nations* (Washington, DC: Brookings).

Krueger, Anne O. (1966) 'Some economic costs of exchange control: the Turkish case', *Journal of Political Economy*, 74, 466–80.

———— (1972) 'Evaluating restrictionist trade regimes: theory and measurement', *Journal of Political Economy*, 80, 48–62.

———— (1977) 'Growth, distortions and patterns of trade among many countries', *Princeton Studies in International Finance*, 40 (New Jersey: Princeton).

———— (1988) 'The relationships between trade, employment, and development', in G. Ranis and T. P. Schultz (eds), *The State of Development Economics* (Oxford: Basil Blackwell).

Krueger, Anne O. and Sonnenschein, H. (1967) 'The terms of trade, the gains from trade, and price divergence', *International Economic Review*, 8, 121–7.

Krugman, Paul R. (1979) 'Increasing returns, monopolistic competition, and international trade', *Journal of International Economics*, 9, 469–79.

Lal, Deepak (1974) 'Methods of project analysis: a review', *World Bank Staff Occasional Papers*, 16 (Baltimore: Johns Hopkins University Press).

Lardy, Nicholas R. (1992) *Foreign Trade and Economic Reform in China 1978–1990* (Cambridge: Cambridge University Press).

———— (1994) *China in the World Economy* (Washington, DC: Institute for International Economics).

Lary, H. B. (1968) 'Imports of manufactures from less-developed countries', National Bureau of Economic Research (New York: Columbia University Press).

Leamer, Edward E. (1984) *Sources of International Comparative Advantage: Theory and Evidence* (Cambridge, Mass. MIT Press).

Leith, Clark (1976) 'Foreign trade and economic development: Ghana', NBER (New York: Columbia University Press).

Leontief, Wassily (1953) 'Domestic production and foreign trade: the American capital position re-examined', *Proceedings of the American Philosophical Society*, 97, 68–99.

———— (1956) 'Factor proportions and the structure of American trade: further theoretical and empirical analysis', *The Review of Economics and Statistics*, 38, 386–407.

Li Lanqing (1991) 'Reforming foreign trade system and promoting foreign trade development' (Gaige waimao tizhi, cujin waimao fazhan), *People's Daily* (Beijing: 11 November).

Li Lanqing, Zheng Peiyan, He Chunlin and Wu Yi (eds) (1995) *China's Utilization of Foreign Capital* (*Zhongguo liyong waizi jichu zhishi*) (Beijing: China Foreign Economic and Trade Publishing House).

Li Yushi (1991) 'China's foreign trade system reforms' (Zhongguo de waimao tizhi gaige), in Zhang Peiji and Yang Jixiao (eds), 94–123.

Liaoning Statistical Bureau (1987) *Liaoning Economic Statistical Yearbook 1986* (*Liaoning jingji tongji nianjian 1986*) (Beijing: China Statistical Publishing House).

Liesner, H. H. (1958) 'European common market and British industry', *Economic Journal*, 68, 302–16.

Little, I. M. D. and Mirrlees, James A. (1966) *Manual of Industrial Project Analysis in Developing Countries*, 2 (Paris: OECD).

———— (1974) *Project Appraisal and Planning for Developing Countries* (London: Heinemann Educational).

Liu, Xiangdong (ed.) (1994) *The Handbook of China's Foreign Economic and Trade Policies (1994–1995)* (*Zhongguo duiwai jingji maoyi zhengce shouce 1994–1995*) (Beijing: Economic Management Publishing House).

Lu Yunchang (ed.) (1985) *An Introduction to Foreign Economic Relations and Trade* (*Duiwai jingmao changshi*) (Nanjing: Jiangsu Science and Technology Publishing House).

Macgill, S. M. (1977) 'Theoretical properties of biproportional matrix adjustments', *Environment and Planning*, A9, 687–701.

Ma Hong, Liu Zhongyi and Lu Baipu (eds) (1997) *Report of China's Macroeconomic Policy 1997* (*Zhongguo hongguan jingji zhengce baogao 1997*) (Beijing: China Financial and Economic Publishing House).

Ministry of Agriculture (MOA), Planning Office (1989) *Chinese Rural Economic Statistics 1949–1986* (*Zhongguo nongcun jingji tongji daquan 1949–1986*) (Beijing: Agricultural Publishing House).

Ministry of Commerce, General Office (1986) *A Compilation of 1985 Commercial Policies and Regulations* (*Yijiubawu 1nian shangye zhengce fagui huibian*) (Beijing: Chinese Commercial Publishing House).

Ministry of Foreign Economic Relations and Trade (MOFERT) (1992) 'Interim administrative procedure for export commodities' (Chukou shangpin guanli zhanxing banfa), *International Business* (*Guoji shangbao*) (31 December).

Ministry of Foreign Trade, Department of Customs Administration (1961) *Customs Import and Export Tariff Schedule of the People's Republic of China* (*Zhonghua renmin gongheguo jinchukou shuize*) (Beijing).

Monthly Customs Statistics (*Haiguan tongji*) Monthly publication by the General Customs Administration, Beijing.

Naughton, Barry (1992) 'Implication of the state monopoly over industry and its relaxation', *Modern China*, 18, 14–41.

Ningxia Statistical Bureau (1988) *Ningxia Statistical Yearbook 1987* (*Ningxia tongji nianjian 1987*) (Beijing: China Statistical Publishing House).

Ohlin, B. (1993) 'Interregional and International Trade', *Harvard Economics Studies* (Cambridge, Mass.: Harvard University Press).

Panoutsopoulos, Vasilis (1992), 'Export pessimisim and the reality', in Hughes (ed.).

Pearson, Scott R. (1975–6) 'Net social profitability, domestic resource costs, and effective rates of protection', *Journal of Development Studies*, 12, 320–33.

Pearson, Scott R, Akrasanee, Narongchai, and Nelson, Gerrald C. (1976) 'Comparative advantage in rice production: a methodological introduction', *Food Research Institute Studies*, 15, 127–37.

People's Bank of China, General Office (ed.) (1983) *A Compilation of Financial Rules and Regulations 1981* (*Yijiubayi nian jinrong guizhang zhidu xuanbian*), 2 (Beijing: China Finance Publishing House).

————— (1986) *A Compilation of Important Documents on Foreign Exchange Administration 1984* (1984 *nian waihui gongzuo zhongyao wenajian xuanbian*) (Beijing: China Finance Publishing House).

People's Bank of China, State Planning Commission, the State Economic Commission, Ministry of Finance, Ministry of Foreign Economic Relations and Trade, State Administration of Commodity Prices, Bank of China and State Administration of Exchange Control (1984) 'Notice on termination of the trial use of the internal settlement rate of foreign exchange', in the People's Bank of China, General Office (ed.) (1986), 588–9.

People's Daily (*Renmin ribao*) A daily newspaper, Beijing.

Price: Theory and Practice (*Jiage lilun yu shijian*) A monthly journal, Tianjing.

Provincial Statistical Bureaus and Population Sample Survey Offices (1989) *Data on China's 1% Population Sample Survey 1987* (*Zhongguo 1987 nian 1% renko chouyang diaocha ziliao*), various provincial volumes (Beijing: China Statistical Publishing House).

Qinghai Statistical Bureau (1987) *Qinghai Social and Economic Statistical Yearbook 1986* (*Qinghai shehui jingji tongji nianjian 1986*) (Beijing: China Statistical Publishing House).

Qiu Deming (1988) *An Introduction to the Reform of Chinese Foreign Trade System* (*Zhongguo waimao tizhi gaige gailun*) (Xian: Shannxi People's Publishing House).

Ren Ruoen and Chen Kai (1994) 'An expenditure-based bilateral comparison of gross domestic product between China and the United States', *Review of Income and Wealth*, 40.

Roskamp, Karl W. and McKeekin, Gordon S. (1968) 'Factor proportion, human capital and foreign trade: the case of West Germany reconsidered', *The Quarterly Journal of Economics*, 82, 152–60.

Samuelson, P. A. (1962) 'The gains from international trade once again', *Economic Journal*, 72, 820–9.

Secretariat of the Central Committee of the Chinese Communist Party (CCP), Research Office, Economics Division, (ed.) (1985) *A Compilation of Documents on Open Door Policy* (*Duiwai kaifang zhengche wenjian huibian*) (Beijing: Party School Publishing House).

Shaanxi Statistical Bureau (1987). *Shaanxi Statistical Yearbook 1986* (*Shaanxi tongji nianjian 1986*) (Beijing: China Statistical Publishing House).

Shan, Weijian (1989) 'Reforms of China's foreign trade system: experiences and prospects', *China Economic Review*, 1, 33–55.

Shandong Statistical Bureau (1990) *Shandong Statistical Yearbook 1989* (*Shandong tongji nianjian 1989*) (Beijing: China Statistical Publishing House).

Shanghai Statistical Bureau (1987) *Shanghai Statistical Yearbook 1986* (*Shanghai tongji nianjian 1986*) (Beijing: China Statistical Publishing House).

Shanxi Statistical Bureau (1987) *Shanxi Statistical Yearbook 1986* (*Shanxi tongji nianjian 1986*) (Beijing: China Statistical Publishing House).

Sichuan Statistical Bureau (1989) *Sichuan Statistical Yearbook 1988* (*Sichuan tongji nianjian 1988*) (Beijing: China Statistical Publishing House).

Song, Ligang, (1996) *Changing Global Comparative Advantage: Evidence from Asia and the Pacific* (South Melbourne: Longman)

Specialized Farm Household Business Newspaper (*Zhuanyehu jingyingbao*) A daily newspaper, Beijing.

Squire, Lyn and van der Tak, Herman G. (1975) *Economic Analysis of Projects* (Baltimore: Johns Hopkins University Press).

Srinivasan, T. N. and Bhagwati, Jagdish N. (1978) 'Shadow prices for project selection in the presence of distortions: effective rates of protection and domestic resource costs', *Journal of Political Economy*, 86, 97–116.

State Administration of Commodity Prices (SACP), (1985) 'A notice on issues concerning the domestic pricing of imported commodities' (Guanyu jinkou shangpin guonei zhuojia wenti de tongzhi), in Ministry of Commerce, General Office (1986), 292.

————, Foreign Affairs Prices Department, and People's University of China, Research Team of Foreign Affairs Prices (1991) 'Issues in price administration for imported goods and suggestions' (Jinkou shangpin jiage guanli wenti ji jianyi), *China Price* (*Zhongguo wujia*), 5, 5–11.

State Administration of Commodity Prices (SACP), Research Institute of Commodity Prices (1984) *A Compilation of Selected Documents on Commodity Prices 1979–1983* (*Wujia wenjian xuanbian 1979–1983*) (Beijing: Chinese Fiscal and Economic Publishing House).

———— (1985) 'A comparison between Chinese agricultural procurement and industrial ex-factory prices and their international trade prices' (Woguo nongchanpin shougoujia he gongyepin chuchangjia yu guojimaoyi jiage bijiao), *Cost and Price* (*Chengben jiage ziliao*), 7; also in Zhang Zhuoyuan, *et al.* (1988), 374–91.

———— (1986) *A Compilation of Selected Documents on Commodity Prices 1984–1985* (*Wujia wenjian xuanbian 1984–1985*) (Beijing: Chinese Material and Equipment Publishing House).

————— (1988) 'A preliminary comparison between domestic and foreign price levels' (Guoneiwai jiage shuiping de chubu bijiao), *Cost and Price (Chengben jiage ziliao)*, 21, 4–12.

State Administration of Exchange Control and the Bank of China (1980) 'Notice on trial foreign exchange swap', in Guangdong Finance Society and Guangdong Provincial Branch of People's Bank of China, Research Institute of Finance (1984), 542–4.

————— (1981) 'Trial methods on foreign exchange quota swap', in People's Bank of China, General Office (ed.) 2 (1983), 209–13.

State Council (1963). 'Interim regulations on unified pricing methods for imported commodities' (Guanyu jinkou shangpin shixing tongyi zuojia banfa de zanxing guiding), in Wuhan Municipal Archives and Price Bureau (ed.) (1984), 144–6.

————— (1965) 'Interim regulations on unified pricing methods for commodities supplied for export' (Guanyu gongying chukou shangpin tongyi zuojia banfa de zanxing guiding), in Wuhan Municipal Archives and Price Bureau (ed.) (1984), 157–9.

————— (1975). 'Transmittal of the State Planning Commission report on recommendation on revising the pricing methods for imported commodities' (Guowuyuan zhuanfa guojia jihua weiyuanhui guanyu jinkou shangpin zuojia banfa xiougai yijian de baogao), in Wuhan Municipal Archives and Price Bureau (ed.) (1984), 166–70.

————— (1979a) 'Some stipulations on several issues concerning vigorously developing foreign trade and increasing foreign exchange revenues' (Guanyu dali fazhan duiwai maoyi, zengjia waihui shouru ruogan wenti de guiding), in Secretariat of the Central Committee (CCP), Research Office, Economic Division (ed.) (1985), 52–63.

————— (1979b) 'Approval and transmittal of the State Administration of Commodity Prices report requesting instructions on several issues in pricing industrial commodites supplied for export' (Pizhuan guojia wujiaju guanyu chukou gongyeping gongying zuojia de jige wenti), in State Administration of Commodity Prices (SACP), Research Institute, 40–3.

————— (1982) 'Notice on approval and transmittal of the State Import and Export Commission report on revising "Trial Methods of Foreign Exchange Retention through Commodity Exports"' (Pizhuan guojia jinuchukouwei dengdanwei guanyu xiuding 'chukou shangping waihui liucheng shixing banfa' de baogao de tongzhi), in Secretariat of the Central Committee (CCP), Research Office, Economic Division (ed.) (1985), 319–26.

————— (1984a) 'Interim regulations on licensing system for import commodities of the People's Republic of China', Editorial Board of the Almanac of China's Foreign Economic Relations and Trade (1986), 69–73, 433–7.

————— (1984b) 'Notice on approval and transmittal of MOFERT report on recommendations of foreign trade system reforms' (Pizhuan duiwai jingji maoyibu guanyu waimao tizhi gaige yijian de baogao de tongzhi), Guangzhou Municipal Industrial and Commercial Administration and Management Society (1985), 482–92.

————— (1985a) 'Customs Import and Export Tariffs of the People's Republic of China', in State Planning Commission (SPC), Legal Office (1987), 1423–578.

————— (1985b) 'Notice on approval and transmittal of MOFERT, SPC and the State Administration of Exchange Control's "Methods of Foreign Exchange Retention through Commodity Exports"' (Pizhuan duiwai jingji maoyibu, guojia jihua waiyuanhui, guojia waihui guanlijü 'chukou shangpin waihui liucheng banfa' de tongzhi), in Secretariat of the Central Committee (CCP), Research Office, Economic Division (ed.) (1985), 553–8.

————— Office for the Price Research Centre (1985c) *Tabulation of Data on 1983 Enterprise Survey for Estimation of Theoretical Prices (Cesuan lilun jiage yijiu basan nian qiye diaochashu huizongbiao)* (Beijing).

————— Office of Tariff Rate Committee, and the General Customs Administration: the Tariff Department (1996) *Import and Export Customs Tariff Regulation of the People's Republic of China (Zhonghua renmin gongheguo jingchukou guanshui tiaoli)* (Beijing:

Law Publishing House).

——— Office of Tariff Rate Committee, and the General Customs Administration: the Tariff Department (1997) *Tabulation of Import and Export Tariff Rate Adjustments* (*Jingchukou guanshui shuilu tiaozhengbiao*) (Beijing: Law Publishing House).

State Council, Office for the Leading Group of National Industrial Census, (1988) *Data on the 1985 Industrial Census of the People's Republic of China* (*Zhonghua renmin gongheguo 1985 nian gongye pucha ziliao*), 3, All Industrial Enterprises (Beijing: Chinese Statistical Publishing House).

——— (1989a) *Data on 1985 Industrial Census of the People's Republic of China* (*Zhonghua renmin gongheguo yijiubawu nian gongye pucha ziliao*), 10: Output Quantities of Major Industrial Products (Beijing: Chinese Statistical Publishing House).

——— (1989b) *Data on 1985 Industrial Census of the People's Republic of China* (*Zhonghua renmin gongheguo yijiubawu nian gongye pucha ziliao*), Summary Volume (Beijing: Chinese Statistical Publishing House).

State Council, Population Census Office, and State Statistical Bureau (1985) Statistical Department of Population, *1982 Population Census of China* (*Computer Tabulation*) (Beijing: China Statistical Publishing House).

State Import and Export Commission and the MFT (1980a) 'Interim Procedure of the System of Export Licensing' (Chukou xuke zhidu zhanxing banfa), in Editorial Board of the Almanac of China's Foreign Economic Relations and Trade (ACFERT) (1985), 25–32, 407–14.

——— (1980b) 'Notice on issuing "Interim Method of Import Administration in Foreign Trade" and "Interim Method of Local Import Administration in Foreign Trade"' (Yinfa 'duiwai maoyi jinkou guanli shixing banfa', 'duiwai maoyi difang jingkou guanli shixing banfa' de tongzhi), in Secretariat of the Central Committee (CCP), Research Office, Economic Division (ed.) (1985), 123–32.

State Planning Commission (SPC) (1987) 'Parameters of construction projects economic evaluation' (Jianshe xiangmu jingi pingjia canshu), State Planning Commission, Economic Laws and Regulations Office (1989), 438–88.

——— (1994) *Methods and Parameters of Construction Projects Economic Evaluation* (*Jianshe xiangmu jingji pingjia banfa yu canshu*), 2nd edn. (Beijing: China Plan Publishing House).

——— Centre for Economic Forecasting, and State Statistical Bureau, Department of Balances of National Economy (1986) *National Input–Output Table 1981* (*Quanguo toru chanchu biao 1981*) (Beijing: China Statistical Publishing House).

——— Economic Laws and Regulations Office (1989) *A Compilation of Planning Laws and Regulations in the People's Republic of China* (*Zhonghua renmin gongheguo jihua jingji fagui huibian 1986–1987*) (Beijing: Chinese Fiscal and Economic Publishing House).

——— Legal Office (1989) *Compendium of Important Economic Laws and Regulations 1977–1986* (*Zhongyao jingji fagui ziliao huibian* 1977–86) (Beijing: China Statistical Publishing House).

State Science and Technology Commission (SSTC) Research Team (1989) *Outward-Oriented Economic Development Strategy for Coastal Open Cities* (*Yanhai kaifang chengshi waixiangxing jingji fazhan zhanlue*) (Beijing: Economic Management Publishing House).

State Statistical Bureau (SSB) (1981–98) *Statistical Yearbook of China*, annual (Beijing: China Statistical Publishing House).

——— (1989b) *Economic Studies and Statistics on Economic Open Coastal Areas* (*Yanhai jingji kifangqu jingji yanjiu he tongji ziliao*) (Beijing: China Statistical Publishing House).

——— (1996b) *China Regional Economy: A Profile of 17 Years of Reform and Opening-Up* (*Gaige kaifang shiqi nian de zhongguo diqu jingji*) (Beijing: China Statistical Publishing House).

————— Department of Balances of National Economy and Office of National Input–Output Survey (1991) *Input-Output Table of China 1987* (*Zhongguo touru chanchu biao 1987*) (Beijing: China Statistical Publishing House).

————— Department of National Economic Accounting (1998) *The Gross Domestic Product 1952–1996* (*Abstract*) (Beijing: China Statistical Publishing House).

————— Information Centre for International Statistics (1989) *A Compilation of World Industrial Statistics 1988* (*Shijie gongye tongji huibian 1988*) (Beijing: China Statistical Publishing House).

————— Office for the Third National Industrial Census (1996) *Summary Survey of the Third National Industrial Census of the People's Republic of China* (*1995*) (*Zhonghua renmin gongheguo 1995 nian disanci quanguo gongye pucha ziliao zhaiyao*) (Beijing: China Statistical Publishing House).

————— Statistical Department of Commodity Trade and Prices (1984) *China's Commodity Trade and Price Statistics 1952–1983* (*Zhongguo maoyi wujia tongji ziliao 1952–1983*) (Beijing: China Statistical Publishing House).

————— Statistical Department of Industry and Communications (1988–95) *Statistical Yearbook of the Chinese Industrial Economy* (*Zhongguo gongye jingji tongji nianjian*) (Beijing: China Statistical Publishing House, annual).

————— Statistical Department of Society (1987) *China's Labour and Wage Statistics 1949–1985* (*Zhongguo laodong gongzi tongji ziliao 1949–1985*) (Beijing: China Statistical Publishing House).

————— Statistical Department of Society (1989) *China's Labour and Wage Statistics 1978–1987* (*Zhongguo laodong gongzi tongji ziliao 1978–1987*) (Beijing: China Statistical Publishing House).

————— Statistical Department of Rural Areas (1986–96) *Rural Statistical Yearbook of China* (*Zhongguo nongchun tongji nianjian*) (Beijing: China Statistical Publishing House, various issues).

————— Statistical Department of Trade and Materials (1990) *China's Commerce and Foreign Trade Statistics 1952–1988* (*Zhongguo shangye waijing tongji ziliao 1952–1988*) (Beijing: China Statistical Publishing House.

————— Urban Social and Economic Survey Team (1988) *Statistical Yearbook of China's Commodity Prices 1988* (*Zhongguo wujia tongji nianjian 1988*) (Beijing: China Statistical Publishing House).

Stone, Richard (1961) *Input–Output and National Accounts* (Paris: Organization for European Economic Cooperation).

Stone, Richard and Brown, A. (1962) *A Computable Model of Economic Growth, 1, A Programme for Growth* (London: Chapman & Hall).

Sun Shangqing (ed) (1989) *Markets in China* (*Zhongguo shichang*) (Beijing: Science Publishing House).

Sung, Yun-Wing (1991a) *The China–Hong Kong Connection: The Key to China's Open-door Policy,* (Cambridge: Cambridge University Press)

————— (1991b) 'The re-integration of Southeast China', paper prepared for the conference on China's Reforms and Economic Growth at the Australian National University (11–14 November)

Taylor, J. R. (1986) 'China's price structure in international perspective', *CIR Staff Paper,* (Washington, DC).

Tianjing Statistical Bureau (1987) *Tianjing Statistical Yearbook 1986* (*Tianjing tongji nianjian 1986*) (Beijing: China Statistical Publishing House).

Tibet Statistical Bureau (1990) *Tibet Social and Economic Statistical Yearbook 1989* (*Xizang shehui jingji tongji nianjian 1989*) (Beijing: China Statistical Publishing House).

Tong Zhiguang (1992) 'Chinese government wishes to restore its status as a GATT treaty member country' (Zhongguo zhengfu xiwang zaori huifu guanmao zongxieding diyueguo de hefa diwei), *Intertrade* (*Guoji maoyi*), 7.

Toren, B. (1957) 'Criterion for examining investment programs' (Jerusalem: Hebrew University), mimeo.

Tower, E. (1985) 'Effective protection, domestic resource costs, and shadow prices: a general equilibrium perspective', *World Bank Staff Working Papers*, 664 (Washington, DC).

Tower, E. and Pursell, Garry (1986) 'On shadow pricing', *World Bank Staff Working Papers*, 792 (Washington, DC).

United Nations (1950) *The Economic Development of Latin America and its Principal Problems*, by Paul Prebisch, Lake Success (New York).

————— (1960) *Standard International Trade Classification*, revised (New York).

————— (1965) *Planning the External Sector: Techniques, Problems and Policies* (New York).

————— (Annual) *Yearbook of International Trade Statistics* (New York).

————— (Annual) *Commodity Trade Statistics* (New York).

United Nations Conference on Trade and Development (UNCTAD) (1990) *Monthly Commodity Price Bulletin, 1970–1989 Supplement* (New York).

United Nations Industrial Development Organization (UNIDO) (1972) *Guidelines for Project Evaluation*, by P. Dasgupta, A. Sen and S. Marglin (New York).

————— (1978) *Guide to Practical Project Appraisal: Social Benefit–Cost Analysis in Developing Countries*, by John R. Hansen (ed.) (New York).

————— (1982) *Changing Patterns of Trade in World Industry: A Empirical Study on Revealed Comparative Advantage* (New York).

————— (1986) *International Comparative Advantage in Manufacturing: Changing Profiles of Resources and Trade* (New York).

United Nations Statistical Office, External Trade Statistics Section (1965–97) *International Trade Data* (New York). (The data are provided by the International Economic Data Bank, Australian National University, Canberra.)

Wang Linshen (1990) 'Review and introspection on the reform of China's foreign trade system' (Waimao tizhi gaige de huigu yu zhanwang), *Science and Technology Herald* (*Keji daobao*), 1, 34–8.

Wang Shaoxi (1989) 'An assessment on ten years of foreign trade system reforms' (Shinian waimao tizhi gaige de pingjia), *International Trade Issues* (*Guoji maoyi wenti*), 12, 2–7.

Wang Shaoxi, Wang Shouchun and Xu Yi (eds) (1989) *An Introduction to China's Foreign Trade* (*Zhongguo duiwai maoyi gailun*) (Beijing: Foreign Trade Education Publishing House).

Wang Shouchun and Li Kanghua (1986) *New Developments in China's Foreign Economic Relations and Trade* (*Zhongguo duiwai jingji maoyi de xinfazhan*) (Beijing: Foreign Trade Education Publishing House).

Wang Zhengzhi and Qiao Rongzhang (1988) *Review and Prospect of China's Price Reform* (*Zhongguo jiage gaige de huigu yu zhanwang*) (Beijing: Chinese Material Publishing House (Zhongguo wuzi chubanshe)).

Warr, Peter G. (1983) 'Domestic resource cost as an investment criterion', *Oxford Economic Papers*, 35, 302–6.

————— (1991) 'Comparative advantage and protection in Indonesia: methodology and results', *Working Papers in Trade and Development*, 91/6, Department of Economics and National Centre for Development Studies, The Australian National University (Canberra).

World Bank (1985a) *China: Economic Structure in International perspective* (Washington, DC).

————— (1985b) *China: Long-Term Development Issues and Options* (Washington, DC).

————— (1986) *Commodity Trade and Price Trend* (Washington, DC).

————— (1988) *China: External Trade and Capital* (Washington, DC).

————— China Department (1988) 'Economic prices for project evaluation in China',

Report, 7365–CHA.

Wu Nianlu and Cheng Quangeng (1987) *A Study on Renminbi Exchange Rates* (*Renminbi Huilu yanjiu*) (Beijing: China Fiscal Economics Publishing House)

Wuhan Municipal Archives and Price Bureau (ed.) (1984) *Compendium of Documents on Commodity Prices 1949–1983* (*Wujia wenjian xuanbian 1949–1983*) (Wuhan)

Xinjiang Statistical Bureau (1990) *Xinjiang Statistical Yearbook 1989* (*Xinjiang tongji nianjian 1989*) (Beijing: China Statistical Publishing House).

Xiong Meihua (1991) 'A comparison between domestic and foreign price levels' (Guoneiwai jiage shuiping bijiao), *China Price* (*Zhangguo wujia*), 1, 52–8.

Xu Feiqing (ed.) (1988) *China's Economic System Reforms* (*Zhangguo de jingji tizhi gaige*) (Beijing: Chinese Fiscal and Economic Publishing House).

Yahr, Merle I. (1968) 'Human capital and factor substitution in the CES production function', in Kenen and Lawrence (eds), 70–99.

Yang Fan (1993) 'A study on the trend of RMB foreign exchange rates' (Renminbi zoushi yanjiu), *China Price* (*Zhongguo wujia*), 3, 3–6.

Yang Songhao (ed.) (1988) *Introduction to Heavy Industry Prices, Transport and Post-Telecommunication Charges* (*Zhonggong jiaotong jiage wenda*) (Beijing: Cultural and Arts Publishing House).

Yang Xingbing (ed.) (1987) *Foreign Country Related Prices and International Market Prices* (*Shewai jiage he guoji shichang jiage*) (Beijing: Chinese People's University Press).

Yeats, Alexander (1991) 'China's foreign trade and comparative advantage', *World Bank Discussion Paper*, 141 (Washington: DC).

Yunnan Statistical Bureau (1991) *Yunnan Statistical Yearbook 1990* (*Yunnan tongji nianjian 1990*) (Beijing: China Statistical Publishing House).

Zhang Guanghua (1991) 'Foreign exchange adjustment markets and the reform of the foreign trade system' (Waihui tiaoji shichang yu waimao tizhi gaige), *Intertrade* (*Guoji maoyi*), 8, 39–41.

Zhang Peiji and Yang Jixiao (eds) (1991) *China's Policies of Opening to the Outside World and Economic Development* (*Zhongguo duiwai kaifang yu jingji fazhan zhengce*) (Beijing: China Foreign Economic Relations and Trade Publishing House).

Zhang Xiaohe (1991) 'The classification of China's industries by factor intensity and the corresponding trade pattern of China', in Chinese Students' Society for Economic Studies (Australia), 122–43.

Zhang Yichun, Zhao Lei and Zheng Zhenlong (1990) *Financial Markets and Investment in China* (*Woguo jinrong shichang yu touzi*) (Beijing: China Social Science Publishing House).

Zhang Yigeng *et al.*(1988) *Introduction to Foreign Economic Statistics* (*Duiwai jingji tongji jichu zhishi*) (Beijing: China Statistical Publishing House).

Zhang Zhuoyuan and Yang Shengming (eds) (1992) *China's Reforms in the Price of the Means of Production Materials* (*Zhongguo shengchan ziliao jiage gaige*) (Beijing: Economic Sciences Publishing House).

Zhang Zhuoyuan *et al.* (1988) *A Study on China's Price Structure* (*Zhongguo jiage jiegou yianjiu*) (Beijing: China Social Science Publishing House).

Zhejiang Provincial Committee (CCP) (1987) Policy Research Office, and Provincial Government, Research Centre for Technological, Social and Economic Development, *Almanac of Zhejiang Economy 1986* (*Zhejiang jingji nianjian 1986*) (Hangzhou: Zhejiang People Publishing House).

Zheng Dunshi (1990) *China's Foreign Trade Statistics* (*Zhongguo duiwai maoyi tongji*) (Beijing: China Foreign Economic and Trade Publishing House).

Zhong Pengrong (1990) *Ten Years of Economic Reforms* (*Shinian jingji gaige*) (Zhengzhou: Henan People Publishing House)

Zhou Shude, Wang Guofu and Zhi Yuanfang (1989) 'On the reform of China's export licensing system' (Lun woguo chukou xukezheng zhidu de gaige), *Guangzhou School of Foreign Trade* (*Guangzhou duiwai maoyi xueyuan xuebao*), 3, 9–14.

Zhou Taihe, *et al.* (eds) (1984) *China Today: Structural Economic Reform* (*Dangdai zhongguo de jingji tizhi gaige*) (Beijing: Chinese Social Science Publishing House).

Zhu Rongji, *et al.* (eds) (1985) *China Today: Economic Management* (*Dangdai zhongguo de jingji guanli*) (Beijing: Chinese Social Science Publishing House).

Zhou Xiaochuan and Yang Zhigang (1996) Transition of Mode of Thinking for an Open Economy (Maixiang kaifangxing jingji de siwei zhuanbian) (Shanghai: Shanghai Yuan dong Publishing House).

Index